The Northern Question

Figure 1

Italy's Regions and Capitals

The Northern Question
Italy's Participation
in the European Economic Community
and the Mezzogiorno's Underdevelopment

Adrian Nicola Carello

Newark: University of Delaware Press
London and Toronto: Associated University Presses

© 1989 by Adrian Nicola Carello

All rights reserved. Authorization to photocopy items for internal or personal use, or the internal or personal use of specific clients, is granted by the copyright owner, provided that a base fee of $10.00 plus eight cents per page, per copy, is paid directly to the Copyright Clearance Center, 27 Congress Street, Salem, Massachusetts 01970. [0-87413-342-4/88 $10.00 + 8¢ pp, pc.]

Associated University Presses
440 Forsgate Drive
Cranbury, NJ 08512

Associated University Presses
25 Sicilian Avenue
London WC1A 2QH, England

Associated University Presses
P.O. Box 488, Port Credit
Mississauga, Ontario
Canada L5G 4M2

The paper used in this publication meets the requirements of the American National Standard for Permanence of Paper for Printed Library Materials Z39.48-1984.

Library of Congress Cataloging-in-Publication Data

Carello, Adrian Nicola, 1957–
  The northern question.

  Bibliography: p.
  Includes index.
  1. Italy, Southern—Economic conditions—1945–
2. European Economic Community—Italy. I. Title.
HC307.S69C374 1989   330.945'7092   87-40642
ISBN 0-87413-342-4 (alk. paper)

Printed in the United States of America

Dedico questo libro
ai miei genitori
che mi hanno dato i mezzi
e mostrato la via
per completarlo
ed anche
agli Italiani del Sud
affinchè sappiano
che il sottosviluppo
del Mezzogiorno
non riflette
la loro immagine
bensì quella
della gente del Nord
sia d'origine italiana
che straniera.

Figure 2

Italy's Three Economic Systems

THE NORTHWEST
Piemonte, Valle d'Aosta
Liguria, Lombardia,

THE CENTER/NORTHEAST
Emilia-Romagna, Friuli-Venezia Giulia,
Alto Lazio, Marche, Toscana,
Trentino-Alto Adige, Umbria, Veneto

THE MEZZOGIORNO
Abruzzo, Basilicata, Basso Lazio,
Calabria, Campania, Molise,
Puglia, Sardegna, Sicilia

Contents

List of Tables 9
Preface 13
Acknowledgments 17
Abbreviations 19

PART I: *The Analytical Framework*

1 For a Political Conceptualization of History and
   Underdevelopment 25

PART II: *A Historical Prelude to Italy's Participation in the European Economic Community*

2 Italy from the Mezzogiorno's Origin to American
   Hegemony 33
3 The Mezzogiorno after World War II: Underdevelopment
   Renewed 42
4 Italy and Western Europe's Integration under American
   Hegemony 55

PART III: *The European Economic Community's Unbalanced Integration and Italy in the International Division of Labor*

5 The European Economic Community and Italy's
   Commercial Exchange 65
6 The European Economic Community and the Italian Lira 72
7 The European Economic Community and Foreign Capital
   in Italy and in the Mezzogiorno 81
8 The European Economic Community and the
   Northwestern Elite's Investment in the Mezzogiorno's
   Underdevelopment 98

PART IV: *The European Economic Community's Unbalanced Integration and the Mezzogiorno's Underdevelopment*

9	The Consequences of the Mezzogiorno's Underdevelopment	115
10	The State of Affairs and Future Prospects	136

Appendixes
A. Statistical Appendix to Chapter 6, "The European Economic Community and the Italian Lira" (tables 45–46)   141
B. Statistical Appendix to Chapter 9, "The Consequences of the Mezzogiorno's Underdevelopment" (tables 47–76)   146

Notes	178
Select Bibliography	194
Index	207

List of Tables

1. Capital Allocation I of the CASMEZ, by Sector — 46
2. Yearly Expenditure of the CASMEZ, 1950–1958 — 47
3. Capital Allocation II of the CASMEZ, by Sector — 50
4. Percent Change of Italy's Commercial Exchange, 1957–1964 — 66
5. Commercial Exchange (Goods and Services) as Percentage of GDP — 67
6. Percent Change of Italy's Commercial Exchange, 1951–1971 — 67
7. Intra-EEC Commercial Exchange, 1952–1971, as Percentage of Italy's Commercial Exchange — 68
8. Intra-EEC Commercial Exchange 1958–1980, as Percentage of Total Commercial Exchange (Goods Only) — 68
9. World Exports of Manufactured Goods — 69
10. Importation of Citrus Fruit by Area and Italy's Export Quota of This Exchange — 70
11. Percentage of Mediterranean Agricultural Products Imported by the EEC from the Mezzogiorno, 1969–1975 — 70
12. Italy's Percent Distribution of Imports and Exports, by Geographic Area, 1970–1978 — 71
13. Percent Distribution of Currencies Used as International Means of Payment in Commercial Exchange — 76
14. Average Dollar/Lira Exchange Rate, 1983–1984, by Categories of the Italian Economy — 77
15. Adjusted Index of the Prices of Goods on the International Market — 78
16. Contribution of the EEC Currencies to the Value of the EUA/ECU, May 1975–May 1984 — 79
17. Eight Largest Sources of Foreign Capital Invested in Italy — 82
18. Companies Producing Goods and Services in Italy with Capital Predominantly or Entirely Foreign, by Source of Foreign Capital — 84
19. Level of Foreign Participation in Industrial Activities in Italy by Eight Largest Sources of Foreign Capital — 85
20. Italian Companies Purchased by Foreign Investors in 1984 — 86

21. Companies and Plants Producing Goods and Services in the Mezzogiorno with the Participation of Foreign Capital in 1981, by Source of Foreign Capital — 87
22. Percentage of Companies in the Mezzogiorno with Foreign Capital by Eight Largest Sources of Foreign Capital in Italy — 88
23. Distribution by Region of Plants Producing Goods and Services in the Mezzogiorno with Participation of Foreign Capital — 89
24. Percentage of the Number of Plants in Southern Lazio and Campania with Foreign Capital Invested in the Mezzogiorno, by Source of Foreign Capital — 90
25. Consumer and Taxpayer Loss Compared to the Producer Gain Caused by the CAP in 1978, by Country — 94
26. Percent Self-Sufficiency Rate of Italy's Agricultural System, 1956–1974 — 94
27. Percent Composition of Agricultural Production, 1973–1977 — 95
28. Structure of EIB's Investments in Italy, 1958–1982, by Sector — 96
29. Distribution of EIB's Investments in the Mezzogiorno, 1958–1982, by Region — 97
30. Percent Distribution of Turnover, Real Property, and Employees of Italy's Leading Businesses, by Their Financial Holding Companies and by Region, 1973 — 99
31. Percent Employment Distribution, 1961–1981, by Region — 102
32. Evolution of CASMEZ's Capital Allocation — 104
33. Selected Labor Force Characteristics in North-Central Italy and the Mezzogiorno — 109
34. Percent Distribution of Fixed Investments in the Mezzogiorno, 1970 and 1980, by Sector — 110
35. Public Works Investments, by Region — 111
36. CASMEZ's Commitments and Expenditures, 1950–1983 — 112
37. Income Formation in the Mezzogiorno — 118
38. Investments in the Mezzogiorno's Industries and Parastate Industries as a Percentage of Italy's Total, 1951–1981 — 120
39. Composition of Internal Demand in the Mezzogiorno and in North-Central Italy in 1976 — 121
40. Extra-EEC and Intra-EEC Immigrant Workers, 1957–1970 — 125
41. Countries Preferred by Would-be Emigrants — 126
42. Italian Citizens Emigrating from Their Regions in January 1984 — 127
43. Mafia Extortion in Italy, 1983 — 134
44. Productivity and Cost of Labor per Unit, by Country — 138

List of Tables

45.	Percent Contribution of EEC Currencies to the Value of EUA/ECU, May 1975–May 1984	142
46.	Contribution of EEC Currencies to Value of ECU, September 1984–May 1985	145
47.	Key Economic Indicators: EEC Averages, 1955–1983	147
48.	Sectoral Distribution of Gross Value Added at Market Prices in 1970 in MIA LIT	150
49.	Sectoral Distribution of Gross Value Added at Market Prices in 1970 in Percentages	151
50.	Sectoral Distribution of Gross Value Added at Market Prices in 1974 in MIA LIT	152
51.	Sectoral Distribution of Gross Value Added at Market Prices in 1974 in Percentages	153
52.	Sectoral Distribution of Gross Value Added at Market Prices in 1979 in MIA LIT	154
53.	Sectoral Distribution of Gross Value Added at Market Prices in 1979 in Percentages	155
54.	Sectoral Distribution of Gross Value Added at Market Prices in 1981 in MIA LIT	156
55.	Sectoral Distribution of Gross Value Added at Market Prices in 1981 in Percentages	157
56.	Growth Rate of Gross Value Added at Market Prices, 1970–1974, by Sector	158
57.	Growth Rate of Gross Value Added at Market Prices, 1974–1979, by Sector	159
58.	Growth Rate of Gross Value Added at Market Prices, 1979–1981, by sector	160
59.	Sectoral Distribution of Employment, 1970, in Thousands	161
60.	Sectoral Distribution of Employment, 1970, in Percentages	162
61.	Sectoral Distribution of Employment, 1974, in Thousands	163
62.	Sectoral Distribution of Employment, 1974, in Percentages	164
63.	Sectoral Distribution of Employment, 1979, in Thousands	165
64.	Sectoral Distribution of Employment, 1979, in Percentages	166
65.	Sectoral Distribution of Employment, 1981, in Thousands	167
66.	Sectoral Distribution of Employment, 1981, in Percentages	168
67.	Distribution of Per Capita Income among Italy's Twenty Regions	169
68.	Distribution of Average Monthly Income per Family and Per Capita Income among Italy's Twenty Regions	170
69.	Unemployment Rate in Italy	171
70.	Inflation Rate in Italy	171
71.	EEC-Harmonized Unemployment Rates for Italy, April 1983 and April 1984	172

72. Family Consumption of Goods and Services, 1970–1980   173
73. Distribution of Resources of the Common Regional Fund among Italy's Fifteen Ordinary Regions   174
74. Distribution of Resources of the Common Regional Fund among Italy's Three Economic Systems, Ordinary Regions Only   175
75. Accounts of Italy's Regional Institutions of Government: 1977 and 1979   176
76. Accounts of Italy's Regional Institutions of Government: Total Expenditure as Percentage of Total Revenue, 1977 and 1979   177

Preface

THIS book proposes to explain underdevelopment by analyzing the underdevelopment of the economic system of southern Italy, the Mezzogiorno, in the context of Italy's participation in the European Economic Community (EEC). The historical subjects of this book are Italy's most powerful social groups and political organizations (e.g., Italy's financial and industrial leadership, the Christian Democratic Party [DC], the Italian Communist Party [PCI]), the EEC's politically dominant member states (West Germany and France), and the United States (the superpower that has thus far exercised hegemony over the EEC). The theoretical subjects are the concepts of power and integration.

The analysis of the relationships between these historical and theoretical subjects depends on an analytical framework—that is, an interpretative model of analysis that attempts to explain why things are the way they are. Only an analytical framework based on the most rigorous elaboration of theoretical concepts placed in the fullest possible historical context has validity because only it can explain realistically why things are the way they are. In essence, history and a realistic analytical framework complement each other: history has no meaning without the interpretation provided by an analytical framework and an analytical framework has no validity outside the context provided by history.

This analysis, and the analytical framework on which it is based, do not attempt to explain everything. They attempt instead to interpret history realistically by integrating only the historical information and the theoretical concepts necessary to explain reality. For this reason, the analysis can seem precipitate and the framework schematic. In fact, they deal only with the sine qua non.

This study makes an unorthodox and, I hope, an original and useful contribution to the study of underdevelopment in general and of the Mezzogiorno's underdevelopment in particular. Nonetheless, it owes much to the many works cited in the notes and in the Select Bibliography. It is left to the reader to deduce and ponder the many differences and similarities between the ideas expressed in this work and those expressed in others.

This book is divided into four parts. Part 1, "The Analytical Framework," provides the book's conceptual base. In it I contend that the distribution of power among political actors determines the consequences of the integration of their economic systems. The strong benefit at the expense of the weak and determine preponderantly their destiny. With regard to the development of the integrating economic systems, the systems of the strong experience generally positive, balanced development at the expense of the weak; the former cause the latter to underdevelop.

Part 2, "A Historical Prelude to Italy's Participation in the European Economic Community," examines integrative processes from a historical perspective. As for the Mezzogiorno's integration in the Italian economy, I contend that Italy's unification under the Kingdom of Sardinia transformed the organic development of capitalism in southern Italy, under way long before the country's unification, into the Mezzogiorno's underdevelopment. The Kingdom of Sardinia's ruling class became Italy's ruling class, identified its interests territorially with the economic system of northwestern Italy (most of which belonged to the Kingdom of Sardinia), and placed the Mezzogiorno in a subaltern position in the Italian economy.

As for the Italian economy's integration in the international economy, through its participation in the EEC, I assert in part 2 that the United States, hegemonic over Western Europe, attempts to maintain the international balance of power in part by giving political and economic predominance in the EEC to West Germany and France, Western Europe's two most important states in the strategic equilibrium between the United States and the Soviet Union. The predominance of West Germany and France in the EEC induces Italy's current ruling class, heir to the Kingdom of Sardinia's, to protect its traditional position of dominance and its interests by intensifying the Mezzogiorno's underdevelopment to the advantage and benefit of the economic system of northwestern Italy.

In part 3, "The European Economic Community's Unbalanced Integration and Italy in the International Division of Labor," I examine integrative processes in the contemporary period from a functional perspective. I contend that Italy's participation in an EEC dominated politically by West Germany and France under American hegemony gives to the Italian economy a subsidiary role in the upper ranks of the international division of labor. This role manifests itself most clearly in Italy's commercial exchange, in the exchange relationships between the Lira and other currencies, and in the movements of capital and labor.

In part 4, "The European Economic Community's Unbalanced

Integration and the Mezzogiorno's Underdevelopment," I examine the consequences of Italy's participation in the EEC for the Mezzogiorno. I believe that the participation of an Italy under its current ruling class in an EEC dominated by other states economically exacerbates the Mezzogiorno's underdevelopment, more functional than ever to the positive, balanced development of north-central Italy. The Mezzogiorno's underdevelopment manifests itself most clearly in its economic development without employment, rural exodus, economic deserts, social disintegration, anomalous urbanization, anomalous consumerism, hypertertiarization, emigration, and in the existence of the entrepreneurial mafia and the mafia model of capitalist accumulation.

Four concepts inform the present analysis and the analytical framework on which it is based. First, political actors are self-interested. Second, power and self-interest are at the base of politics. Third, political and economic development cannot be understood outside the context of the distribution of power among political actors. Last, in politics it never pays to be weak. In this book I contend that history shows these concepts to be fundamental truths.

Acknowledgments

THIS book is the product of two personal experiences: years of study in the United States and a year-and-a-half of research (from mid-1982 to the end of 1983) in Italy. Of these experiences, the latter was by far the more important because it made me aware of the inadequacy of the former. In the United States, Italy is poorly studied, misunderstood, and misrepresented. Before attending graduate school I had to learn about Italy on my own, outside formal academic confines and in a general environment of ignorance and, therefore, bias. While attending graduate school, I studied Italy entirely on my own initiative. Were it not for the cultured domestic environment created by my parents, I would have been unable to understand what the formal and informal systems of education and socialization in the United States intended me to learn about Italy, and why. Nor would I have had the means to profit from my sojourn in Italy without the help of my parents.

I owe much to the many people who in various ways helped me to realize this work. Some of these people were especially helpful. My dissertation committee, Professors Gerard Braunthal and Eric S. Einhorn of the department of political science and Roland Sarti of the department of history, the University of Massachusetts at Amherst, offered useful observations on the text and the opportunity to develop myself. Professors Eileen L. McDonagh, Suzanne Ogden, and Minton F. Goldman of the department of political science, Northeastern University, Boston, provided me wise counsel, generous support, and their own example. While a visiting professor at the University of Massachusetts, Mr. Christopher Brown, reader in political science, the University of Kent, United Kingdom, caused me to conceive this work by introducing me to many development theories and their various conceptualizations of underdevelopment. Professor Vera Zamagni of the "Cesare Alfieri" Department of Political Science, University of Florence, helped me to orient myself in my research in Italy. Ms. Jenny Hopkins and Mr. Wolfgang Knuppel of the Statistical Office of the European Communities (EUROSTAT), Luxembourg, and Dr. Roberta Faggian of the Documentation Service, Public Spending Office, Veneto Regional Council, provided me the data presented in the statistical appendix to chapter 9. Last, Lisa Rivard, a graphic illustrator for the U.S. military newspaper *Stars and Stripes*, was helpful in preparing the maps for this book. I am also grateful to the many other persons who helped in the research for this book and whose names are too numerous to list here.

Abbreviations

CAP	Common Agricultural Policy
CASMEZ	Cassa per il Mezzogiorno (Southern Development Fund)
CEE	Comunità Economica Europea (European Economic Community)
CIPE	Comitato Interministeriale per la Programmazione Economica (Interministerial Committee for Economic Programming)
CNPE	Comitato Nazionale per la Programmazione Economica (National Committee for Economic Programming)
DC	Democrazia Cristiana (Christian Democratic Party)
ECU	European Currency Unit
EEC	European Economic Community
EIB	European Investment Bank
EMS	European Monetary System
ERDF	European Regional Development Fund
EUA	European Unit of Account
FECOM	European Monetary Cooperation Fund
FEOGA	The Guidance and Guarantee Sections of the CAP
IASM	Istituto per l'Assistenza allo Sviluppo Meridionale (Institute for Assistance to Southern Development)
ICE	Istituto Commercio Estero (Foreign Trade Institute)
INSOR	Istituto Nazionale di Sociologia Rurale (National Institute of Rural Sociology)
PCI	Partito Comunista Italiano (Italian Communist Party)
PSI	Partito Socialista Italiano (Italian Socialist Party)
SME	Sistema Monetario Europeo (European Monetary System)

The Northern Question

Part I
The Analytical Framework

1
For a Political Conceptualization of History and Underdevelopment

An Inconclusive Debate

THE INTELLECTUAL DEBATE on underdevelopment has two traditional sides. "Orthodox" Marxists (such as Geoffrey Kay) and liberals (such as Joseph Schumpeter) do not conceptualize underdevelopment as a problem. Marxist "theoreticians of underdevelopment" (such as Paul Baran, André Gunder Frank, Immanuel Wallerstein, Arghiri Emmanuel, and Samir Amin) distinguish between development and underdevelopment and ascribe the latter's causes to monopoly exchange, production, or pricing.

Thus far, the debate has established what underdevelopment is not by eliminating the false answers to the questions posed about it: each side has pointed up the shortcomings of the other's arguments.[1] Although this may be a necessary and important contribution, the debate has not yet established what underdevelopment is because its participants, wittingly or not, subordinate history to ideology by conceptualizing development in accordance with their intellectual traditions, unfortunately more ideological than historical or political. Marxist theoreticians ultimately ascribe the fundamental catalyst of development to impersonal "iron laws" that concern the forces of production and the class struggle. Liberal theoreticians ultimately ascribe the fundamental catalyst of development to impersonal "market forces" that concern the "invisible hand" of supply and demand and competition among businesses.

The ideological bases of the Marxist and liberal intellectual traditions sanction the creation and historicization of an ahistorical, secular human telos: in the ambit of these traditions, the term *human history* refers to an abstract process of constant progress identified with the historical evolution of modes of production. Although Marxists and liberals alike may consider this evolution to the the telos's historical manifestation and realization, liberals consider the capitalist mode of production to be the telos's fulfillment, while Marxists foresee this fulfillment in capitalism's transcendence by socialism and communism. Nonetheless, both ideological groups affirm that the teleological process cannot be blocked; however, it can be accelerated by means of "scientific development" (understood not as the development of an episteme but rather as the development of that knowledge based on the "scientific method" that fosters technological development by employing experiments to test the veracity of hypotheses).

Marxists and liberals produce a tautological conceptualization of history by historicizing their ahistorical, secular human telos. On the one hand they define history as the telos's manifestation and realization, not as indeterminate relationships established among political actors on the bases of power and self-interest. On the other hand, they identify the telos's highest expression with political and economic dominance: the strongest are a priori the most "advanced," the most "developed."

In short, Marxists and liberals deny indeterminate "power politics" a priori in the name of the telos but evaluate the telos's progress ex post facto in terms of "power politics." For this reason, they misinterpret the role of politics in development by underestimating at the least and by ignoring at the most the significance of human agency in history. In essence, Marxists and liberals subordinate human agency to modes of production and their "laws of development" ("iron laws," "market forces") by subordinating history to the Marxist and liberal ideologies.

Under these circumstances, the participants of the intellectual debate on underdevelopment produce ambiguous concepts—that is, concepts ahistorical (ideological) and historical (political)—at the same time. In the ambit of the Marxist and liberal intellectual traditions, *development* refers both to an ideologically sanctioned abstract process of constant progress and to the type of development realized in history by the international economy's "central" or "core" areas, which are its "developed" areas. This conceptual ambiguity manifests itself clearly in the failure of the debate's participants to explain underdevelopment: they recognize its existence as a historical phenomenon characteristic of the international economy's "peripheral" areas but they cannot express it with conceptual rigor in a way that corresponds effectively with historical reality.

The participants instead create a dichotomy between development and underdevelopment and argue among themselves about the relationship between the two moments.[2] On the one hand, both orthodox Marxists, who love to insist that capitalism as a mode of production will revolutionize itself by means of its own development and will lead to a "higher" historical epoch, and liberals hold two points in common: they ascribe underdevelopment's causes to factors such as the periphery's "historical backwardness" and its "cultures poorly suited to modernization and modernity", and they affirm the center to be the periphery's future. On the other hand, Marxist "theoreticians of underdevelopment" affirm underdevelopment to be a product of capitalism itself, a problem tied to the existence of capitalism as a mode of production and a problem unresolvable for as long as capitalism exists.

According to both sides, the mode of production determines human history, conceptualized as a linear teleological process. Both sides distinguish between humanity as "backward" and "developed." The only difference between the sides concerns the (alleged) teleological function of capitalism as a mode of production: for orthodox Marxists and liberals, it is the agent that will make humanity whole;[3] for Marxist theoreticians of underdevelopment it is the means by which humanity is torn apart and which must therefore be supplanted by socialism, a more human and more progressive mode of production.

Moreover, both sides employ ideological metaphysics in order to provide human history with a telos that naturalist philosophy (which sustains that "science" is the only source of true knowledge) cannot express. Problems manifest themselves when Marxists and liberals attempt to explain human history by using theories based on ahistorical foundations. Their failure to explain underdevelopment is the most salient characteristic of the inconclusive intellectual debate on the subject.

The Liberation of History from Ideology

In order to properly conceptualize development and therefore underdevelopment—that is, with conceptual rigor in a way that corresponds effectively with historical reality, it is necessary to separate and thus to liberate history from ideology by repudiating the ideological foundations of the Marxist and liberal intellectual traditions. Such a repudiation establishes that development does not depend ultimately on impersonal "iron laws" and "market forces" allegedly (according to the Marxist and liberal ideologies) superior to human agency but rather on human agency itself. In short, history understood as politics (or human agency) and not as ideology determines development.[4]

The liberation of history (politics) from ideology produces five fundamental consequences—two negative and three positive. As for the negative consequences, the liberation of history (politics) from ideology destroys the identification between development as an ideologically sanctioned abstract process of constant progress on the one hand and as the type of development realized by the international economy's central areas on the other: the latter is not development but rather a particular historical, and therefore politically determined manifestation of development. Second, it falsifies the development/ underdevelopment dichotomy: underdevelopment is not opposed to development. It too is a type of development, a particular historical and therefore politically determined manifestation of development.

As for the positive consequences, the liberation of history from ideology establishes development as a process that increases the labor productivity of economic systems[5] and that manifests itself historically as two moments, each opposed to and organically united with the other: the type of development realized by the center and the type of development experienced by the periphery—that is, underdevelopment. Second, it establishes that each moment determines the other according to the historical, politically determined relationships between them. Last, it establishes that together these moments express the international economy.

Integration and Underdevelopment

The international economy's central and peripheral areas are integrated in that the political actors that manage and influence the economic systems located in these areas are interdependent. That is, they are reciprocally dependent: the decisions taken by one actor create repercussions in the others.[6] However, the international economy's integration is unbalanced in that the interdependence among political actors is asymmetrical: political actors in the international system are not equally interdependent because power is not distributed equally among them.[7] The dominant actors are at the political center of the international economy while the subaltern actors are at its political peripheries.

The maldistribution of power in the international system creates disequilibria in the international economy: the dominant political actors use their greater power to organize the international economy's means of production to their own advantage and benefit.[8] The economic systems under the jurisdiction of the dominant political actors become dominant or central and experience positive, balanced development—greater productivity—together with a greater diversification of internal production.[9] The economic systems under the jurisdiction of the subaltern political actors become peripheral and experience negative, unbalanced development or underdevelopment, or greater productivity without a greater diversification of internal production.[10]

Underdevelopment can also be called dependent development because the development of the peripheral economic systems depends preponderantly on the decisions taken by political actors outside the confines of these systems.[11] The productive capacity of the peripheral systems is oriented more toward the needs of the dominant external actors than toward the needs of the internal populations. Under these circumstances, an insufficient part of the real income produced by these systems is saved for internal reinvestment, and that part that is saved is often not reinvested as productively as possible, while an excessive part is consumed in a way that does not increase the demand for a wide range of internally produced goods and services.[12] Moreover, a growth in the real income produced by peripheral economic systems causes an excess of unproductive internal investments and an increase in demand that does not stimulate the diversification of internal production. Rather it stimulates the excessive consumption of imports, which limits increases in productivity to the export-oriented sectors of these systems.

Underdevelopment is the type of development experienced by economic systems occupying positions of political and therefore economic subordination in the international economy. Underdevelopment is not a nonproblematic stage of development through which peripheral economic systems must pass in order to obtain the type of development realized by central systems, whose systematic, and presumably beneficent, exploitation would ultimately create the periphery in the center's image.[13] Nor is underdevelopment an inevitable and perpetual condition of inferiority to which peripheral systems are relegated as a consequence of their contact with central systems, whose systematic and often nefarious exploitation would seem to condemn the periphery to eternal subordination. Instead, underdevelopment is a consequence of a power imbalance among political actors and reflects the inability of subaltern actors to determine the consequences of the political and economic relationships established by dominant actors.[14] The economic systems under the jurisdiction of subaltern actors will experience underdevelopment unless and until these actors acquire sufficient political autonomy to be able to determine the political organization of the means of production of and the use of the real income produced by their systems.[15]

PART II
A Historical Prelude to Italy's Participation in the European Economic Community

2
Italy from the Mezzogiorno's Origin to American Hegemony

The Kingdom of Sardinia, the Kingdom of Italy

THE EMERGENCE OF the Kingdom of Italy, proclaimed formally by the first Italian Parliament on 18 February 1861, marked the emergence of the modern Italian state. The Kingdom of Italy was the product of a particular process of unbalanced integration dominated politically by the Kingdom of Sardinia, whose initiatives to unify Italy were favored by the international balance of power during the second half of the nineteenth century.

The Kingdom of Sardinia's political predominance in Italy's unification gave to the Kingdom of Sardinia's ruling class, an emergent autochthonous bourgeoisie, control of the state apparatus, in fact an extension of the Kingdom of Sardinia's administrative and fiscal systems to the rest of Italian territory. This ruling class used its control of the state apparatus in order to consolidate its political predominance in two ways: first, by coopting the ruling classes of the political actors absorbed into the new state, the strongest of whom was the Kingdom of the Two Sicilys' autochthonous bourgeoisie, and all other social groups that might contend for an equal or dominant measure of control of the state apparatus;[1] and second, by establishing alliances with social groups that accepted subordinate positions of political tutelage.[2]

One Economy, Three Economic Systems

The Kingdom of Sardinia's political predominance in Italy's unification did not reflect a commensurate economic stature with respect to the economies of the actors absorbed into the new state. In 1861 the kingdom's economy was not developed enough to occupy the rest of

Italian territory by means of simple economic expansion. Moreover, the Kingdom of the Two Sicilys' economy was as developed structurally, if not productively, as that of the Kingdom of Sardinia.[3]

The Kingdom of Sardinia's ruling class used its control of state apparatus to establish its predominance in the Italian economy by politically reorganizing the means of production on Italian territory and by employing the real income produced by the economy to its own advantage and benefit. This political reorganization of the country's means of production created the three distinct economic systems comprising the Italian economy and determined the function of each one.[4] In short, the Kingdom of Sardinia determined Italy's political order and economic structure.

The economic system of the northwest became the Italian economy's center—that is, the system that conditions the other systems' development by determining the political organization of their means of production.[5] This system sustains not only small and medium enterprises but the greater part of Italy's large enterprises as well because its centrality allows it to create within itself the conditions for greatest development. The economic system of the northwest experiences positive, balanced development.

The Kingdom of Sardinia's native bourgeoisie, once the Kingdom of Sardinia's ruling class, now became the Italian bourgeoisie's politically dominant component—the bourgeoisie of the economic system of the northwest. This bourgeoisie's highest expression, the industrial and financial leadership, became Italy's northwestern elite, a ruling class that identifies its interests territorially with the economic system of the northwest.

The economic system of the center/northeast became the Italian economy's semicenter, or the system that sustains principally the small and medium enterprises serving as the external economies of the large enterprises of the economic system of the northwest, together with some large enterprises of its own.[6] Like the economic system of the northwest, it experiences positive, balanced development.

The Mezzogiorno became the Italian economy's periphery, or the economic system whose means of production are politically organized in nearly total dependence on external exigencies that change over time.[7] It has provided the more central, dominant economic systems a market for their manufactured goods, an outlet for their surplus investment capital and a reservoir of capital, cheap labor, and cheap agricultural products.[8] Under such circumstances, the Mezzogiorno cannot and does not develop in a positive, balanced way but instead experiences underdevelopment.

The Question of The "Southern Question"

Italy's unification under the Kingdom of Sardinia deprived the Mezzogiorno of a ruling class endowed with the political autonomy and the organizational capacity needed to define, defend, and promote its best interests. The Kingdom of the Two Sicilys' bourgeoisie, which had become that kingdom's ruling class, could have become the standard-bearer of the Mezzogiorno's best interests, had either a process of balanced or even unbalanced integration in favor of the Kingdom of the Two Sicilys determined Italy's unification.

However, the northwestern elite used its control of the state apparatus to install as the Mezzogiorno's new ruling class a politically subordinate ally who would serve the best interests of the economic system of the northwest in exchange for political dominance in the Mezzogiorno. The northwestern elite displaced the Kingdom of the Two Sicilys' bourgeoisie and replaced it with the landlord class of the Mezzogiorno's great estates.[9] The Mezzogiorno's new ruling class expressed the northwestern elite's political and economic interests in the Mezzogiorno more than it expressed the Mezzogiorno's own interests and organized the Mezzogiorno's means of production accordingly.

The Kingdom of Sardinia's political dominance in Italy's unification subordinated and impoverished the Mezzogiorno. The Kingdom of Italy's fiscal policies imposed on the Mezzogiorno proportionately higher taxes and a proportionately greater share of the public debt, but allocated to the Mezzogiorno proportionately less public monies in comparison with the rest of Italy. The Kingdom of Italy's banking system, always firmly in the hands of the northwestern elite and represented principally by the Banca Nazionale (transformed into the Banca d'Italia in 1898), choked off credit to the Mezzogiorno's industries by draining the reserves of precious metals from the Mezzogiorno's banking system, represented principally by the Banco di Napoli and the Banco di Sicilia. Moreover, the Kingdom of Italy's agricultural policies oriented the Mezzogiorno's agriculture toward the cultivation of Mediterranean agricultural products (locally produced wines and olive oil, citrus fruits, fresh and dried fruits) for external markets but oriented agriculture in the rest of Italy toward the cultivation of grain and other crops with stable internal demand. Although Mediterranean agricultural products may have been highly remunerative on the international market at that time, their dependence on external demand made the Mezzogiorno's agriculture more vulnerable to damage by protectionism than agriculture in the rest of

Italy—as was proved when the Kingdom of Italy imposed the tariffs of 1878 and 1887.[10]

The Mezzogiorno has never been the master of its own destiny, let alone the Italian economy's center. The northwestern elite has traditionally taken advantage of the Mezzogiorno's political dependence by organizing social consensus in the area as political ballast in support of an Italian economy whose structure has produced positive, balanced development for the economic systems of the northwest and the center/northeast and underdevelopment for the Mezzogiorno. It is ironic that traditional historiography refers to the Mezzogiorno's underdevelopment as the "southern question." In reality, it is a northern question, a phenomenon whose causes are found more outside the Mezzogiorno than within and whose roots are found in the political and economic relationships established between the Mezzogiorno and the rest of the international economy.

Italian Fascism and the Mezzogiorno

The political and ideological biases that inform historiography have greatly impeded the elaboration of an objective political analysis of Italy's Fascist regime (28 October 1922–25 July 1943), especially in determining if Fascist Italy's political leadership actually might have tried to change the structural relationships between Italy's three economic systems with the goal of eliminating the Mezzogiorno's underdevelopment.[11] Unfortunately, traditional historiography indiscriminately presents Fascism as an ideological abstraction and as a historical experience by attributing to the ideology the inherent evil attached to the regime by those who did not benefit from it or could not make use of it. Moreover, it attributes to the Fascist experience the ineluctability of war, defeat, and all its negative consequences, presumably born of an allegedly evil ideology. On the other hand, recent critical historiography has timidly begun to revalue Fascism by distinguishing ideology from history and by suggesting that the Fascist leadership may have attempted a positive and pragmatic reorganization of the means of production on Italian territory but that World War II may have put a premature end to such a reorganization.[12]

The northwestern elite has always viewed with apprehension any prospect of a territorial reorganization of the Italian economy because a reorganization would put into question the traditional centrality of the economic system of the northwest. The northwestern elite did not grieve at Fascism's downfall in World War II because Fascism's development bode ill overall for the northwestern elite's political and economic interests. Italy's industrial and financial leadership entered into a marriage of convenience with the Fascist leadership: each tried to manipulate the other for its own ends.[13]

Fascism's development had earlier benefited the northwestern elite's political and economic interests because Fascism had quelled the Left in Italy after the "revolution that failed" of 17 April 1920; in this way, Fascism preserved the northwestern elite's political autonomy and power.[14] Moreover, the country's ill-fated participation in World War II favored the northwestern elite's interests in that the war effort's immediacy and priority necessitated an intensive utilization of the national economy's existing structure and precluded the possibility of a territorial reorganization of the economy, for example, to the Mezzogiorno's benefit.[15]

However, Fascism's development more than offset these advantages. First, the regime's endemic instability made constant the possibility that the leadership might at some point organize social consensus in a way that might subordinate the northwestern elite politically. The industrial and financial leadership had to struggle constantly and diplomatically to impede the Fascist leadership from politically reorganizing the means of production on Italian territory in any way that might have compromised its own political autonomy or privileged political and economic position. Second, although the northwestern elite may have largely prevented Fascism from realizing its revolutionary potential, Fascism succeeded in breaking the power of the Mezzogiorno's landlord class by encouraging the development of a class of small peasant proprietors. In this way, Fascism greatly weakened the system of organized social consensus established by the northwestern elite in the Mezzogiorno soon after Italy's unification. Last, Austria's annexation by Germany (the Anschluss) on 12 March 1938 marked Italy's subordination to Germany in the Rome-Berlin Axis (24 October 1936–25 July 1943). Had the Axis won World War II, Italy's victory would have been Pyrrhic because Germany intended to suffocate Italian industry and to make Italy into an agrarian client state.[16]

Military Defeat and Political Conflict

The Anglo-American military destruction of the Fascist regime jeopardized the northwestern elite's traditional political dominance in Italy. When these forces destroyed the Fascist regime, the northwestern elite found itself precariously atop a political order now lacking legitimacy and a stable institutional structure. In this unstable situation, the northwestern elite had to confront challenges in all parts of Italy. For example, in the economic systems of the northwest and the center/northeast, where Italian capitalism and the Left, which criticized it, had most developed, many workers struck and joined the anti-Fascist resistance movement; in the Mezzogiorno, where Fascism had broken the political dominance of the landlord class, many landless peasants and day laborers occupied the great estates in order to expropriate the land and divide it among themselves.[17]

The Left took advantage of this instability to regain the power lost under Fascism by championing political disaffections and by transforming them into opposition to the Fascist regime and into positive political support. The Left, now represented principally by the Italian Communist Party (PCI), better organized and more coherent politically than the Italian Socialist Party (PSI) that had dominated the Left before Fascism, succeeded in organizing more consensus among the northern workers than among the southern peasants. In northern Italy, the Left easily put itself at the vanguard of the workers' movement because that area was its traditional stronghold and because the Axis's stubborn resistance to the Allied advance northward provided it with an opportune cause around which to rally popular support. On the other hand, in the Mezzogiorno, the Left belatedly (in 1948) put itself at the vanguard of the 1944 peasants' movement because it was not as well established there as in other parts of Italy and because the rapid Allied advance through the area precluded the necessity of organized anti-Fascist partisan resistance. The Left wanted to subordinate the northwestern elite on behalf of the working class.[18]

American Hegemony and Its Limits

The United States used its hegemony over Italy to give victory to the northwestern elite in its battle with the Left at the end of World War II. The United States perceived that the destabilization of the country's traditional political order caused by Fascism and by World War II would make a regime dominated by the northwestern elite more dependent upon American support and therefore more congenial to its tutelage than a regime dominated by the Left, which promised to give to Italy greater autonomy in the international system than the United States desired. Moreover, the United States wanted to secure its strategic military posture against its rival, the Soviet Union, in the Mediterranean region by making use of Italy's suitable location.

The United States was hegemonic but not omnipotent in that it could not control all the variables that would determine the future course of events in Italy. The preconditions for the attenuation of American hegemony accompanied its establishment. Two factors beyond the United States' control conditioned it in the exercise of its hegemony over Italy at the end of World War II: the renewed strength of the Left in Italy and Italy's geographic location in the context of the East-West conflict.

The Left, whose communist component, the PCI, had succeeded in maintaining clandestine organizations during Fascism, emerged from World War II stronger than it had ever been previously. The Left's political resolve and its dogged paramilitary activities against the Axis in Italy as the principal component of the anti-Fascist partisan resistance movement had gained for it considerable popularity.[19] By 1947, it had organized enough political consensus to contend seriously, if not successfully, for control of the Parliament.[20] In short, the Left at the end of World War II was a major political force in Italy and a valid electoral rival of the political Center-right.

In the context of the East-West conflict, Italy is located approximately four thousand miles from the United States, separated by the Atlantic Ocean but is about five hundred miles from the Soviet Union, separated by south-central Europe. Although the Anglo-American occupation of Italy may have secured for it a place under American hegemony, its place was on the geographic periphery of the American sphere of influence. In geographic terms, the United States faced difficult logistics necessary to maintain both hegemony over Italy and a viable strategic posture in the Mediterranean region.

These factors forced the United States to secure Italy's political allegiance by legitimizing to Italian society the reestablishment of its country's traditional political order and economic structure. To this end, the United States had to temper the exercise of its hegemony by allowing the northwestern elite to organize mass social consensus, principally through the Christian Democratic Party (DC), so that the northwestern elite might offset the strength of the Left. Moreover, the United States had to allow to Italy the economic capacity to create conditions of increasing prosperity so that the regime might justify its existence and might seem more appealing to Italian society than a regime dominated by the Left.

The United States found itself in a paradoxical and delicate situation: paradoxical because, in order to maintain its hegemonic position, the United States had to aid Italy in developing the capacities that could potentially allow it to regain lost political autonomy and delicate because the excessive development of these capacities would make Italy under the northwestern elite too strong and independent for comfort while insufficient development of these capacities could help the Left to displace the northwestern elite at the top of Italy's political order. Under these circumstances the United States needed to influence the development of Italy's capacities so that they might disadvantage American interests only minimally. The United States used its hegemony to attempt to manage the balanced development of the economic systems of the northwest and the center/northeast, and the Mezzogiorno's underdevelopment, by assigning Italy to a subsidiary role in the upper ranks of the international division of labor so that the northwestern elite might retain power yet remain under American tutelage.

The Northwestern Elite and the United States: A Problematic Relationship

At the end of World War II the United States exacted as the price for its military conquest the severe limitation of Italy's political autonomy. Italy had to swear allegiance to the United States in return for needed support. In short, the northwestern elite had to submit to tutelage from abroad in order to rule at home. Moreover, the United States limited the northwestern elite's ability to organize the means of production on Italian territory to its advantage and benefit by assigning Italy to a subsidiary role in the international division of labor.

Nonetheless, the northwestern elite, which never renounced its interest in political autonomy nor resigned itself to a political existence under American tutelage, fostered the development of its capacity to organize mass social consensus and to create conditions of increasing prosperity. The political power derived from the DC's organizational strength, together with an unprecedented strengthening of the Italian economy, allowed Italy to increase its autonomy gradually and modestly. This allowed Italy to modify its position in the international system: a commitment toward an autonomous united Europe, together with independent foreign policy initiatives toward the Soviet Union, the Eastern bloc, the countries of the Middle East, and many underdeveloped countries, replaced unswerving allegiance to the United States.[21]

In all probability, the consequence of a tempered American hegemony that most distresses the northwestern elite (and the United States) is the opportunity afforded the Left to emulate the northwestern elite in the ability to organize mass social consensus. Although the DC may have to take the Left's strength into serious consideration, the political divisions between the PCI and the PSI, which culminated in the dissolution in 1957 of the Unity of Action Pact of 1934, have thus far prevented the Left from consolidating its strength enough to gain control of the government.[22]

The tempered American hegemony, which helps the northwestern elite to retain its traditional political and economic dominance in Italy, also creates the conditions that could provoke its downfall. This situation could persuade the northwestern elite to pursue its best interests by reducing dependence on the United States rather than trust that the advantages of a tempered American hegemony will always outweigh the disadvantages. For its part, the Left desires to displace the northwestern elite at the top of Italy's political order and to increase the country's autonomy by organizing social consensus based on counterbalanced American and Soviet influence. In any case, foreign interests will largely determine the type and degree of development experienced by the Italian economy unless and until a ruling class acquires sufficient political autonomy to organize the means of production on Italian territory more in accordance with its own exigencies than in dependence of external exigencies.

3
The Mezzogiorno after World War II: Underdevelopment Renewed

The Ideological Legitimation of the Mezzogiorno's Underdevelopment

AT THE END OF World War II, the Mezzogiorno's traditional political and economic relationships with the rest of the Italian economy were in crisis. Fascism had effectively undermined the northwestern elite's system of political control over the Mezzogiorno by fostering the development of a class of small peasant proprietors. As a result the northwestern elite's subordinate political ally, the landlord class of the Mezzogiorno's great estates, was greatly weakened. Moreover, the Mezzogiorno's military occupation by Anglo-American forces provoked nearly four years of mass political instability (1944–48). It eliminated the Fascist regime's socio-political and institutional structures implemented to manage the area's agricultural transformation. Peasants and landless day laborers occupied and appropriated land.[1]

The balance of power in the international system determined the outcome of the crisis in the relationships between the Mezzogiorno and the rest of the Italian economy long before the political instability in the Mezzogiorno ended. First, American hegemony over Italy guaranteed the Mezzogiorno's continued subordination in the Italian economy by reestablishing the northwestern elite's traditional dominance in Italy. Second, the factors that caused the United States to temper its hegemony over Italy required the northwestern elite to legitimize its dominance by organizing social consensus and by creating conditions of increasing prosperity. Last, the United States constrained the northwestern elite to face intense international competition by integrating the Italian economy into the international economy under the banner of the "free enterprise" ideology, which promoted an increase in industrial activity, commerce, and mobility of capital and labor. In this situation the northwestern elite had to devise a new system of control over the Mezzogiorno because the landlord class, discredited in the eyes of the peasants and the workers, was no longer a viable instrument for the area's political subordination. Had the northwestern elite attempted to reestablish the landlord class's political and economic dominance in the Mezzogiorno, the Left would have had an opportune cause around which to rally popular support.

The northwestern elite confronted the Mezzogiorno's political instability by availing itself of the modified "free enterprise" ideology adopted as an expedient by the United States and by the United Kingdom during the 1930s to reconcile their common abstract ideological principles with the reality of their economically depressed areas. The modified free enterprise ideology, whose manifestations include the creation of the Tennessee Valley Authority in the United States (1933) and the enactment of the Depressed Area Laws of 1934 and 1937 in the United Kingdom, posits the need of industrialization to overcome underdevelopment and the idea that underdevelopment is a technical problem to be solved within a given economic structure by means of systematic state intervention. Accordingly, private investment in an underdeveloped area is induced by developing the area's infrastructure and by offering capital incentives to businesses (i.e., advantageous credit terms and tax exemptions). Moreover, this ideology disparages the direct industrialization of an underdeveloped area by the state.[2]

The Left contested the modified free enterprise ideology's conceptualization of underdevelopment by maintaining that, far from being a technical problem to be solved within an economic structure, underdevelopment is caused by that same structure and is primarily a political problem because the organization of the means of production is sanctioned, if not determined, politically. In short, a reorganization of the means of production to the benefit of an underdeveloped area is necessary in order to overcome underdevelopment.

As for the Mezzogiorno's underdevelopment, the Left maintained that the modified free enterprise ideology would merely allow the northwestern elite to legitimate its use of the state's resources to establish a system of control over the Mezzogiorno suited to the northwestern elite's new place and function in the international economy under a tempered American hegemony. Moreover, according to the Left, an essential precondition to the solution of the problem of the Mezzogiorno's underdevelopment was a reorganization of its means of production: it would be necessary to modernize the Mezzogiorno's agricultural system so that the area might begin to produce more efficiently the capital to be accumulated to finance self-sustained development.³ In an Italy dominated by the northwestern elite under American tutelage, the Left had to operate from a position of political inferiority.

The Instruments of Political Control: Land Reform and Public Works

The northwestern elite used the modified free enterprise ideology to legitimize the conceptualization of the Mezzogiorno's underdevelopment as a technical problem to be solved within Italy's traditional economic structure by means of systematic state intervention designed to induce private capital to undertake industrial investments. This allowed the northwestern elite to reestablish its control over the area by legitimizing the use of the state's resources in a way that feigned to remedy the Mezzogiorno's underdevelopment. In reality, so that it might better sustain international competition and impede the development of effective competition from the Mezzogiorno's entrepreneurs, the northwestern elite reestablished its control over the Mezzogiorno in such a way as to increase the area's involvement in the process of capital accumulation in the Italian economy. It expanded the Mezzogiorno's productive base without changing the area's place in the national economy through policies of land reform and public works.⁴

The northwestern elite used these policies to replace the Mezzogiorno's landlord class with a group of subordinate allies better able to meet its new exigencies. Political stability in the Mezzogiorno and in Italy best served the interests of these subordinate allies because the dominance they enjoyed in the Mezzogiorno depended upon the northwestern elite's dominance in Italy. The land reform, which effected a limited redistribution of property ownership by expropriating the poorest agricultural land in the areas of greatest political instability, consolidated the development of a class of small peasant proprietors;⁵ the public works policy, which established in the Mezzogiorno a system of political patronage and clientelism, created a bureaucratic "middle class," known more commonly as the "state bourgeoisie."⁶

Three laws governed land reform in the Mezzogiorno. The Parliament enacted law no. 230 of 12 May 1950 (known as the Law for the Sila [Legge Sila], named after an extensive mountainous zone and high plateau of Calabria) and law no. 841 of 21 October 1950 (known as the Summary Law [Legge Stralcio]). The Sicilian Regional Government enacted the other law, no. 104 of 27 December 1950 (known as the Sicilian Law [Legge Siciliana]). These laws created eight reform districts embracing 8,558,000 hectares (21,147,673 acres) of cultivated land in thirty-six provinces, equivalent to 30 percent of Italian territory and 41 percent of Italy's cultivated land.[7]

It was up to the Land Reform Agencies (Enti di Riforma) to carry out the land reform by determining the land to be expropriated, the compensation to be awarded and the distribution of the expropriated land, and by providing the grantees with the financial and technical aid necessary to make their land productive. These agencies expropriated a total 767,000 hectares, of which 673,000 lay within the eight reform districts and equaled a mere 7.9 percent of the land to be expropriated; the remaining 94,000 hectares expropriated lay elsewhere. Nearly 89 percent (682,000 hectares) of the expropriated land was distributed to 109,103 families, of whom 8 percent were small proprietors, 40 percent sharecroppers and 52 percent agricultural laborers. Approximately 75 percent of these families lived in the Mezzogiorno. The high cost of the redistribution and improvement reflects the poor quality of the land expropriated. The Land Reform Agencies, which employed the greater part of their resources to clear land, acquire farm machinery, and construct irrigation systems, roads, schools, and agricultural villages, spent $940 million, or an average $1,200 per hectare and an average $10,600 for the settlement of each family.[8]

The northwestern elite's public works policy, in conformity with the modified free enterprise ideology, was not a development policy with precise goals but rather a general preindustrialization policy calculated to induce the expansion of private economic activity and to increase employment in the Mezzogiorno by developing agriculture, improving infrastructure, and providing capital incentives to business. The principal instrument was the Cassa per il Mezzogiorno (CASMEZ, or Southern Development Fund), charged with formulating and implementing public works projects and with coordinating them with the ordinary institutions of government. It also sought to attract private investment capital to the Mezzogiorno from within and without Italy. American hegemony over Italy manifested itself in the CASMEZ's activities through the legitimation provided by the modified free enterprise ideology and, financially, through the World Bank, dominated by the United States. The bank provided 30 percent of the CASMEZ's funds in its first decade. Moreover, Americans and Italians jointly drew up the CASMEZ's initial disbursement plan.[9]

Law no. 949 of 25 July 1952 extended the CASMEZ's term, established originally by law no. 646 of 10 August 1950 at ten years, to twelve years and increased the CASMEZ's original appropriation of LIT

Table 1

Capital Allocation I of the CASMEZ by Sector

	Under Law No. 646		Under Law No. 949	
	LIT (billions)	% of total	LIT (billions)	% of total
Agriculture	770.0	77.0	887.5	69.3
Transportation/ Communication	90.0	9.0	190.0	14.8
Aqueducts/ Sewerage	115.0	11.5	177.5	13.9
Industry	---	---	---	---
Artisan trades	---	---	---	---
Tourism	25.0	2.5	25.0	2.0
Fisheries	---	---	---	---
Vocational training	---	---	---	---
Institutions of social character	---	---	---	---
Total	1,000.0	100.0	1,280.0	100.0

Source: Joseph A. Martellaro, *Economic Development in Southern Italy, 1950-1960* (Washington, D.C.: Catholic University of America Press, 1965), 11.

1,000 billion (to be disbursed at an average annual rate of LIT 100 billion) to LIT 1,280 billion, to be disbursed at an average annual rate of LIT 110 billion from the fourth to the twelfth year.[10] Table 1 shows how the CASMEZ allocated its funds from fiscal year 1950–51 to fiscal year 1957–58. In this period, the CASMEZ spent LIT 1,035.7 billion, or an average LIT 129.5 billion per year.

The Mezzogiorno's "Programmed" Underdevelopment

During the 1950s, the northwestern elite became increasingly aware that the exigencies of international economic competition would overwhelmingly influence the political organization of the means of production on Italian territory because American hegemony over Western

Europe promised to promote the institutionalized market policy integration of the major West European economies. For this reason, the northwestern elite urgently addressed itself to the preparations needed to make the economic system of the northwest as competitive as possible in the international economy. To this end, between 1950 and 1957 the Italian state spent four times more for capital incentives to businesses in north-central Italy than to those in the Mezzogiorno.[11] Moreover, the northwestern elite now wanted to increase the Mezzogiorno's involvement in the process of capital accumulation in the Italian economy beyond what the public works and the land reform policies might allow. Although the northwestern elite may have succeeded in reestablishing its political control over the Mezzogiorno by means of these policies, it considered them inadequate to allow the economic system of the northwest to meet the exigencies of international economic competition.

Once again the northwestern elite made ideological virtue of political necessity, this time by partially repudiating the modified free

Table 2

Yearly Expenditure of the CASMEZ, 1950-1958

Fiscal Year	LIT (in billions)
1950-51	4.0
1951-52	50.3
1952-53	116.9
1953-54	157.1
1954-55	181.7
1955-56	197.4
1956-57	173.8
1957-58	154.5
Total	1,035.7

Source: George H. Hildebrand, *Growth and Structure in the Economy of Modern Italy* (Cambridge: Harvard University Press, 1965), 66.

enterprise ideology's conceptualization of underdevelopment. It contended that such a conceptualization might impede the state from dealing effectively with the problem of the Mezzogiorno's underdevelopment because, under the resultant preindustrialization policy, the state could merely attempt to promote the area's industrialization by developing infrastructure and agriculture. It still maintained that the Mezzogiorno's underdevelopment was a technical problem to be solved within Italy's traditional economic structure but now advocated that the state might take a more active role in the political organization of the area's means of production.

The northwestern elite legitimized the state's more active role by incorporating the problem of the Mezzogiorno's underdevelopment into the elaboration of national economic programs, more symbolic than substantive. Through the DC the elite availed itself of the economic programming concept (*programmazione economica*) to create the impression that the state intended to realize a series of declared socioeconomic objectives by carrying out a predetermined and systematic plan. In order to maintain ideological purity against the Left, the northwestern elite scrupulously refrained from using the phrase *economic planning (pianificazione economica)*.

The Italian government adopted its first national development program in 1954. Elaborated for the period 1955–64, the Vanoni Plan (*Schema Vanoni*) sought to reduce unemployment in the Mezzogiorno, remedy its underdevelopment without sacrificing economic growth in the rest of the Italian economy, and improve Italy's international balance of payments. By remaining abstract declarations, these goals symbolized the northwestern elite's true attitude toward the problem of the Mezzogiorno's underdevelopment.[12]

The Mezzogiorno's Modernized Underdevelopment: Incentives and Dependent Industrialization

The Italian government specified the state's more active role in the political organization of the Mezzogiorno's means of production by enacting law no. 634 of 29 July 1957, which made the state an agent of industrialization with the task of directing and controlling capital investments in the Mezzogiorno. Law no. 634 established two contradictory policies: one charged the state to industrialize the Mezzogiorno directly by concentrating large industrial and infrastructural investments in "areas of industrial development"; the other charged the state to industrialize the Mezzogiorno indirectly by implementing an incentives policy that might encourage the dispersion of small and medium businesses outside the "areas of industrial development."[13]

An "area of industrial development" is a conglomeration of "industrial nuclei" or areas in which large businesses are concentrated, together with the infrastructure necessary to support and to join them. Law no. 634 charged the Committee of Ministers for the Mezzogiorno to approve the projects for industrialization submitted for judgment by a consortium of communes in each industrial area. Under this law each consortium must attempt to attract industry by developing the necessary infrastructure, up to 50 percent of whose cost the CASMEZ would cover. Moreover, law no. 634 obliged north-central Italy's large parastate industries to locate 40 percent of their total investments and 60 percent of their new investments in the Mezzogiorno.

The incentives policy tried to reduce the production costs of small and medium businesses in the area by providing for tax reductions and exemptions, advantageous credit terms, and capital grants offered by the CASMEZ. Law no. 634 increased the capital available to these businesses by allowing medium-term credit institutions based in north-central Italy to operate in the Mezzogiorno for the first time. The incentives policy encouraged the dispersion of small and medium businesses by implying that reduced fiscal obligations to the state might lower production costs and therefore increase competitiveness automatically and might substitute adequately the infrastructure and the external economies lacking outside the "areas of industrial development."

The contradictory policies established by law no. 634 benefited north-central Italy's large parastate industries more than the small and medium businesses in the Mezzogiorno because the policy of direct industrialization prevailed over the policy of indirect industrialization for two reasons. First, the northwestern elite, through the DC, politically dominated the parastate industries, the Committee of Ministers for the Mezzogiorno and CASMEZ. Second, the parastate industries, already more productive than the small and medium businesses in the Mezzogiorno, disposed of greater capital resources and operated in areas equipped with adequate infrastructure. Moreover, the incentives policy did not encourage the establishment of many small and medium businesses in the Mezzogiorno for another two reasons: first, because reduced fiscal obligations to the state did not lower production costs and did not adequately substitute the infrastructure and the external economies lacking outside the "areas of industrial development," and second, because the Italian government subsequently eliminated any incentive for small and medium businesses to locate in the Mezzogiorno by implementing a similar incentives policy for the rest of Italy.

In reality, north-central Italy's large parastate industries benefited most from the incentives policy designed originally to promote the establishment of small and medium businesses in the Mezzogiorno. Law no. 634 defined such businesses as those whose personnel totaled less than five hundred and whose total fixed investments did not exceed LIT 1.5 billion. Following the enactment of law no. 555 of July 1959, which modified law no. 634, the Committee of Ministers for the Mezzogiorno, in December 1959, extended the incentives policy to those businesses whose personnel totaled less than five hundred and whose total fixed investments did not exceed LIT 3 billion. In May 1961 the committee extended the incentives policy to businesses of all sizes, provided the value of no single productive unit exceeded LIT 6

Table 3

Capital Allocation II of the CASMEZ by Sector

	Under Law No. 634		Under Law No. 622	
	LIT (billions)	% of total	LIT (billions)	% of total
Agriculture	1,138.0	55.6	1,150.0	55.4
Transportation/ Communication	259.0	12.6	259.0	12.5
Aqueducts/ Sewerage	312.0	15.2	312.0	15.0
Industry	245.0	12.0	245.0	11.8
Artisan trades	5.0	0.2	5.0	0.2
Tourism	44.5	2.2	56.5	2.7
Fisheries	5.0	0.2	5.0	0.2
Vocational training	38.0	1.9	43.5	2.1
Institutions of social character	2.0	0.1	2.0	0.1
Total	2,048.5	100.0	2,078.0	100.0

Source: Joseph A. Martellaro, *Economic Development in Southern Italy, 1950-1960* (Washington, D.C.: Catholic University of America Press, 1965), 11.

billion; in this way, a business of any size whose assets might be opportunely distributed could take advantage of the incentives policy. Finally, law no. 1462 of September 1962 extended the incentives policy to all businesses, provided that they were established with an initial investment no greater than LIT 6 billion.

Moreover, law no. 634 refinanced the CASMEZ and extended its life to fifteen years—that is, until 1965. The government appropriated additional monies to the CASMEZ under law no. 622 of 24 July 1959 but did not further extend the CASMEZ's life. Under law no. 622, the funds for vocational training included LIT 8,500 million from American agricultural surpluses accepted by the Italian government under law no. 1349 of 28 December 1957.[14] Following its refinancing, the CASMEZ greatly increased its yearly expenditure. For example, in FY 1958–59 the CASMEZ spent LIT 221.4 billion and in FY 1959–60 the CASMEZ spent LIT 239.7 billion.[15]

The Mezzogiorno in the Italian Economy 1950–1961

The following statistics reflect the gap in economic development that existed between the Mezzogiorno and north-central Italy (i.e., the economic systems of the northwest and the center/northeast) in 1951. The percent distribution by sector of employment (1) and gross domestic product (2) was:

	Agriculture		Industry		Tertiary		Public[a] Administration	
	(1)	(2)	(1)	(2)	(1)	(2)	(1)	(2)
Mezzogiorno	56.7	34.0	21.1	23.7	23.2	42.3	5.8	12.8
Italy	43.8	22.0	29.5	36.7	26.7	40.5	5.8	9.4

[a] as part of the tertiary
Source: Del Monte and Giannola, *Il Mezzogiorno nell'economia italiana*, 359.

Thirty-seven percent of Italy's population resided in the Mezzogiorno at that time. The distribution of *per capita* income, with Italy at 100, showed the Mezzogiorno at 58.2 and north-central Italy at 126.1. The average income (in thousands of LIT) per hectare of farmland showed the Mezzogiorno at 230, Italy at 265 and north-central Italy at 290. Industrial workers in the Mezzogiorno numbered 709,788, against 3,456,466 in north-central Italy.[16] In Italy, 19.7 million people were employed, of whom 13.2 million lived in north-central Italy and 6.5 million in the Mezzogiorno. For every person employed, 1.3 people were unemployed in north-central Italy, against 1.6 in the Mezzogiorno.[17] Fifteen percent of Italy's industrial investments and 19.7 percent of its industrial employment were located in the Mezzogiorno.[18] Business employed an average 6.9 people in north-central Italy, against 2.6 in the Mezzogiorno. In the latter, there were 3.7 million agricultural workers, or 43 percent of the national agricultural work force.[19]

The capital infused into the Mezzogiorno by the public works and the land reform policies, together with the expenditure of the ordinary institutions of government and private capital, increased the area's involvement in the process of capital accumulation in the national economy by developing its productive apparatus. The public works policy developed its infrastructure and, together with the land reform, increased agricultural productivity by disseminating better farming techniques, mechanizing farms, and fertilizing and irrigating the land. In 1958 the percent distribution by sector of employment (1) and gross domestic product (2) was:

	Agriculture		Industry		Tertiary		Public[a] Administration	
	(1)	(2)	(1)	(2)	(1)	(2)	(1)	(2)
Mezzogiorno	45.6	27.6	26.1	24.7	28.3	48.1	6.6	14.3
Italy	34.2	18.5	34.6	35.9	31.2	45.6	6.4	10.3

[a] as part of the tertiary
Source: Del Monte and Giannola, *Il Mezzogiorno nell'economia italiana*, 359.

The Mezzogiorno's development increased demand there for manufactured goods. North-central Italy's industries satisfied more of the Mezzogiorno's demand than the Mezzogiorno's own industries because the former, located in the more dominant economic systems of the northwest and the center/northeast, were already more diversified and more productive. The Mezzogiorno's most advanced industries succeeded in sustaining the competition of similar industries based in north-central Italy but were too few in number to affect significantly the Mezzogiorno's development. The increase in productivity of the Mezzogiorno's agriculture complemented the increase in productivity of north-central Italy's industries because the Mezzogiorno, in relation to the rest of the Italian economy, became a net importer of manufactured goods and a net exporter of agricultural products, predominantly Mediterranean (wines and citrus fruits).[20]

The Mezzogiorno's industries most affected by the increased demand for manufactured goods were the labor-intensive ones; therefore, less productive, small, traditional industries that produced for local markets had no competition from north-central Italy's industries.

Of the workers who left agriculture to seek industrial employment, the Mezzogiorno's small traditional industries absorbed a greater share of this group in its area than north-central Italy's industries did in its area. However, the Mezzogiorno's relatively inefficient industries could not match the increase in productivity of the industries in the more dominant economic systems of the northwest and the center/northeast. Between 1951 and 1958, value added in the industrial sector increased by 6.15 percent in Italy but only by 5.98 percent in the Mezzogiorno. In this period, *per capita* income in the Mezzogiorno fell from 64.5 percent to 62.5 percent of Italy's average.[21] Between 1951 and 1959, value added in the Mezzogiorno's manufacturing sector was 12.5 percent of the value added in the Italian economy's manufacturing sector.[22]

The increased employment in the Mezzogiorno's labor-intensive industries was insufficient to absorb all the unemployed and underemployed people in the area's work force. The northwestern elite compensated partially for the lack of industrial employment opportunities in the Mezzogiorno by absorbing workers into the tertiary sector and public administration at a rate higher in the Mezzogiorno than in the more productive systems of the northwest and the center/northeast. The majority of unemployed and underemployed people in the Mezzogiorno remained a reserve work force for the industrial expansion of more dominant economic systems within and outside Italy.[23] The increase in the productivity of the Mezzogiorno's agricultural system permitted agricultural laborers to seek industrial employment without reducing the Mezzogiorno's agricultural production, which was exchanged for manufactured goods produced in north-central Italy.

Between 1951 and 1961 the percent distribution by sector of employment in the Mezzogiorno evolved in the following manner:

	1951	1954	1959	1961
Agriculture	56.3	51.0	42.4	39.4
Industry	19.1	23.8	29.1	29.0
Tertiary	15.9	—	—	23.0
Public administration	8.7	—	—	8.6
Combined tertiary and public administration	24.6	25.2	28.5	31.6

Sources: Data from Del Monte and Giannola, *Il Mezzogiorno nell'economia italiana;* Bagnasco, *Tre Italie;* and Martellaro, *Economic Development in Southern Italy.*

In this period agricultural productivity increased by 5.25 percent in the Mezzogiorno but by 5.40 percent in north-central Italy,[24] while value added in the manufacturing sector increased by an average 6.17 percent per year in the Mezzogiorno but by an average annual rate of 8.36 percent in Italy.[25]

4
Italy and Western Europe's Integration under American Hegemony

The Juridical Dimension of Integrative Processes

THE CONSEQUENCES FOR the Mezzogiorno of Italy's participation in the European Economic Community (EEC) derive from the area's integration in the Italian economy, which in turn is integrated in the international economy through the country's participation in the EEC. It is necessary to recognize the juridical dimension of these integrative processes for two reasons. First, it exposes the structure of authority within which the political actors under study establish the political and economic relationships affecting the Mezzogiorno. Second, it exposes their professed political and economic objectives, as well as the means by which they attempt to realize them and upon which they bestow juridical legitimacy.

Two sets of juridical relationships affect the Mezzogiorno in the context of Italy's participation in the EEC: those between Italy and the EEC and those between the Mezzogiorno and the Italian state.

As for the relationship between Italy and the EEC, the Treaty of Rome of 25 March 1957 declared the continuous, balanced, and harmonious economic development of the EEC states to be the EEC's objective and affirmed that it would attempt to realize this objective by increasing the mobility of capital, labor, and commerce among the EEC states and by establishing common customs tariffs and a common commercial policy toward non-EEC states.[1] Under the treaty, the authority of the EEC's institutions in many cases superseded the legislative authority of the member states' parliaments with regard to foreign policy, agricultural policy, the regulation of economic competition, fiscal policy, social policy, labor policy, and the EEC budget.[2] Moreover, the protocol concerning Italy affirmed that the Mezzogiorno's economic development was the EEC's concern.[3]

As for the relationship between the Mezzogiorno and Italy, Italy's republican constitution of 1948 affirms the concept of regional political autonomy by recognizing explicitly the existence of subnational administrative regions and by affirming the concept of regional legislative autonomy.[4] The subnational administrative regions that are part of the Mezzogiorno are the juridical nexus between it and the Italian state (besides the fact that the Mezzogiorno is sovereign Italian territory). Italy's constitution legally limits the political autonomy of its regions by denying them the authority to regulate interregional commerce and by granting them only as much fiscal autonomy and therefore only as much economic authority as the state desires. Moreover, the state legally affirms its particular role in the Mezzogiorno's economic development by creating instruments of extraordinary intervention for the area such as the CASMEZ, designed to formulate and to implement special public works projects.[5]

It remains to be seen whether or not the means (e.g., greater mobility of capital, labor and commerce, common customs tariffs and a common commercial policy, a protocol to a treaty, regional legislative autonomy, instruments of extraordinary economic intervention) and the professed objectives (e.g., balanced and harmonious economic development, regional political autonomy) of the political actors under study correspond effectively in reality. To this end, it is necessary to place the legal relationships established between these political actors against the historical record by examining their political and economic relationships in the context of the distribution of power among them. Such an examination will show if the means, in the historical context in which they are adopted, lead to the political actors' professed objectives, and indeed if these objectives are even their true objectives.

The Basic Premises

After World War II the United States promoted the institutionalized market policy integration of Western Europe's major economies. The resultant EEC contributed to the stabilization of the strategic equilibrium between the superpowers in two ways. First, it stabilized Western Europe politically by creating greater interdependence between its major economies than between those of other areas. Second, it consolidated West Germany's and France's predominance over Western Europe's other states because the uniform limitation of market policy authority among the EEC member states effectively sanctioned the existing distribution of power that advantages West Germany and France.[6]

The EEC interests West Germany and France because it promises to sanction their political predominance over a Western Europe under a tempered American hegemony. The two countries exercise their political predominance over Western Europe's other states by fostering the EEC's development only in the ways that satisfy principally the exigencies of their own economies. They perceive that their interests may best be served by a minimum redistribution of power to the EEC's institutions because a strong EEC jeopardizes their political predominance in Western Europe. However, should the costs of American hegemony seem to West Germany and France greater than the benefits, and should the prospect of an autonomous Western Europe under their political predominance seem unlikely, West Germany and France would have to accept a strengthening of the EEC's institutions as the means to repudiate American hegemony.

West Germany, France and the Rewards of Political Predominance

West Germany and France derive three fundamental advantages from their political predominance over Western Europe's other states. First, they have greater political autonomy and therefore a greater capacity to organize the means of production of their economies according to internal exigencies, to create the composition of internal demand, and to orient the productive capacity of their economies to meet the needs of their own populations. Second, they have a greater capacity to concentrate within their borders the accumulation and the investment of capital and therefore to establish the levels of productivity to which the entrepreneurs of Western Europe's other states must adapt themselves. As a consequence, West German and French entrepreneurs are more competitive than other West European entrepreneurs and are better able to establish the remunerative value of the goods and services exchanged with those produced elsewhere in Western Europe.[7] Third, West Germany and France have a greater capacity to determine the division of labor among Western Europe's states—that is, to determine which goods and services produced in Western Europe's other economies will be exchanged for their own goods and services.[8]

These advantages allow West Germany and France to determine the political organization of the means of production of Western Europe's other states by conditioning the ways in which they may accumulate, invest, and consume the real income produced by their economies and therefore the ways in which they may use their labor forces. West Germany and France can do this by offering to the politically dominant entrepreneurs of the other states the prospect of the greatest remuneration for the production of goods and services that principally satisfy the exigencies of the West German and French economies. Such a prospect conditions the consumption of real income in Western Europe's other economies because their politically dominant entrepreneurs seek to give themselves the greatest competitive advantage in the West German and French markets by using their political power to ensure the consumption of their products in their domestic markets. This allows the real income produced by their economies to accrue to them as earnings to be used as investment capital. The concentration of investment capital in the hands of the politically dominant entrepreneurs of Western Europe's other states in turn allows these entrepreneurs to control the demand for labor by investing capital in the most profitable ways.

West Germany and France also affect the consumption of the real income produced by the other West European economies and the use of the labor forces in these economies by producing goods and services for export and by investing capital. The two states affect this consumption by penetrating the others' domestic markets with goods and services generally more remunerative than those imported from them and by investing capital in Western Europe's other economies in order to produce goods and services that satisfy some of the demands of their populations. West Germany and France affect the use of the labor force by creating a demand for labor that their domestic labor forces alone can not satisfy and that therefore requires the importation of labor.

West Germany and France will determine the political organization of the means of production on the territories of Western Europe's other states unless and until these states acquire greater political autonomy. Without such autonomy, those West European states whose domestic political and economic exigencies are most compatible with those of West Germany and France will fare best and will least desire change. On the other hand, those West European states whose domestic political and economic exigencies are least compatible with those of West Germany and France will fare worst and will desire change most. In any case, for as long as the distribution of power remains to their advantage, West Germany and France will have high levels of productivity, high *per capita* incomes, and very diversified internal production.[9]

The EEC and the CAP

West Germany and France made the Common Agricultural Policy (CAP) the EEC's pivot because agriculture is the basis of economic activity and its costs are the basis of wages and the cost of living and, therefore, of industrial costs.[10] The CAP's fundamental purpose is to insure that the EEC's agriculture may be a viable source of surplus capital to be accumulated and invested according to the EEC's political dictates, or according to the demands created principally by West Germany and France. For this reason, the two states made the EEC the CAP's custodian.

The CAP is a policy of international agricultural protectionism that makes the EEC a closed economic system within the international economy for the accumulation of capital through the agricultural sectors of the EEC states. It reserves their domestic markets for the nearly exclusive consumption of EEC agricultural products.[11]

By opposition and neglect West Germany and France have retarded the equivalent development of the EEC's other policies such as competition and industrial, energy, fiscal, fisheries, monetary, regional, and social and transport, because their development—with perhaps the exception of energy, fisheries, and transport—could undermine severely the two states' political dominance over Western Europe's other states by transferring authority to the EEC's institutions that would be influenced by the other EEC states. These institutions could develop "European interests" different from West German or French interests.

In addition, West Germany and France made the CAP the EEC's pivot because it satisfied their reciprocal interests. Besides securing the political support of West German and French farmers for their countries' regimes, the CAP's price supports and protectionism for the EEC's agricultural products guaranteed to French farmers—whose 1957 production already exceeded domestic demand—a market for their surpluses, a high and stable price for their products, and therefore a high return on their investments. In return, France accepted the elimination of barriers to commerce within the EEC, which therefore allowed the EEC to become a market open to West German industrialists, already net exporters in 1957.

The CAP minimizes the EEC's dependence on external food supplies by guaranteeing the viability of the EEC's agriculture. Moreover, the export of the surpluses created by the CAP's excessive price supports aids the EEC states in offsetting the high cost of energy, approximately 70 percent of which is imported.

West Germany and France could undermine their dominance over the other EEC states by mismanaging the CAP. Should the CAP's price supports and protectionism for the EEC's agricultural products oblige the EEC to expend more capital to maintain the CAP than the EEC's agriculture can provide the EEC, the CAP would become counterproductive. In such a situation the EEC's agriculture would no longer provide the EEC with surplus capital but would instead drain capital from the other sectors of the EEC states' economies. Such a depletion of capital would adversely affect the performance of these economies by hindering the accumulation of capital for productive investment and could, consequently, create political unrest among the EEC states.

The EEC, or the De Jure Rules of the Game

When Italy, as an original signatory of the Treaty of Rome, became one of the EEC's six founding members, its integration into the international economy under American hegemony reached its highest expression to date. The political and economic relationships of institutionalized market policy integration established by the treaty are the *de jure* "rules of the game" that determine how the EEC states may legitimately respond to the exigencies of international economic competition. The two fundamental rules concern intra-EEC competition and competition between the EEC and other states. For the former, the EEC states agreed to eliminate barriers to trade and to the mobility of capital and labor. For non-EEC states, the EEC states agreed to establish common customs tariffs and a common commercial policy.[12] Moreover, the treaty establishes the EEC's two principles of integration: the prohibition of falsified economic competition and the equalization of progress.[13]

For the EEC states the Treaty of Rome gives to the prohibition of falsified economic competition de facto prevalence over the equalization of progress. The treaty's "rule" concerning intra-EEC competition (implicitly legitimized by the free enterprise ideology) limits the EEC states' market policy authority and therefore their effective political control over the relationships established between their economies. This limitation of political control determines before the fact the way in which the EEC's institutions and states can legitimately attempt to equalize progress in the EEC. The equalization of progress is thus an ideological palliative in a treaty whose dominant free enterprise ideology reflects American hegemony over Western Europe. It also legitimizes an economic system that in practice rewards the EEC's strong states by giving them the greater share of the benefits derived from their relationships with the EEC's weak states.

The De Facto Rules of the Game Imposed on Italy under the Northwestern Elite

Western Europe's integration under American hegemony offered Italy's northwestern elite political security and economic uncertainty by forcing it to accept two existing conditions that affected its management of the Italian economy. The first condition obliged the elite to expose entrepreneurs to intense international economic competition by increasing the mobility of commerce, capital, and labor between the Italian economy and other economic systems, principally those of Western Europe. Through the principal exponent of its interests, the DC, the second condition made the elite legitimize its dominance in Italy by organizing mass social consensus and by increasing prosperity.

These conditions affected the northwestern elite's management of the Italian economy by establishing the actual "rules of the game" that determine how it might respond to the exigencies of international economic competition and political legitimation. The first condition limited its market policy authority and therefore its effective political control over the relationships established between the Italian economy and other economic systems by determining which measures of economic intervention it might be able to implement legitimately. The second condition obliged it to risk its political legitimacy by accepting responsibility for the national economy's performance and by promising its positive performance. Its response to the exigencies of international economic competition and political legitimation, within the context of the established rules, determined the political organization of the means of production on Italian territory.

These conditions put the northwestern elite in a paradoxical situation since the first condition limited its control over the Italian economy's performance, for which the second condition obliged it to accept responsibility. On the one hand, the second condition obliged the northwestern elite to develop its political capacity to create increasing prosperity; the northwestern elite hoped to legitimize its dominance in Italy by gaining the greatest possible benefits from the relationships established between the Italian economy and other economic systems. On the other hand, the first condition undermined its efforts to allow the Italian economy to sustain the competition of economic systems initially more developed or managed by initially more dominant states; the first condition rewarded the superior strength of these systems by giving them the greater share of the benefits derived from their relationships with the Italian economy.

Therefore the northwestern elite had to concern itself more with the exigencies of international economic competition than with the domestic demands of political legitimation. In order to legitimize its dominance in Italy, the northwestern elite had to legitimize a political organization of the means of production on Italian territory that might give to the economic system of the northwest the greatest possible competitive advantage in the international economy.[14] Were the economic system of the northwest unable to sustain such competition because the first condition undermined excessively the system's competitiveness, or were the northwestern elite unable to legitimize a suitable political organization of the means of production on Italian territory, with its domestic repercussions, the northwestern elite's political legitimacy would suffer greatly. Such a situation could persuade it to pursue its best interests by changing or breaking the established rules. However, constrained to accept Western Europe's integration under American hegemony, the northwestern elite could only hope that the measures taken to sustain international competition would not create disaffections that the Left could champion.

PART III
The European Economic Community's Unbalanced Integration and Italy in the International Division of Labor

5

The European Economic Community and Italy's Commercial Exchange

THE VOLUME OF Italy's commercial exchange reflects the development stimulated by the increased mobility of capital, labor, and commerce between Italy and the other EEC states. Between 1953 and 1963, the annual value of Italian exports increased from LIT 942 billion to LIT 3,706 billion (or from $1.5 billion to $5.9 billion yearly).[1] One-third of this increase occurred between 1953 and 1957, two-thirds between 1958 and 1962.[2] Italian exports, if set at 100 in 1953, reached 180 in 1957 and 205 in 1964. Italian exports of manufactured goods doubled between 1953 and 1957 and then tripled between 1957 and 1964, while world exports increased by 30 percent between 1953 and 1957 and by 56 percent between 1957 and 1964.[3] Moreover, between 1953 and 1963, Italian exports to European countries rose from little more than LIT 600 billion to more than LIT 2,000 billion yearly, while annual exports to Africa and Asia increased from LIT 200 billion to LIT 450 billion.[4] On the other hand, the volume of Italian exports to the United States and Canada remained practically unchanged at about 10 percent of total exports.[5] In 1963, in terms of value, 67 percent of Italian exports satisfied European demand, while the remaining 33 percent satisfied North American demand (see table 4).

The Italian economy's performance was conditioned by its commercial exchange in general but especially by its exchanges with other EEC member states and less so with Western Europe's other countries, as the data in tables 5 through 8 indicate.

From 1954 to 1971, Italy's share of world exports of manufactured goods increased from 2.7 to 6.8 percent, while the EEC's portion rose from 31.9 to 43.6 percent.[6]

During the 1970s, Italian exports reached an average 6.4 percent of the export markets of all industrial countries (see table 9). In this period, the average volume of exports exceeded imports but the average value of imports exceeded exports.

The structure of Italy's commercial exchange, both in terms of the

Table 4

Percent Change of Italy's Commercial Exchange, 1957–1964
(in Constant 1963 Prices)

	1957–58	1959–60	1961–62	1963–64
Imports from the EEC	3.3	42.9	21.5	11.2
Imports from the rest of the world	8.7	20.1	13.5	7.8
Exports to the EEC	11.4	37.0	23.9	14.2
Exports to the rest of the world	18.9	15.3	11.8	7.8

Source: Franca Falcone, "Effetti dell'integrazione economica europea sulla struttura delle esportazioni italiane" (The effects of European economic integration on the structure of Italian exports), Rassegna economica, no. 5 (September/October 1975): 1144.

types of goods and services exchanged and in terms of their geographic distribution, reflects the economy's subsidiary role in the upper ranks of the international division of labor. Demand in the EEC for the manufactured goods produced by Italy's traditional or labor-intensive sectors was the primary cause of increased exports; in 1963, exports of manufactured goods produced by the capital-intensive sectors represented only 15 percent of total exports.[7] During the 1960s and 1970s, Italy imported primarily raw materials and intermediate goods and exported primarily medium-value-added consumer and investment goods.[8]

During the 1960s, Italian exports of agricultural products as a part of total exports increased in absolute terms but decreased in relative terms. During the 1970s, they decreased in absolute terms because demand in the EEC for Italian products concerned principally traditional manufactured goods and because the CAP favored both Continental agricultural products and the agricultural producers, already more efficient and productive, of the EEC's more dominant economic systems. External demand for north-central Italy's processed agricultural products caused the increase in agricultural exports during the 1960s. During the 1960s and 1970s, exports of the Mezzogiorno's (or Mediterranean) agricultural products first increased little, then decreased (see tables 10 and 11). During the 1970s and 1980s, Italy imported progressively greater quantities of agricultural products.

Italy effects the principal share of its commercial exchange with the countries of Western Europe, especially the other EEC member states. The United States provided 10 percent of Italy's commercial exchange

Table 5

Commercial Exchange (Goods and Services)
as Percentage of GDP

	1958		1965		1973		1977		1981	
	Imp.	Exp.	Imp.	Exp.	Imp.	Exp.	Imp.	Exp.	Imp.	Exp.
Italy	12.0	11.0	13.0	13.9	20.2	17.0	24.5	24.0	28.5	24.7
EEC	17.9	19.0	18.4	18.5	22.5	23.0	26.7	27.4	29.6	29.1

Source: Helen Wallace, William Wallace, and Carole Webb, eds., *Policy-making in the European Community*, 2d ed. (Chichester: John Wiley and Sons, 1983), 122.

Table 6

Percent Change of Italy's Commercial Exchange, 1951-1971
(in Constant 1963 Prices)

	1951-54	1954-58	1958-62	1962-65	1965-68	1968-71
Imports from the EEC	26.5	4.4	32.2	6.3	16.5	17.8
Imports from the rest of the world	6.0	11.3	16.8	6.5	9.5	10.6
Total imports	9.5	9.8	20.0	6.4	11.5	12.9
Exports to the EEC	5.8	17.2	30.4	18.8	20.1	13.3
Exports to the rest of the world	11.1	15.9	16.6	10.9	8.8	7.2
Total exports	10.2	16.1	16.5	12.9	11.7	8.9

Source: Franca Falcone, "Effetti dell'integrazione economica europea sulla struttura delle esportazioni italiane" (The effects of European economic integration on the structure of Italian exports), *Rassegna economica*, no. 5 (September/October 1975): 1142-43.

Table 7

Intra-EEC Commercial Exchange, 1952-1971,
as Percentage of Italy's Commercial Exchange

	1952	1955	1958	1962	1966	1971
Imports from the EEC as % of total imports	16.5	21.8	18.4	27.1	27.6	34.3
Exports to the EEC as % of total imports	15.1	16.1	15.4	23.6	27.6	36.8

Source: Franca Falcone, "Effetti dell'integrazione economica europea sulla struttura delle esportazioni italiane" (The effects of European economic integration on the structure of Italian exports), *Rassegna economica,* no. 5 (September/October 1975): 1142-43.

Table 8

Intra-EEC Commercial Exchange, 1958-1980,
as Percentage of Total Commercial Exchange (Goods Only)

	1958		1965		1973		1977		1980	
	Imp.	Exp.	Imp.	Exp.	Imp.	Exp.	Imp.	Exp.	Imp.	Exp.
Italy	29.4	33.7	37.3	48.8	49.4	52.4	43.5	48.6	44.1	49.0
EEC	33.9	35.5	43.3	46.9	52.2	53.9	49.8	51.7	47.9	53.6

Source: Helen Wallace, William Wallace, and Carole Webb, eds., *Policy-making in the European Community,* 2d ed. (Chichester: John Wiley and Sons, 1983), 123.

Table 9

World Exports of Manufactured Goods

	Quota percentage of Italian exports in the export markets of all industrial countries	Volume		Value (LIT)		Value ($)		Price (LIT)	
		Imp.	Exp.	Imp.	Exp.	Imp.	Exp.	Imp.	Exp.
1970	6.3	15.6	7.1	20.0	12.6	20.0	12.6	3.8	5.2
1971	6.5	0.4	7.6	5.8	13.4	5.8	13.4	5.5	5.4
1972	6.7	10.9	12.7	13.8	15.9	22.3	24.6	2.6	2.8
1973	5.9	11.2	1.2	45.1	19.8	44.0	19.5	30.4	18.4
1974	6.0	- 5.5	7.7	61.9	52.6	47.0	36.8	71.3	41.7
1975	6.5	-10.7	3.7	- 5.7	15.3	- 6.1	14.8	5.6	11.2
1976	6.2	15.6	11.7	45.8	36.3	14.4	7.0	26.2	22.0
1977	6.7	- 0.3	7.6	15.1	28.2	9.0	20.9	15.8	19.2
1978	6.9	7.4	10.8	12.8	18.8	17.1	23.4	5.0	7.2
Avg.	6.4	5.0	7.8	23.9	23.7	19.3	19.2	18.5	14.8

Source: Data from Donald C. Templeman, *The Italian Economy* (New York: Praeger Publishers, 1981), 180, 181, and 185. For Templeman, "industrial countries" include Austria, Belgium, Canada, Denmark, the United Kingdom, France, Italy, Japan, the Netherlands, Norway, Sweden, Switzerland, the United States, and West Germany.

during the 1960s; the American share declined to 7 percent during the 1970s and remained constant in the 1980s.[10] During the 1960s, Italy's commercial exchange with the oil-producing and exporting countries increased because it became increasingly dependent on foreign sources for its energy supplies, 82 percent of which are imported (see table 12).[11]

An ever-greater number of Italian entrepreneurs produce goods not for the Italian market but rather for foreign markets (those of states both weaker and stronger than Italy). Italy's participation in an EEC dominated politically by West Germany and France under a tempered American hegemony increases the nation's involvement in the process of capital accumulation among the EEC states principally to the advantage and benefit of the West German and French economies. This reduces the prospects of maximum remuneration and of a stable demand in the Italian market relative to many foreign markets.

According to a study issued in July 1985 by the Istituto Commercio Estero (ICE), Italy's foreign trade institute, the number of Italian businesses selling goods abroad increased from 48,321 in 1972 to slightly more than 86,000 in 1985 (an increase of about 78 percent).

Table 10

Importation of Citrus Fruit by Area
and Italy's Export Quota of This Exchange

	EEC		EFTA			USSR/Central Europe		
	Total	From Italy		Total	From Italy		Total	From Italy	
	.000 T	.000 T	%	.000 T	.000 T	%	.000 T	.000 T	%
1961-63	1,670	79	4.7	726	99	13.6	162	10	6.2
1964-66	1,975	74	3.7	811	97	12.0	362	16	4.9
1967-69	1,923	65	3.4	813	83	10.2	485	31	6.4

Source: Marcello Gorgoni, "Agrumicoltura italiana e mercato estero" (Italian citrus fruit production and the foreign market), *Rassegna economica*, no. 3 (May/June 1973): 772.

Table 11

Percentage of Mediterranean Agricultural Products
Imported by the EEC from the Mezzogiorno,
1969-1975

	Citrus Fruits	Vegetables	Dried Fruits
1969-70	7.7	19.6	25.5
1974-75	4.9	17.2	17.0

Source: Data from Vincenzo Guizzi, *Comunità europea e sviluppo del Mezzogiorno* (The European community and the Mezzogiorno's development) (Milan: Giuffrè, 1978), 183.

Table 12

Italy's Percent Distribution of Imports and Exports, by Geographic Area, 1970-1978

	Percent Distribution	
	Imports	Exports
EEC	43	45
Non-EEC Western Europe	19	22
Oil-producing and exporting countries	17	10
United States	7	7
Canada	1	1
Japan	1	1
Others	12	14

Source: Data from Donald C. Templeman, *The Italian Economy* (New York: Praeger Publishers, 1981), chap. 7.

The geographic distribution of these businesses reflects the Mezzogiorno's subaltern position in the Italian economy: 70 percent are located in northern Italy, 20 percent in central Italy, and 10 percent in the Mezzogiorno.

In recent years a growing number of the entrepreneurs of central Italy and the Mezzogiorno has sought higher remuneration by penetrating foreign markets rather than selling greater quantities of products in the Italian market. Of the more than 86,000 Italian businesses selling goods abroad, the export earnings of the 30 percent located in central Italy and in the Mezzogiorno increased from 21.2 percent of Italy's total export earnings in 1978 to 24.1 percent in 1983. The export earnings of the 70 percent located in northern Italy decreased correspondingly from 78.8 percent of Italy's total export earnings in 1978 to 75.9 percent in 1983. Between 1978 and 1983, the number of businesses selling goods abroad increased more in Campania and in Puglia (two of the Mezzogiorno's regions), and to a lesser extent in the Veneto (a region of the economic system of the center/northeast), than in the country's other regions.[12]

6
The European Economic Community and the Italian Lira

The Italian Lira and the International Monetary Hierarchy

THE ITALIAN LIRA is an authentic currency because nation-states accept it as a unit of account, an instrument of exchange and a fund of value.[1] The lira derives its value from the political organization of the means of production on Italian territory. Consequently its value compared to other currencies derives from and reflects Italy's ability (1) to influence the political organization of the international economy's means of production and (2) to influence the political organization of the means of production on Italian territory. In short, the lira's value reflects the Italian economy's place and function in the international economy and therefore its role in the international division of labor.

The lira's value compared to the United States dollar and the West German mark indicates most clearly the Italian economy's subsidiary role in an EEC politically dominated mainly by West Germany because the United States and West Germany have more ability than Italy to influence both the political organization of the means of production on Italian territory and of the international economy's means of production. The dollar, which forms the largest part of the official reserves held by central banks in the world, is currently the only authentic reserve currency in the international economy. It is the currency considered the most valid international means of payment by other states for two reasons: (1) the United States is the state most able to influence the international economy and therefore to determine the international division of labor; and (2) the United States is the only state that can use its own currency to finance its deficits in the international economy.[2] The West German mark is an actual reserve currency in the international economy. That is, it is a valid international means of payment second only to the dollar because West Germany's political and economic dominance in Western Europe gives this state a great ability to influence the political organization of the international economy's means of production and therefore to determine the international division of labor.³

The most common indicator of the lira's value compared to the dollar and the mark is the exchange rate between these currencies—that is, their politically accepted ratio of value expressed as each currency's price in the others' monetary denominations. Such an indicator is misleading, however, because it expresses the ratio of the extrinsic value between these currencies (or each currency's buying power in the others' economies), not the ratio of the intrinsic value between them (that is, an adjusted comparison of their buying power within their respective economies). The difference between the ratio of the extrinsic and intrinsic values between these currencies, called seigniorage, accrues to the United States and to West Germany at Italy's expense because Italy occupies a subaltern position compared to these countries in the international economy.⁴

American hegemony over Western Europe insured that the United States and West Germany had the ability to appropriate seigniorage from Italy. The United States exercised its power in the international system in such a way as to foster the creation of a politically acceptable complex of the ratios of value between the various currencies in the world. Thus emerged an international monetary regime whose institutional mechanics and formal political commitments obliged the world's various states to maintain the fluctuations of the exchange rates between their currencies within politically accepted margins, but did not oblige the dominant states to compensate the weaker states for the value lost in the form of seigniorage. In short, the United States fostered the creation of an international monetary regime that maintained both the stability of exchange rates between currencies and the advantages and benefits enjoyed by the dominant states. The resultant Bretton Woods international monetary regime (22 July 1944–15 August 1971), which became fully operative in 1946, had three fundamental characteristics: (1) the convertibility of the United States Dollar for gold; (2) the convertibility of the currencies of Western Europe's major states for gold beginning in December 1958; and (3) fixed exchange rates between currencies, whose extrinsic value could fluctuate no more than ± 1 percent from parity except in cases of official devaluation.⁵

An international monetary nonregime began on 15 August 1971 when the United States unilaterally terminated the Bretton Woods regime by devaluing the dollar and suspending its convertibility for gold. Under the Smithsonian Agreement of December 1971, the central banks of the Group of Ten (that is, the major industrialized countries in the world: Belgium, Canada, France, Italy, Japan, the Netherlands, Sweden, the United Kingdom, the United States, and West Germany) committed themselves to maintain the fluctuations of the exchange rates between their currencies within a margin of ± 2.25 percent compared to the dollar. On 19 March 1973 the Group of Ten, together with Switzerland (then an associate member, now a full member) and the minor EEC member states (Denmark, Ireland, and Luxembourg), renounced the Smithsonian Agreement because it established fluctuation margins without establishing the institutional mechanics and formal political commitments that might govern how the central banks of the adhering countries might collectively maintain the prescribed parity between their currencies.[6] In the meantime, under the Basle Accord of 21 March 1972, the EEC member states established "central exchange rates" between their currencies, put these exchange rates into effect on 10 April 1972, and agreed to maintain their fluctuations within a margin of ± 2.25 percent. In 1973, Sweden and Norway committed themselves to the Basle Accord, but Italy renounced it in February 1973 for the same reason for which it had renounced the Smithsonian Agreement.[7] In April 1973 the EEC states created the European Monetary Cooperation Fund (FECOM), which was charged to regulate the financial operations undertaken by the central banks of the EEC states to maintain the parity of their currencies relative to the "central exchange rates" established under the Basle Accord.[8]

Under the Kingston Agreement of January 1976, the Group of Ten, together with Denmark, Ireland, Luxembourg, and Switzerland, terminated the international monetary nonregime by establishing a new international monetary regime based on the coordination by their central banks of flexible exchange rates between currencies.[9] Under the Brussels Accord of 5 December 1978, the EEC states created the European Monetary System (EMS), which became effective on 13 March 1979 and recommitted them to maintain the fluctuations of the exchange rates between their currencies within a margin of ± 2.25 percent, relative to the "central exchange rates" of these currencies, except in the cases of the Irish pound and the Italian lira, which were accorded fluctuation margins of ± 6 percent.[10] Since 1984 the Bank of Italy has been favorably disposed toward a reduction of the lira's fluctuation margin from ± 6 percent to ± 2.25 percent. However, the Italian government has made the reduction contingent upon the United Kingdom's full participation in the European Monetary System, something that, as of 1988, had not yet come about.[11]

The Italian Lira and the United States Dollar

Neither the exact amount of seigniorage gained by the United States and by West Germany at Italy's expense, nor the correct ratio of the intrinsic value between the dollar, the mark, and the lira can be readily ascertained because the field of economics has invented neither a scientific formula that may quantify the relationship between value and price nor a concrete and universal model of analysis. In short, economics lacks universal criteria and means with which currencies may be compared in order to determine their real ratio of value. The ability to determine their ratio presupposes the ability to make a universal comparison between currencies that derive their value from the political organization of different, particular means of production. The ability to determine correctly the exact amount of seigniorage gained by the dominant states at the expense of the subordinate states presupposes the ability to differentiate, especially quantitatively, between the intrinsic and the extrinsic value of currencies.

Nonetheless, the political and economic relationships established between Italy and the United States allow some observations on the comparative value of the lira and the dollar and therefore some observations on the Italian economy's place and function in the international economy. Although Italy's commercial exchange is mainly with Western Europe, especially the EEC states, it has become more dependent than the other EEC states on the dollar as an international means of payment and calculates the value of a greater share of its imports than its exports in dollars.[12] A study issued in July 1984 by the Commercial Bank of Italy compares the payment structure of Italy's commercial exchange with that of the EEC (see table 13).

The payment structure of Italy's commercial exchange ties its balance of payments to the dollar, whose extrinsic value, more than that of any other currency, determines the cost of Italian imports. On the one hand, for every ten lire lost by the dollar in its exchange rate with the lira, the cost of Italian imports decreases by LIT 480 billion.[13] On the other hand, a strong dollar relative to the lira, by increasing the price of Italian imports, produces three consequences. First, an econometric study issued in December 1983 by the Bank of Italy revealed that, under the conditions then prevailing, when valued at LIT 1,600, the dollar was responsible for three percentage points of Italy's inflation rate.[14] Second, the average dollar/lira exchange rate in 1984 ($1 = LIT 1,750) against the dollar/lira exchange rate in 1983 ($1 = LIT 1,519) constrained Italy to disburse LIT 2,935 billion more in 1984 than in 1983 to cover the cost of imports (see table 15). Last, a

Table 13

Percent Distribution of Currencies Used as
International Means of Payment in Commercial Exchange

	Country's Own Currency	U.S. Dollar	Other Currencies
Imports:			
Italy	20.0	43.0	37.0
EEC Average	28.3	28.5	43.2
Exports:			
Italy	32.0	34.0	34.0
EEC Average	50.7	16.6	32.7

Source: *La Repubblica*, 26 July 1984, 27.

strong dollar hinders Italy's ability to take advantage of the reductions of the prices of raw materials (see table 15): although fewer dollars may be needed to purchase raw materials, more lire are needed to purchase dollars.

American influence over an Italy dominated politically and economically by its northwestern elite has made the dollar Italy's principal international means of payment. The dollar drains value in the form of seigniorage from the Italian economy through Italy's commercial exchange with the international economy, and especially through its importation of petroleum, because the dollar's extrinsic value relative to the lira determines the cost of Italian imports. Should the dollar prove too costly for the Italian economy, the northwestern elite, or another future ruling class, could decide to replace the dollar with another international means of payment.

Italy and the ECU

The European Currency Unit (ECU), created by the Brussels Accord of 5 December 1978 to replace the European Unit of Account (EUA), could in all probability replace the dollar as Italy's principal international means of payment. In the 1980s the ECU was not an authentic currency but rather another EEC unit of account—that is, a redenomination of a part of the gold and dollars already held as reserve assets by the central banks of the EEC states.[15] The ECU's value derives from and reflects the composite value of the currencies of the EEC states: each currency contributes a portion of the ECU's value according to a coefficient prescribed collectively by the finance ministers of the EEC states (except Italy, which is represented by its treasury minister).

All the EEC states except West Germany have been disposed to transform the ECU from the EEC's unit of account into the EEC's authentic currency because such a transformation would allow them to terminate their dependence on the dollar by making the ECU equal, if not superior, to the dollar. West Germany has been consistently opposed to such a transformation since it would deprive the West German economy of the advantages derived from the mark's dominance over the other EEC currencies by terminating its role as a de facto reserve currency in the international economy. Should the political and economic costs of an EEC divided monetarily against the dollar outweigh the advantages gained for the West German economy by the

Table 14

The Average Dollar/Lira Exchange Rate, 1983-1984, by Categories of the Italian Economy (in Billions of LIT)

	1983 ($1=LIT 1,519)				1984 ($1=LIT 1,750)		
			Of which lira value calculated in dollars		Cost added to Imports	Potential gain for Exports	Loss or gain
	Imports	Exports	Imports	Exports			
Agriculture/Zootechny	10,000	3,000	4,240	389	644	69	- 575
Foodstuffs and Related Processing	10,000	4,800	2,000	1,536	300	234	- 66
Textiles	3,900	9,300	780	2,139	120	325	205
Clothing	931	4,900	232	1,470	36	223	187
Footwear	221	4,600	91	368	14	56	42
Furniture and Wood Products	1,727	3,000	345	768	53	117	64
Transportation Vehicles	9,000	12,000	1,035	5,484	157	834	677
Machines and Appliances	8,360	19,720	1,546	8,874	235	1,349	1,114
Precision Mechanics	4,600	3,300	1,480	963	225	147	- 78
Ferrous Metallurgy	2,958	4,956	393	2,656	235	404	169
Non-Ferrous Met.	6,073	4,214	3,692	2,162	562	329	- 233
Chemicals	11,800	7,900	2,478	3,318	377	504	175
Petroleum and Derivatives	36,203	5,812	35,630	5,521	5,5420	804	-4,616
Total							-2,935

Source: *La Repubblica*, 9-10 September 1984, 3.

mark's dominance over the other EEC currencies, West Germany would have to accept the ECU's transformation from the EEC's unit of account to the EEC's authentic currency.[16]

Italy remains one of the EEC's principal proponents of such a transformation because it could aid the northwestern elite in minimizing the negative consequences of the EEC's unbalanced integration for the Italian economy. It would allow Italy to terminate both its dependence on the dollar and the mark's dominance over the lira. In order to terminate the mark's dominance over the other EEC currencies, Italy must attempt to overcome West German resistance to the ECU's transformation by organizing among the EEC states the broadest possible political consensus for such a transformation.

The Italian Lira, the EUA/ECU, and the West German Mark

The relationship between the percent contribution of the lira and the mark to the value of the EUA/ECU is the most accurate indicator

Table 15

Adjusted Index of the Prices of Goods
on the International Market
(1977=100)

	Prices in Dollars	Prices in Lire
December 1982	195.17	313.41
January 1983	194.41	307.41
February	178.83	286.98
March	177.22	289.97
April	177.59	295.81
May	178.84	301.30
June	179.93	312.02
July	179.64	325.32
August	181.16	327.40
September	180.88	330.22
October	180.74	326.29
November	180.38	335.48

Source: *La Repubblica*, 10 January 1984, 31.

Table 16

Contribution of the EEC Currencies
to the Value of the EUA/ECU, May 1975–May 1984
(in Percentages)

	May 1975(1)	May 1984(2)	Absolute change(3) (2)-(1)=(3)	Relative Change (4) $\frac{(3) \times 100}{(1)} = (4)$
DM	27.10	37.03	9.93	36.64
FF	21.83	16.72	-5.11	-23.41
L	15.72	14.99	-0.73	- 4.64
HFL	9.13	11.35	2.22	24.32
LIT	13.40	7.89	-5.51	-41.12
FB	8.03	7.92	-0.11	- 1.37
DKR	3.05	2.65	-0.40	-13.11
IRL	1.30	1.04	-0.26	-20.00
FLUX	.31	.30	-0.01	- 3.23

Note: This table is an elaboration of the data presented in Appendix A (table 45).

DM = West German mark HFL = Dutch florin DKR = Danish crown
FF = French franc LIT = Italian lira IRL = Irish pound
L = British pound FB = Belgian franc FLUX = Luxembourg franc

of the comparative value of these currencies because a fixed and stable coefficient mediates each currency's contribution. Between May 1975 and May 1984 the mark's contribution to the value of the EUA/ECU increased by 9.93 percent (from 27.10 percent to 37.03 percent), while the lira's contribution decreased by 5.51 percent (from 13.40 percent to 7.89). The lira's contribution to the value of the EUA/ECU was 49.95 percent of the mark's contribution in May 1975, 21.31 percent in May 1984. In short, between May 1975 and May 1984, the lira's value decreased by 15.44 percent in absolute terms and 112.70 percent in relative terms against the mark's value; the value of the lira's percent contribution to the value of the EUA/ECU as a percentage of the mark's percent contribution decreased by 28.14 percent in absolute terms, 132.05 percent in relative terms.

West Germany's dominance over the other EEC states manifests itself in the value relationships between the mark and the other EEC currencies in two ways: first, the mark's contribution to the value of the EUA/ECU is clearly the greatest among the contributions of the EEC currencies, and second, between May 1975 and May 1984 the mark's contribution to the value of the EUA/ECU increased greatly, mainly at the expense of the Italian lira and French franc, whose contributions—together with those of the other EEC currencies, except the Dutch florin—decreased, as table 16 shows.

The comparative value of the lira and the other EEC currencies reflects the Italian economy's subordinate position among the economies of the other major EEC states in that between May 1975 and May 1984 (and not only in this period) the other EEC currencies gained value on the lira (see tables 17–20). Between 1973 and 1976, the lira's depreciation cost the Italian economy, through its commercial exchange, $7.3 billion, while the mark's appreciation earned for the West German economy $2 billion.[17]

7
The European Economic Community and Foreign Capital in Italy and in the Mezzogiorno

Foreign Investments in the Mezzogiorno

THE FOREIGN CAPITAL invested in the Mezzogiorno comes from the United States, the EEC states, Australia, Canada, Japan, Lebanon, Liechtenstein, Sweden, Switzerland, and the EEC's agencies.[1] Italy's law no. 43 of 7 February 1956, modified by law no. 169 of 11 March 1965, regulates the investments of foreign capital on Italian territory and provides that investors may transfer out of the country all the capital invested productively, together with all the dividends and profits realized.[2]

Foreign investors operate in Italy so that the country may continue to play its traditional role in the international division of labor and so that one or more of its three economic systems may serve either as a market for the goods and services produced by their investments or as a territorial base for the production of goods and services to be exchanged elsewhere. The principal determinant of foreign investments in the Mezzogiorno, in comparison with the economic systems of the northwest and the center/northeast, is the policy of incentives. Before the Italian government abolished salary discrimination between the Mezzogiorno and the rest of Italy in 1969, foreign investors operated in the Mezzogiorno in order to take advantage of the lower cost of labor.[3]

These investors consider the Mezzogiorno not a market but rather a territorial base for the production of goods and services to be exchanged elsewhere, two-thirds of which are exported principally to north-central Italy and to Western Europe's other states, especially the EEC states. One-quarter of the businesses producing goods and services in the Mezzogiorno with the participation of foreign capital produce primarily for export; two-thirds export a sizable portion of their goods, while only 10 percent produce for the Mezzogiorno. The quality of the foreign investments in the Mezzogiorno reflects the area's inferior position in the international economy. Investors employ their capital not to promote research and development, reserved for the more dominant economic systems, but rather to produce and assemble parts of some products.[4]

Private Foreign Capital in Italy

Although the EEC states collectively, in comparison with the United States, may manage more plants and may own and participate in more companies in Italy, the United States, responsible for 75 percent of the foreign capital invested in the Mezzogiorno and LIT 10,000 billion of investments in the Italian economy, is by far the single largest source of the foreign capital invested in Italy.[5] Foreign investors, as independent entrepreneurs or as minority or majority participants with Italian investors, produce goods and services in Italy according to the figures in table 17, which refer to the eight largest sources of foreign capital invested in Italy.

Table 17

Eight Largest Sources of Foreign Capital Invested in Italy

	Companies		Branches
	Number	% of Total	
Belgium	33	2.1	58
France	171	11.2	311
Netherlands	48	3.1	100
United Kingdom	206	13.5	372
West Germany	271	17.8	389
EEC Subtotal	729	47.7	1,230
Sweden	47	3.1	80
Switzerland	174	11.4	288
United States	576	37.8	1,048
Total	1,526	100.0	

Source: *La Repubblica*, 2 January 1985, 35.

The European Economic Community and Foreign Capital 83

In Italy there were 820 companies in 1984 whose capital is predominantly or entirely foreign (see table 18). These companies employ 424,000 people.[6] Investors from the eight largest sources of foreign capital provide at least 50 percent of the capital in 797 (52 percent) of the 1,526 companies producing goods and services on Italian territory with the participation of foreign capital according to table 19.

The influx of foreign capital into Italy in 1983, 1984, and 1985 reflects the country's strategic importance to investors, who want to influence as much as possible the political organization of the means of production on Italian territory so that Italy may continue to play its traditional role in the international division of labor. These investors legitimized their interest by creating a perception of Italy as a most desirable site for the investment of capital.[7] They demonstrated their interest in many significant ways. For example, on 25 July 1984, the EEC approved the expenditure of LIT 1,084 billion of investment capital in north-central Italy and LIT 800 billion in the Mezzogiorno, principally through north-central Italy's private oligopolies, in order to facilitate the restructuring of Italy's automotive industry.[8] On 7 August 1984, Electrolux (Sweden) became Zanussi's controlling shareholder by purchasing 49 percent of Zanussi's stock for LIT 32 billion.[9] On 4 September 1984 a consortium of foreign banks covered $500 million of bonds issued by Italy's Ministry of the Treasury, which had placed these bonds on the Eurodollar market one month earlier in order to facilitate the reconstruction of some of the Mezzogiorno's areas affected by the earthquake of 23 November 1980.[10] From 28 to 30 March 1985, more than one hundred of the world's largest private investment agencies attended a "summit meeting" organized by Euromobiliare in Florence to elaborate programs for the future investment of capital in Italy.[11] On 2 April 1985 a consortium of London's banks covered another $500 million of bonds issued by Italy's Ministry of the Treasury,[12] and on 14 April 1985 the European Investment Bank placed LIT 150 billion of bonds on the Italian market to finance Italian businesses.[13]

The largest share of the foreign capital invested in Italy and in Western Europe is American. In 1983 the United States, by investing $3.8 billion abroad, surpassed its 1980 record of $2.1 billion of foreign investments.[14] In Western Europe it invested $2.2 billion (compared to $797 million in 1982), which represents 57.9 percent of total foreign investments. In London it invested $1.1 billion, 50 percent of the $2.2 billion invested in Western Europe.[15] On 22 December 1983 AT&T (United States) became Olivetti's largest shareholder by purchasing 25 percent of Olivetti's stock for LIT 440 billion ($260 million) with an option to purchase up to 40 percent of its stock.[16] On 24 October 1984

Table 18

Companies Producing Goods and Services in Italy
with Capital Predominantly or Entirely Foreign
by Source of Foreign Capital

	Companies	
	Number	% of Total
Belgium	24	2.9
France	109	13.3
Luxembourg	5	.6
Netherlands	38	4.7
United Kingdom	120	14.6
West Germany	97	11.8
EEC Subtotal	393	47.9
Canada	5	.6
Japan	6	.7
Liechtenstein	7	.9
Sweden	31	3.8
Switzerland	95	11.6
United States	278	33.9
Others	5	.6
Total	820	100.0

Source: La Repubblica, 4/5 March 1984, 30.

Table 19

Level of Foreign Participation in Industrial Activities in Italy
by Eight Largest Sources of Foreign Capital

	Companies in Italy with Capital Predominantly or Entirely Foreign / Companies in Italy with Foreign Capital	% of Total
Belgium	24/33	72.7
France	109/171	63.7
Netherlands	38/48	79.2
United Kingdom	120/206	58.3
West Germany	97/271	35.8
EEC Subtotal	388/729	53.2
Sweden	31/47	66.0
Switzerland	95/174	54.6
United States	278/576	48.3
Total	792/1,526	51.9

Source: Data from *La Repubblica*, 4/5 March 1984, 30, and 2 January 1985, 35.

the Merrill Lynch investment firm (United States), at the head of an international consortium of banks, placed $1 billion of bonds on international money markets on behalf of Italy's Ministry of the Treasury.[17] After a twenty-year absence, in 1984 the United States started to invest again in the Italian stock exchange,[18] and on 8 January 1985 Bechtel (USA) purchased Elc-Elettroconsult.[19]

Foreign investors purchased thirty Italian companies in 1984. Data relative to the seventeen largest are presented in table 20.

Private Foreign Capital in the Mezzogiorno

In 1981, 258 plants employing 78,667 people produced goods and services in the Mezzogiorno with the participation of foreign capital provided by 195 companies, as the data in table 26 show. These statistics compare to 16 plants in 1950, 50 in 1959, 104 in 1964, 150 in 1969, and 223 in 1974.[20]

Table 20

Italian Companies Purchased by Foreign Investors in 1984

Company	Turnover (LIT in billions)	Shares Ceded (%)	Prices Paid[a] (LIT in billions)	Buyers (Country)
Cartiere Fabbri	280	100	210	Mandl Group (U.K.)
Elettronica	180	35	47	Plessey (U.K.)
Fotomec	16	100	8	Ciba (Switzerland)
Isf	90	100	-	Smithkline (USA)
Italchemi	in liquidation	100	20	Glaxo (U.K.)
Landy Freres	45	100	-	Winefoods (USA)
Lazzaroni	55	50	6	Campbell (USA)
Lepetit [b]	272	8	48	Dow Chemical (USA)
Magrini	100	100	76	Merlin Gerin (France)
Maserati	112	5	-	Chrysler (USA)
Neopharmed	17	75	8	Merck (USA)
Pierrel	132	52	80	Fermenta (Sweden)
Ras	2,855	100	700	Allianz (West Germany)
Selvi	10	100	-	3M (USA)
Siel	131.6	100	80	Isc (USA)
Zamberletti	1,566	49	32	Electrolux (Sweden)

Source: *La Repubblica*, 2 January 1985, 35.

[a]The price paid refers only to the purchase price of the stock and does not include the subsequent expenditures necessary to restructure the company.

[b]Dow Chemical already owned 92 percent of the stock.

Table 21

Companies and Plants Producing Goods and Services
in the Mezzogiorno with the Participation of
Foreign Capital in 1981, by Source of Foreign Capital

	Companies		Plants		Employees	
	No.	%	No.	%	No.	%
Belgium	5	2.6	8	3.1	1,071	1.3
France	19	9.7	40	15.5	11,173	14.2
Luxembourg	2	1.0	2	.8	668	.9
Netherlands	8	4.1	13	5.0	4,766	6.1
United Kingdom	21	10.8	21	8.1	2,551	3.2
West Germany	20	10.3	24	9.3	6,787	8.6
EEC Subtotal	75	38.5	108	41.9	27,016	34.3
Australia	2	1.0	9	3.5	837	1.1
Canada	3	1.5	3	1.2	1,852	2.3
Japan	3	1.5	3	1.1	510	.7
Lebanon	1	.5	1	.4	80	.1
Liechtenstein	9	4.6	10	3.9	2,331	3.0
Sweden	3	1.5	6	2.3	2,055	2.6
Switzerland	24	12.3	22	8.5	6,107	7.8
United States	75	38.5	96	37.2	37,879	48.1
Total	195	100.0	258	100.0	78,667	100.0

Source: *Iniziative industriali a partecipazione estera nel Mezzogiorno* (Industrial initiatives with the participation of foreign capital in the Mezzogiorno) (Rome: IASM, 1981), 11.

The quantity of the foreign investments in the Mezzogiorno reflects the area's subordinate position in the international economy. The investors from the eight largest sources of foreign capital in Italy have located only 175 (11.5 percent) of their 1,526 companies in the Mezzogiorno, as table 22 shows.

Foreign investments in the Mezzogiorno have thus far exacerbated the area's disequilibria in part because investors have concentrated their plants in southern Lazio and Campania so that these investments might benefit both from the infrastructure located around and between Rome and Naples and from the geographic proximity of southern Lazio and Campania to the markets of Western Europe, especially the EEC states.[21] Of the 258 plants that produce goods and services in the Mezzogiorno with the participation of foreign capital, 167 (64.7

Table 22

Percentage of Companies in the Mezzogiorno with Foreign Capital by Eight Largest Sources of Foreign Capital in Italy

	No. of Companies in the Mezzogiorno / No. of Companies in Italy	% of Total
Belgium	5/33	15.2
France	19/171	11.1
Netherlands	8/48	16.6
United Kingdom	21/206	10.2
West Germany	20/271	7.4
EEC Subtotal	73/729	10.0
Sweden	3/47	6.4
Switzerland	24/174	13.8
United States	75/576	13.0
Total	175/1,526	11.5

Source: Data from *La Repubblica,* 2 January 1985, 35, and *Iniziative industriali a partecipazione estera nel Mezzogiorno* (Industrial initiatives with the participation of foreign capital in the Mezzogiorno) (Rome: IASM, 1981), 11.

Table 23

Distribution by Region of Plants Producing
Goods and Services in the Mezzogiorno
with Participation of Foreign Capital

	Plants		Employees	
	No.	%	No.	%
Abruzzo	24	9.3	5,089	6.5
Basilicata	3	1.2	445	.6
Calabria	5	1.9	1,234	1.6
Campania	78	30.2	26,315	33.5
Southern Lazio	89	34.5	31,611	40.2
Marche[a]	4	1.6	1,781	2.3
Molise	0	---	0	---
Puglia	22	8.5	6,535	8.3
Sardegna	15	5.8	2,762	3.5
Sicilia	18	7.0	2,895	3.7

Source: *Iniziative industriali a partecipazione estera nel Mezzogiorno* (Industrial initiatives with the participation of foreign capital in the Mezzogiorno) (Rome: IASM, 1981), 12.

[a]The province of Ascoli-Piceno is an area of competence of CASMEZ.

percent) are located in southern Lazio and Campania, 46 (17.8 percent) in Abruzzo and Puglia, 33 (12.8 percent) in Sicilia and Sardegna, 12 (4.7 percent) in Calabria, Marche (Ascoli-Piceno province), and Basilicata, but none in Molise (see table 23).

The percentage of the foreign investments in southern Lazio and in Campania as a percentage of the foreign investments in the 258 plants located in the Mezzogiorno is as follows (in descending order): North America (Canada and the United States), 81 percent; Western Europe non-EEC (Liechtenstein, Sweden, and Switzerland), 79 percent; Western Europe (EEC and non-EEC), 58 percent; EEC, 50 percent; and Oceania/Middle East (Australia, Japan, and Lebanon), 23 percent. The highest concentrations in southern Lazio and in Campania of this foreign capital derive from the investments coming from Lebanon (100 percent), Liechtenstein (90 percent), Switzerland (82 percent), and the United States (81 percent). The concentration in southern Lazio and in Campania of the capital invested in the Mezzogiorno from other countries is less than 70 percent (see table 24).

Table 24

Percentage of the Number of Plants in Southern Lazio
and Campania with Foreign Capital Invested in the Mezzogiorno,
by Source of Foreign Capital

	Number of Plants in Southern Lazio and Campania / Number of Plants in the Mezzogiorno	% of Total
Belgium	$\frac{4}{8}$	50.0
France	$\frac{20}{40}$	50.0
Luxembourg	$\frac{0}{2}$	0.0
Netherlands	$\frac{9}{13}$	69.2
United Kingdom	$\frac{12}{21}$	57.1
West Germany	$\frac{9}{24}$	37.5
EEC Subtotal	$\frac{54}{108}$	50.0
Australia	$\frac{2}{9}$	22.2
Canada	$\frac{2}{3}$	66.7
Japan	$\frac{0}{3}$	0.0
Lebanon	$\frac{1}{1}$	100.0
Liechtenstein	$\frac{9}{10}$	90.0
Sweden	$\frac{3}{6}$	50.0
Switzerland	$\frac{18}{22}$	81.8
United States	$\frac{78}{96}$	81.2
Total	$\frac{167}{258}$	64.7

Source: *Iniziative industriali a partecipazione estera nel Mezzogiorno* (Industrial initiatives with the participation of foreign capital in the Mezzogiorno) (Rome: IASM, 1981).

The European Regional Development Fund, Italy, and the Mezzogiorno

The EEC directs its part of the foreign capital invested in Italy and in the Mezzogiorno principally through the European Regional Development Fund (ERDF), the Guidance and Guarantee Sections (FEOGA) of the Common Agricultural Policy (CAP), and the European Investment Bank (EIB).

The ERDF is the EEC's principal instrument of regional policy; its objectives are to induce the creation of new positions of employment and to maintain existing positions by financing regional development projects. In its original form (18 March 1975–6 February 1979), the ERDF was a passive political instrument in that it could only supplement the regional development initiatives already assisted financially by the member states concerned by disbursing its resources not to various regions but rather to states according to the following quotas: Italy 40 percent, the United Kingdom 28 percent, France 15 percent, West Germany 6.4 percent, Ireland 6 percent, the Netherlands 1.7 percent, Belgium 1.5 percent, Denmark 1.3 percent, and Luxembourg 0.1 percent.

Under regulation no. 214 of 6 February 1979, the EEC's Council of Ministers made the ERDF a more active political instrument by creating a "nonquota" section. The resources of this section, limited in 1980 to 5 percent of the ERDF's total appropriation, are not supplements to the regional development initiatives of the member states but rather funds at the EEC's disposal that are disbursed to realize the EEC's regional development initiatives in conjunction with, or independently from, the member states' initiatives. Simultaneously, the Council of Ministers slightly modified the ERDF's disbursement quotas: Italy 39.39 percent, the United Kingdom 27.03 percent, France 16.86 percent, West Germany 6.4 percent, Ireland 6 percent, the Netherlands 1.5 percent, Belgium 1.39 percent, Denmark 1.2 percent, and Luxembourg 0.09 percent. The ERDF's "quota" section, which supplements the member states' regional development initiatives, finances two types of investments: (1) industrial and service investments, by covering 20 to 50 percent of the cost incurred by the member states; and (2) infrastructural investments, by covering 30 to 40 percent of the cost incurred by the member states. Regulation no. 214 also assigns the financing of the ERDF to the EEC's budget.

Between 1975 and 1983 the EEC's Regional Policy Committee approved 21,729 projects in the EEC, of which 15,901 (74 percent) were to develop infrastructure and 5,578 (26 percent) to develop industry and services. It approved 8,008 projects in Italy (37 percent of the total in the EEC), of which 6,675 (83 percent) were to develop infrastructure and 1,333 (17 percent) for industry and services. The projects in Italy promoted investments of ECU 19,772.46 million, equal to 28 percent of the ECU 70,141.60 million of investments promoted by the ERDF's contributions in the EEC in this period. Moreover, between 1975 and 1983, the Regional Policy Committee approved ERDF contributions to the projects in Italy of ECU 3,493.55 million, or 38 percent of the ERDF's contributions to projects in the EEC (ECU 9,175.97 million).[22]

The EEC's programs that coordinate the intervention of two or more EEC agencies in a given area (and, when necessary, with the interventions of the appropriate agencies of the EEC states concerned), the so-called integrated operations or integrated programs, represent other potential sources of foreign capital to be invested in the Mezzogiorno. These programs concern the EEC's peripheral economic systems, those located principally in Mediterranean and far north-western Europe. They are designed to insure the survival of inland farming, to create jobs outside the agricultural sector, and to guarantee incomes that may maintain or improve the standard of living. These programs aim to achieve their objectives by improving the infrastructure, rationalizing coastal farming principally through specialization, and modernizing fisheries. In 1985 the EEC implemented two experimental "integrated programs," one in Naples, the other in Belfast.[23]

The ERDF's new regulations, which became effective on 1 January 1985, modify the system that governs the distribution of the ERDF's captial to the EEC states. The quotas, once fixed, are now variable and governed by margins of fluctuation. Under the new regulations, Italy receives a minimum of 31.94 percent and a maximum of 42.59 percent of the ERDF's capital.[24] As before, the EEC's Regional Policy subsidizes the regional policies of the EEC states by means of the ERDF's contributions to the financing of the projects elaborated by the EEC's various regions. However, it does nothing to foster the accumulation and the investment, according to internal exigencies, of the real income produced by the EEC's underdeveloped economic systems. For this reason, the Regional Policy remains incapable of promoting the EEC's positive balanced development.

The Common Agricultural Policy, Italy, and the Mezzogiorno

The Common Agricultural Policy reflects the political dominance of West Germany and France over the other EEC states. It offers greater price support and protection to their (Continental) agricultural products than to Mediterranean agricultural products. It also expends more capital to sustain agricultural prices, based on the production costs of the least efficient producers, than to modernize or to rationalize inefficient producers. In this way the most efficient producers, especially those of the more dominant economic systems, receive the greatest return on their investments, retain their advantage in terms of productivity over less efficient ones, and produce more surplus capital to be transferred to other sectors of the economy. For example, between 1962 and 1968, FEOGA's Guidance Section, in order to modernize and to rationalize inefficient agricultural producers, expended the equivalent of LIT 230 billion. This represented only 3.5 percent of the LIT 6,500 billion expended by FEOGA's Guarantee Section to sustain agricultural prices between 1968 and 1972.[25] Between 1965 and 1974 the expenditures of FEOGA's Guidance Section equaled only 10.4 percent of FEOGA's total expenditure.[26]

Such a policy disadvantages Italy's agricultural system within the EEC because, in comparison with the agricultural systems of the politically dominant EEC states and for reasons of topography and climate, Italy produces a proportionately greater quantity of Mediterranean agricultural products and a proportionately lesser quantity of Contintental agricultural products. Therefore, under the CAP's price regime, which favors Continental agricultural products, Italy receives a smaller share of the FEOGA's monies and a smaller stimulus to produce surplus capital to be transferred to its other economic sectors.

Three examples indicate some of the detrimental consequences for its agricultural system of Italy's participation in the CAP. First, with respect to capital contributed and received, the CAP cost Italy LIT 175,209 million between 1962 and 1970: Italy lost 224,977 million to FEOGA's Guarantee Section and gained 49,768 million from FEOGA's Guidance Section.[27] Second, Italy's agricultural producers, in comparison with the producers of the other EEC states, benefit least from the CAP, as the statistics in table 25 show. Last, the CAP has aggravated Italy's deficit relating to the commercial exchange of agricultural products: Italy's agricultural exports in 1983 were less than LIT 7,000 billion, while its agricultural imports were more than LIT 16,000 billion, with a resulting deficit of more than LIT 9,000 billion (LIT 10,126 billion in 1984;[29] see also table 26). Moreover, the CAP disadvantages most the Mezzogiorno's agricultural system within Italy and the EEC because Mediterranean products, disadvantaged under the CAP, form 56 percent of the Mezzogiorno's agricultural production, as is evident in table 27.

Table 25

Consumer and Taxpayer Loss Compared to the Producer Gain
Caused by the CAP in 1978, by Country

	Consumer and Taxpayer Loss Per Capita	Producer Gain Per Person Employed in Agriculture	Per Capita Change in Resources	Change in Resources as % of GDP
Belgium	93.2	5,100	-25.4	-0.5
Denmark	81.6	3,200	64.8	1.2
United Kingdom	45.0	1,700	-24.5	-0.9
France	74.5	1,800	-5.4	-0.1
Ireland	66.8	1,700	64.8	3.2
Italy	68.1	700	-27.6	-1.3
Netherlands	87.4	4,900	15.0	.3
West Germany	93.4	2,400	-28.2	-.5
EEC	71.2	1,700	-15.9	-.4

Source: Gisele Podbielski, "The Common Agricultural Policy and the Mezzogiorno," *Journal of Common Market Studies* 19 (June 1981): 337.

Table 26

Percent Self-Sufficiency Rate of
Italy's Agricultural System, 1956-1974

	Wine	Cereals	Bovine Meat	Milk	Cheese	Butter	Sugar	Oils and Fats
1956-60	105	87	75	100	98	81	103	54
1973-74	137	63	61	96	88	61	57	57

Source: Rosemary Galli and Saverio Torcasio, *La partecipazione italiana alla politica agricola comunitaria* (Italy's participation in the Common Agricultural Policy) (Bologna: Il Mulino, 1976), 48.

The European Investment Bank, Italy, and the Mezzogiorno

The European Investment Bank (EIB) is the EEC's credit institution. One of its objectives is to promote the EEC's harmonious and balanced development in three ways: (1) by financing regional development projects, above all in the economically weakest regions; (2) by financing projects of interest to the EEC and projects necessary to

Table 27

Percent Composition of Agricultural Production, 1973-1977

	EEC less Italy	Italy	Mezzogiorno
	Continental Agricultural Products		
Cereals	11.2	12.1	10.7
Milk	20.3	10.3	5.3
Meat	39.1	25.0	13.3
Other livestock products	4.5	3.9	2.7
Other crops	11.9	9.8	11.8
Total	87.0	61.1	43.8
	Mediterranean Agricultural Products		
Citrus and non-citrus fruits	3.2	10.9	16.9
Olive oil	--	5.3	12.1
Vegetables	5.4	13.0	16.2
Wine	4.4	9.7	11.0
Total	13.0	38.9	56.2

Source: Gisele Podbielski, "The Common Agricultural Policy and the Mezzogiorno," *Journal of Common Market Studies* 19 (June 1981): 333.

Table 28

Structure of the EIB's Investments in Italy,
1958-1982, by Sector

	Investments ECU (in millions)	% of Total
Industry, agriculture, and services	3,048.0	30.8
Energy	2,365.1	23.9
Aqueducts	1,466.5	14.8
Telecommunications	1,388.1	14.0
Transportation	1,243.5	12.6
Other infrastructures	391.6	3.9
Total	9,902.8	100.0

Source: *Venticinque anni 1958-1983* (Twenty-five years) (Luxembourg: Banca Europea per gli Investimenti, 1983), 28.

the realization of the Treaty of Rome's objectives; and (3) by financing the creation, modernization, and reconversion of economic enterprises. A second objective of the EIB is to employ its capital resources in investments whose suitability is determined not by their profitability but rather by their efficaciousness in realizing the objectives of the Treaty of Rome and the EEC, provided such investments may not jeopardize the EIB's credit worthiness by threatening its solvency.[30]

Between 1958 and 1982 the EIB invested in the EEC ECU 22,487.9 million, of which ECU 15,974.4 million (62 percent) was to finance regional development projects and ECU 9,634.3 million (38 percent) to finance projects of interest to the EEC (i.e., the modernization and reconversion of businesses, the development of energy resources, and infrastructures).[31] In this period the EIB invested in Italy ECU 9,902.8 million (see table 28), equal to 44 percent of the ECU 22,487.9 million invested in the EEC. Of the sum invested in Italy, the EIB provided ECU 7,710.4 million (78 percent) to finance regional development projects and ECU 2,194.2 million (22 percent) to underwrite projects of interest to the EEC. These EIB investments annually averaged ECU 40 million between 1958 and 1967, ECU 165 million between 1968 and 1972, ECU 270 million between 1973 and 1977, more than ECU 1,000 million between 1978 and 1982, with ECU 1,450 million in 1982 alone.[32]

Between 1958 and 1982, the EIB invested in the Mezzogiorno ECU

7,293 million, equal to 74 percent of the ECU 9,902.8 million spent in Italy and 95 percent of the ECU 7,710.4 million put into regional development projects in Italy. The geographic distribution of the EIB's investments in the Mezzogiorno has both positive and negative effects on the area's disequilibria. On the positive side, the EIB invested ECU 1,860.1 million (25.5 percent) of the ECU 7,293 million to finance multiregional projects. This sum clearly exceeds the total invested in any single region of the Mezzogiorno. On the negative side, the EIB invested ECU 3,235.4 million (62 percent) of the remaining ECU 5,217.3 million in the area's single regions, in Puglia (19 percent of the EIB's investments), Sicilia (13 percent), and Campania (12 percent). Together these three regions received 44 percent of the EIB's investments. Each of the Mezzogiorno's other regions received less than 10 percent (see table 29).

Table 29

Distribution of the EIB's Investments
in the Mezzogiorno, 1958-1982, by Region

	Investments ECU (in millions)	% of Total
Abruzzo	425.6	5.8
Basilicata	91.3	1.2
Calabria	361.5	5.0
Campania	908.6	12.5
Southern Lazio	340.7	4.7
Marche[a]	57.9	.8
Molise	94.8	1.3
Puglia	1,375.5	18.9
Sardegna	608.4	8.3
Sicilia	951.3	13.0
Toscana[a]	1.7	.0
Multiregional projects	1,860.1	25.5
Loans	215.6	3.0
Total	7,293.0	100.0

Source: *Venticinque anni 1958-1983* (Twenty-five years) (Luxembourg: Banca Europea per gli Investimenti, 1983), 28.

[a] The province of Ascoli-Piceno and the Island of Elba are areas of competence of CASMEZ.

8
The European Economic Community and the Northwestern Elite's Investment in the Mezzogiorno's Underdevelopment

Dependent Industrialization and Social Control

THE POLICIES OF incentives and dependent industrialization modified the political and economic relationships between the Mezzogiorno and the Italian state in two ways: first, they made the Mezzogiorno the territorial base of the complex of parastate industries, and second, the complex of parastate industries became the Mezzogiorno's primary accumulator of capital (see table 30). The economic dominance of the parastate industries in the Mezzogiorno modified the political and economic relationships, mediated by the Italian state, both between the Mezzogiorno and the rest of the Italian economy and between the "state bourgeoisie" and the northwestern elite. This power intensified the Mezzogiorno's underdevelopment by increasing the area's capacity to accumulate capital and by exacerbating its disequilibria. It also transformed the "state bourgeoisie": what was a public managerial class responsible for the functioning of north-central Italy's economically subaltern parastate industries and a bureaucratic "middle class" in the Mezzogiorno became the region's dominant class, one that identified its interests with that area. In short, the policies of incentives and dependent industrialization increased the Mezzogiorno's power in the Italian economy, fused the area's economic exigencies with the state bourgeoisie's political exigencies, increased the state bourgeoisie's power within the state apparatus, and exacerbated the Mezzogiorno's disequilibria.[1]

These consequences offered the northwestern elite economic security and political uncertainty by creating positive and negative repercussions that strengthened and undermined its privileged political and economic position in Italy. One the one hand, the Mezzogiorno's greater power in the Italian economy strengthened the northwestern

Table 30

Percent Distribution of the Turnover, Real Property, and Employees of Italy's Leading Businesses, by Their Financial Holding Companies and by Region, 1973

	Turnover	Real Property	Employees
	Mezzogiorno		
Parastate Industries	37.7	43.9	32.1
Montedison Group	18.9	16.4	31.3
Fiat Group	9.0	14.2	8.0
Independent businesses	34.4	25.5	28.6
Total	100.0	100.0	100.0
	North-Central Italy		
Parastate Industries	10.2	13.5	13.5
Montedison Group	6.1	7.7	8.6
Fiat Group	2.6	3.5	4.3
Independent businesses	81.1	75.3	73.6
Total	100.0	100.0	100.0

Source: Alfredo Del Monte and Adriano Giannola, *Il Mezzogiorno nell'economia italiana* (The Mezzogiorno in the Italian economy) (Bologna: Il Mulino, 1978), 235.

elite's position by allowing it to gain greater advantage and benefit from the Mezzogiorno so that the northwestern economic system might better sustain international economic competition under the adverse conditions created by the EEC's unbalanced integration. On the other hand, the remaining consequences undermined the northwestern elite's position. The fusion of the Mezzogiorno's economic exigencies with the state bourgeoisie's political exigencies, mentioned above, reduced the northwestern elite's control over the state apparatus in favor of a group identifying its interests with the Mezzogiorno. The exacerbation of the Mezzogiorno's disequilibria created unrest that the Left could champion.[2]

These contradictory repercussions forced the northwestern elite to increase its concern for the domestic exigencies of political legitimation. Its dominance in Italy depended on its ability to organize the means of production on Italian territory in such a way as to allow the economic system of the northwest to respond to the exigencies of international economic competition. Therefore the northwestern elite had to devise a way to minimize the costs and maximize the benefits of the policies of incentives and dependent industrialization.

To this end the northwestern elite combined these policies, whose investments expanded the Mezzogiorno's productive base, with a policy of social control. This policy did not expand the Mezzogiorno's productive base; rather, it expended capital unproductively by subsidizing incomes; by commissioning in the area public works projects not functional to the accumulation of capital in the national economy; and, last, by increasing employment in the area's tertiary sector and public administration at a rate disproportionately high compared to that of increased productivity in the area's agricultural and industrial sectors. In short, the northwestern elite responded to the exigencies of international economic competition and to the domestic exigencies of political legitimation by astutely combining the productive and the unproductive expenditure of capital in the Mezzogiorno.[3]

The northwestern elite found itself in a delicate situation in that the mismanagement either of the policies of incentives and dependent industrialization or of the policy of social control could undermine its privileged political and economic position in Italy by hindering the process of capital accumulation in the economy. Too many productive investments by means of the policies of incentives and dependent industrialization could transform the state bourgeoisie into a valid political rival capable of challenging the northwestern elite's control of the state apparatus and therefore of investment capital. Too few productive investments would insufficiently involve the Mezzogiorno in the process of capital accumulation in the Italian economy. Moreover, an excess of unproductive investments through the policy of social control would sharply reduce the quantity of capital available for productive investments in the Italian economy.

The northwestern elite invested in the Mezzogiorno's underdevelopment by implementing the policies of incentives and dependent industrialization. These policies committed the Italian state to the expenditure of huge amounts of capital so that the Mezzogiorno's intensified underdevelopment might allow the economic system of the northwest to sustain international competition under the adverse conditions created by the EEC's unbalanced integration. The northwestern elite receives a good return on its investment only when the state bourgeoisie is subaltern and when the political and economic benefits realized for the economic system of the northwest outweigh the costs of the Mezzogiorno's underdevelopment. The northwestern elite enjoys an inherent advantage in its relationships with the state bourgeoisie: the northwestern elite is an organic class firmly established in civil society and capable of organizing mass social consensus.

On the other hand, the state bourgeoisie is an artificial class superimposed on civil society and incapable of organizing mass social consensus. The northwestern elite enjoys no such advantage in its relationships with the Left, which represents the working class and is capable of championing effectively (the PCI more than the PSI) the political disaffections created by the Mezzogiorno's exacerbated disequilibria. In a political confrontation the northwestern elite would find the state bourgeoisie a much less formidable opponent than the Left.

The Mezzogiorno in the Italian Economy 1961–1965

In 1961 businesses employed an average 9.1 people in north-central Italy, against 3.4 in the Mezzogiorno.[4] For every person employed, 1.3 were unemployed in north-central Italy, against 1.9 in the Mezzogiorno. Industrial workers in the Mezzogiorno numbered 965,000 against 4.5 million in north-central Italy.[4] Value added in the Mezzogiorno's manufacturing sectors was 11.7 percent of that in the national manufacturing sectors.[5] The investments of the parastate industries equaled 29.9 percent of all the industrial investments in the Mezzogiorno in the 1960–64 period, against 15.8 percent in 1957–59. They equaled 12.6 percent of all the industrial investments in north-central Italy from 1960–64, against 10.7 percent for 1957–59.[6] Per capita income in Italy was 60 percent of the EEC average in 1960 and 63 percent in 1963; while in the Mezzogiorno it was 39 percent of the EEC average in 1963.[7] In 1963, the distribution percent by sector of employment (1) and gross domestic product (2) was:

	Agriculture		Industry		Tertiary		Public[a] Administration	
	(1)	(2)	(1)	(2)	(1)	(2)	(1)	(2)
Mezzogiorno	39.2	23.7	29.9	25.9	30.9	50.4	8.3	15.8
Italy	26.7	13.9	40.1	38.9	33.2	47.3	7.7	11.3

[a] as part of the tertiary
Source: Del Monte and Giannola, *Il Mezzogiorno nell'economia italiana*, 359.

At that time the vast majority of businesses located in the Mezzogiorno were small while the distribution of businesses according to size was far more balanced in north-central Italy, as table 31 indicates.

Between 1958 and 1963, the growth rate of the national economy's least productive sectors, the tertiary sector and the public administration, was greater in the Mezzogiorno than in the rest of Italy. The

Table 31

Percent Employment Distribution, 1961-1981, by Region

	Businesses (Number of Employees)			
	Small (10-99)	Medium (100-499)	Medium-large (500-999)	Large (1,000+)
1961				
Mezzogiorno	77.4	12.5	4.8	5.3
North-central Italy	55.1	23.7	5.8	15.5
1971				
Mezzogiorno	65.1	15.2	6.7	13.0
North-central Italy	52.8	23.3	7.7	16.2
1981				
Mezzogiorno	58.3	17.0	8.1	16.6
North-central Italy	58.0	22.5	6.7	12.8

Sources: For 1961 and 1971: Alfredo Del Monte and Adriano Giannola, *Il Mezzogiorno nell'economia italiana* (The Mezzogiorno in the Italian economy) (Bologna: Il Mulino, 1978), 232. For 1981: Salvatore Vinci, "Il quadro macroeconomico per lo sviluppo del Mezzogiorno" (The macroeconomic framework for the Mezzogiorno's development), *Rivista Trimestrale Mezzogiorno d'Europa* (Mezzogiorno d'Europa Quarterly Review), no. 4 (October/December 1984): 547.

growth rate of the national economy's single most productive sector, industry, was greater in the rest of Italy than in the Mezzogiorno. An inverse tendency manifested itself only in the national economy's second most productive sector, agriculture, whose growth rate was greater in the Mezzogiorno than in the rest of Italy. The investments effected by the CASMEZ nourished the Mezzogiorno's agriculture and partially protected it from the adverse conditions created by the CAP, under which north-central Italy's agriculture restructured itself.

A Commitment to the Mezzogiorno's "Programmed Underdevelopment"

During the 1960s, the northwestern elite became increasingly aware that the quality of the productive investments effected by means of the policies of incentives and dependent industrialization would determine the quality of the return obtained from the investment in the Mezzogiorno's underdevelopment. In order to maintain its power in Italy, the northwestern elite needed to make productive investments that might not only benefit the economic system of the northwest but that might also furnish a sufficient quantity of surplus capital to finance an efficacious policy of social control that would not hinder the accumulation of capital for productive investment in the Italian economy. This awareness caused it to intensify the Mezzogiorno's underdevelopment by locating the productive investments of capital in the area's most promising "areas of industrial development"—that is, those areas in which the productive investment of capital promised to most satisfy the needs of the northwestern economic system. Consequently the northwestern elite reorganized the institutional mechanisms governing the accumulation and the investment of capital in the Mezzogiorno.[8]

The northwestern elite, through the DC, legitimized this investment strategy by presenting the resultant reorganization of the state's intervention in the Mezzogiorno as the foundation of a renewed commitment to the "economic programming" concept. In January 1965 the Council of Ministers approved for 1966–70 the so-called First National Economic Program.[9] This program was inspired by the rider to the report on the 1962 budget—better known as the Nota Aggiuntiva La Malfa—and by Professor Pasquale Saraceno's 1963 report on the state of the Italian economy. Like the Vanoni Plan, the First National Economic Program was more symbolic than substantive. The Italian Parliament sanctioned the program in principle in July 1967, after nearly one-third of the programming period had elapsed. Moreover, the program's fundamental goal, the coordination of the CASMEZ's activities with those of the ordinary administration, remained an abstract declaration.

The Italian government reorganized the institutional mechanisms that governed the accumulation and the investment of capital in the Mezzogiorno by enacting law no. 717 of 26 June 1965 and law no. 1523 of 30 June 1965. Law no. 717 increased the states's involvement in the development of the Mezzogiorno's infrastructure by charging the ordinary administration to locate at least 40 percent of its public works projects in the Mezzogiorno. It also increased the state's involvement in the area's industrialization by requiring the CASMEZ to concentrate the greatest part of its resources on the most promising "areas of industrial development" and to concentrate the expenditure of its remaining resources on the Mezzogiorno's most promising agricultural areas. Moreover, law no. 717, aside from extending the CAS-

MEZ's life to 1980, obliged it to cover 85 percent of the cost incurred by the consortiums of communes to develop the infrastructure necessary to attract industries and to cover 40 percent of the cost incurred by individual businesses to equip themselves with an infrastructure. It also located the Committee of Ministers for the Mezzogiorno within the National Committee for Economic Programming (CNPE), replaced in 1969 by the Interministerial Committee for Economic Programming (CIPE).[10] Law no. 1523 of 30 June 1965, known more commonly as the Single Text (Testo Unico) (also more symbolic than substantive and therefore less important than law no. 717), gathered under a single heading the legislation that concerned the institutional mechanisms governing the accumulation and the investment of capital in the Mezzogiorno.[11]

A greater amount of public and private capital invested in the Mezzogiorno, especially in its industrial sector, accompanied the location of the productive investments of capital in its most promising areas. Between 1965 and 1970 the CASMEZ expended LIT 2,800 billion, 40 percent more than the LIT 2,000 billion spent between 1950 and 1965 (see table 32).

The parastate industries increased their investments, which equaled 33.2 percent of all the industrial investments in the Mezzogiorno from 1965–69, against 29.9 percent from 1960–64 and 15.8 percent in 1957–59. They provided 12.4 percent of all the industrial investments in north-central Italy from 1965–69, against 12.6 percent in 1960–64 and 10.7 percent in 1957–59.[12] Moreover, in order to circumvent the efforts of the trade unions to participate in the formulation of a

Table 32

Evolution of CASMEZ's Capital Allocation

	1950–65		1965–70	
	LIT (billions)	% of Total	LIT (billions)	% of Total
Industry	240	12	1,344	48
Infrastructure	660	33	980	35
Subtotal	900	45	2,324	83
Agriculture	1,100	55	476	17
Total	2,000	100	2,800	100

Source: Gisele Podbielski, *Italy: Development and Crisis in the Post-war Economy* (Oxford: Clarendon Press, 1974), 135.

response to the exigencies of international economic competition, north-central Italy's private oligopolies decentralized their production by dispersing some of their productive facilities in the Mezzogiorno.[13]

Between 1963 and 1966, in comparison with 1958-63, the growth rate of the Italian economy's least productive sectors, the tertiary sector and the public administration, remained greater in the Mezzogiorno than in the rest of Italy, although by narrower margins. The growth rate of the national economy's most productive sector, industry, was greater in the Mezzogiorno than in the rest of Italy between 1963 and 1966 because the investments effected by means of the policies of incentives and dependent industrialization nourished the Mezzogiorno's industries while north-central Italy's industries restructured themselves after twelve years of strong, sustained growth (1951-63, especially 1958-63). The growth rate of agriculture was greater in the rest of Italy than in the Mezzogiorno between 1963 and 1966 because north-central Italy's agriculture, in comparison with the Mezzogiorno's, was better able to restructure itself under CAP while the Mezzogiorno's agriculture nearly stagnated after CASMEZ had completed the investments mandated by law no. 622 of 24 July 1959.

Between 1966 and 1970 the growth rate of the industrial sector was greater in the rest of Italy than in the Mezzogiorno following the restructuring of north-central Italy's industries in 1963-66, while the growth rate of agriculture was greater in the Mezzogiorno following the resumption of CASMEZ's investments under law no. 717 of 26 June 1965. For the first time the growth rate of the tertiary sector was greater in the rest of Italy than in the Mezzogiorno because north-central Italy's tertiary sector began to acquire a greater functional complementary with that area's industrial sector by providing employment to Italy's (especially the Mezzogiorno's) unemployed and underemployed and by developing increasingly important ancillary marketable services. The growth rate of the public administration remained greater in the Mezzogiorno than in the rest of the country. In 1970, the distribution percent by sector of employment (1) and gross domestic product (2) was:

	Agriculture		Industry		Tertiary		Public[a] Administration	
	(1)	(2)	(1)	(2)	(1)	(2)	(1)	(2)
Mezzogiorno	30.7	18.0	32.0	29.0	37.2	53.0	10.3	15.6
Italy	18.9	10.2	42.2	40.5	38.9	49.4	9.0	10.8

[a] as part of the tertiary
Source: Del Monte and Giannola, *Il Mezzogiarno nell'economia italiana*, 359.

In 1971, businesses employed an average of ten people in north-central Italy, against 4.1 in the Mezzogiorno. For every person employed, 1.6 were unemployed in north-central Italy, against 2.2 in the Mezzogiorno. Industrial workers numbered 1,059,000 in the Mezzogiorno, against 4,592,000 in north-central Italy.[14] Between 1961 and 1970, value added in the manufacturing sector increased by an average 7.43 percent per year in Italy but an average 9.42 percent per year in the Mezzogiorno.[15] Between 1961 and 1971, agricultural productivity increased by 7.0 percent in the Mezzogiorno but by 8.5 percent in north-central Italy.[16]

The Rationalization of the Mezzogiorno's "Programmed Underdevelopment"

During the 1970s the northwestern elite sought to improve the quality of the return on its investment in the Mezzogiorno's underdevelopment by facilitating the location of the productive investments of capital in the Mezzogiorno's most promising areas. Consequently the northwestern elite rationalized the relationships between the institutional mechanisms governing the accumulation and the investment of capital in the Mezzogiorno. Through the DC it legitimized this rationalization by presenting the resulting institutional reorganization as another example of its commitment to the "economic programming" concept.[17]

The Italian government rationalized these relationships by enacting law no. 853 of 6 October 1971 and law no. 183 of 2 May 1976. Law no. 853 provided for the abolition, effected in November 1971, of the Committee of Ministers for the Mezzogiorno. The duties of the committee were assumed by CIPE, which was charged to insure that the state's interventions in the Mezzogiorno might strictly conform with the objectives of national economic policy (determined preponderantly by the northwestern elite). Law no. 853 also provided for the creation of regional and interregional "special projects," which were designated the pivots of the state's interventions in the Mezzogiorno. It required the parastate industries to locate 60 percent of their total investments and 80 percent of their new investments in the Mezzogiorno. Moreover, it obliged businesses whose proposed investments might exceed LIT 7 billion and companies with capital assets greater than LIT 5 billion to submit their projects intended for the Mezzogiorno to the judgment of CIPE, which, under this law, tacitly approved those projects not explicitly rejected within three months. Law no. 183 reconfirmed the provisions of law no. 853 and charged

CIPE to formulate the five-year programs that might establish the general and the specific objectives of the state's interventions in the Mezzogiorno within the context of the objectives of national economic policy.[18]

Laws no. 853 and 183 include the Mezzogiorno's institutions of regional government among the institutional mechanisms governing the accumulation and the investment of capital in the Mezzogiorno. Under these laws the Minister for Extraordinary Intervention in the Mezzogiorno must submit to the judgment of the CIPE the "special projects" formulated either by the minister, the Mezzogiorno's regional governments, or the CASMEZ, this last charged to implement these projects. A committee of the Mezzogiorno's regional presidents (law no. 853) and two representatives elected by each of the Mezzogiorno's regional councils (law no. 183) advise the CIPE when it evaluates "special projects."

In reality, the participation of the Mezzogiorno's regional governments is inconsequential regarding both the formulation and the evaluation of the "special projects" because the Mezzogiorno's regional governments lack both the authority to determine the fate of the "special projects" and the resources and the technical expertise to formulate them. The CIPE subordinates the Mezzogiorno's interests to the interests of the economic system of the northwest by directing the state's interventions in the Mezzogiorno according to the dictates of a national economic policy that reflects the best interests of the politically dominant northwestern elite: the CASMEZ, controlled by the northwestern elite through the DC, holds a virtual monopoly of the resources and the technical expertise needed to formulate the "special projects."[19]

The growth rate of the industrial sector was greater in the Mezzogiorno than in the rest of Italy between 1970 and 1973 because the investments effected under the policies of incentives and dependent industrialization nourished the Mezzogiorno's industries while north-central Italy's industries restructured themselves after five years of strong, sustained growth (1966–70). The growth rate of the agricultural sector during this time was greater in the Mezzogiorno than in the rest of Italy because the CASMEZ's investments provoked a modest growth of the Mezzogiorno's agriculture while north-central Italy's nearly stagnated under the CAP. The growth rate of the tertiary sector remained greater in the rest of Italy than in the Mezzogiorno because north-central Italy's tertiary sector continued to acquire a greater functional complementarity with its industrial sector. It provided employment (especially in the Mezzogiorno) and developed increasingly important ancillary marketable services. However, the growth rate of the public administration remained greater in the Mezzogiorno than in the rest of Italy. In 1973, the percent distribution by sector of employment (1) and gross domestic product (2) was:

	Agriculture		Industry		Tertiary		Public[a] Administration	
	(1)	(2)	(1)	(2)	(1)	(2)	(1)	(2)
Mezzogiorno	29.3	18.2	32.1	29.0	38.5	52.8	11.2	16.3
Italy	16.9	10.0	41.8	39.3	41.3	50.8	9.9	12.1

[a] as part of the tertiary
Source: Del Monte and Giannola, *Il Mezzogiorno nell'economia italiana*, 359.

The investments of the parastate industries equaled 39.9 percent of all the industrial investments in the Mezzogiorno in the 1970–74 period, 26.5 percent in 1975–76, against 33.2 percent in 1965–69. They equaled 17.2 percent of all the industrial investments in north-central Italy from 1970–74, 17.9 percent in 1975–76, against 12.4 percent from 1965–69.[20] Value added in the manufacturing sector increased by an average 5.81 percent per year in Italy between 1970 and 1974, 0.74 percent annually between 1974 and 1976, but increased by an average 7.08 percent per year in the Mezzogiorno between 1970 and 1974, and 3.29 percent between 1974 and 1976.[21] Value added in the Mezzogiorno's manufacturing sectors was 15.4 percent of the value added in the national economy's manufacturing sectors between 1974 and 1976, 14.1 percent between 1970 and 1976.[22] In 1976, the distribution percent by sector of employment (1) and gross domestic product (2) was:

	Agriculture		Industry		Tertiary		Public[a] Administration	
	(1)	(2)	(1)	(2)	(1)	(2)	(1)	(2)
Mezzogiorno	26.6	14.4	29.6	29.1	43.9	56.4	15.6	16.7
Italy	14.7	8.5	38.0	39.4	47.3	52.1	14.2	11.3

[a] as part of the tertiary
Source: Del Monte and Giannola, *Il Mezzogiorno nell'economia italiana*, 359.

Since 1976 the northwestern elite implements the policies of incentives and dependent industrialization by organizing the institutional

Table 33

Selected Labor Force Characteristics
in North-Central Italy and the Mezzogiorno

	North-Central Italy	Mezzogiorno		
		Entire	Urban	Rural
Activity rate of working-age population	60	54	52	55
Percentage of labor force with stable employment	95.5	88.3	86.5	89.3
Percentage of labor force in search of first job	1.0	4.0	5.5	3.0

Source: Data extracted from Collana Documenti SVIMEZ, *Il Mezzogiorno nell'Europa a dodici* (The Mezzogiorno in the Europe of Twelve) (Rome: SVIMEZ, 1979), 245.

mechanisms that govern the accumulation and the investment of capital in the Mezzogiorno according to law no. 853 of 6 October 1971 and law no. 183 of 2 May 1976 so that the economic system of the northwest may derive the greatest possible advantage and benefit from the Mezzogiorno's underdevelopment. The following statistics in table 33 reflect the Mezzogiorno's subordinate position in the Italian economy in 1979. Industrial employment in the Mezzogiorno equaled 19.7 percent of industrial employment in Italy in 1951, against 17.9 percent in 1979. Although the number of industrial workers may have increased in the Mezzogiorno between 1951 and 1979, the rate of increase was lower than in the rest of Italy.[23]

Between 1970 and 1980, the sectoral distribution of fixed investments in the Mezzogiorno was, on average: 11.5 percent in agriculture, 24.5 percent in industry, 52.0 percent in the tertiary sector, and 12.0 percent in public administration. At the same time, the average sectoral distribution of fixed investments in north-central Italy was 5.0 percent in agriculture, 30.0 percent in industry, 56.5 percent in the tertiary sector, and 8.5 percent in public administration.[24] In this period fixed investments in the Mezzogiorno decreased greatly in industry, increased in agriculture and in the tertiary sector, and remained stable (above the level in north-central Italy) in public administration (see table 34). Public works investments, although relatively

Table 34

Percent Distribution of Fixed Investments
in the Mezzogiorno, 1970 and 1980, by Sector

	Agriculture	Industry	Tertiary	Public Administration
1970	10.0	30.0	48.0	12.0
1980	13.0	19.0	56.0	12.0

Source: Claudio Signorile, *Il nuovo Mezzogiorno e l'economia nazionale* (The new Mezzogiorno and the national economy) (Bari: Laterza, 1982), 68.

greater in the Mezzogiorno than in north-central Italy, were less in absolute terms (see table 35).

In 1980 the percent distribution by sector of employment (1) and gross domestic product (2) was:

	Agriculture		Industry		Tertiary		Public[a] Administration	
	(1)	(2)	(1)	(2)	(1)	(2)	(1)	(2)
Mezzogiorno	24.1	12.2	28.9	30.6	28.9	39.0	18.1	18.2
North-central Italy	8.8	5.2	40.3	42.6	34.8	40.5	16.1	11.7

Source: Data from tables 4-5 of appendix to CASMEZ, *Thirty-year Review.*

In that year, businesses headquartered outside the Mezzogiorno employed 70 percent of the Mezzogiorno's industrial workers.[25]

The CASMEZ "Transformed"

In 1984 the CASMEZ underwent a "transformation" that was potentially significant but in all probability more symbolic than substantive. On 2 August 1984 the Italian Parliament put the CASMEZ into liquidation but at the same time charged it to honor the commitments that it had assumed before 31 July 1984 and to manage the expenditure of the LIT 15,000 billion appropriated to finance the government's three-year program for the Mezzogiorno (law no. 651 of December 1983).[26] The Parliament enabled the CASMEZ to honor its

Table 35

Public Works Investments, by Region
(Billions of LIT in Constant 1970 Prices)

	1951–80	1970–80
Mezzogiorno	18,000	10,200
North-central Italy	22,000	11,100

Source: Claudio Signorile, *Il nuovo Mezzogiorno e l'economia nazionale* (The new Mezzogiorno and the national economy) (Bari: Laterza, 1982), 27.

commitments, which extend to 1995, by transforming the "CASMEZ-in-liquidation" into a "transition CASMEZ," financed with an initial appropriation of LIT 14,000 billion, later increased to LIT 28,000 billion.[27]

The CASMEZ's "transformation" ostensibly marked the beginning of a period of change in which the Italian government reconsidered the ways in which the state intervened in the Mezzogiorno. Initial indications did not augur well for a transformation to mark the end of the area's underdevelopment. First, the government undertook to replace the CASMEZ with a National Fund for the Development of the South, to be financed with an appropriation of LIT 120 thousand billion for 1985–94.[28] Then it created two agencies: one for territorial interventions, charged to formulate and implement public works and infrastructure projects in the Mezzogiorno, and another agency for the development of the Mezzogiorno, needed to induce investment in the area by providing capital grants, financing, and incentives.[29] The National Fund for the Development for the South seems nothing more than the old CASMEZ with a new name, while the two agencies appear to be merely the old CASMEZ divided in two.

Table 36

CASMEZ's Commitments and Expenditures, 1950-1983
(Valued in Constant 1982 Lire and Expressed in Millions of Dollars)

Infrastructures	Commitments	Disbursements
Water mains and sewers	10,039.4	6,775.6
Roadworks	6,775.6	5,074.0
Railways and ferry routes	1,006.1	912.4
Harbors and airports	1,099.5	810.4
Hospitals	1,461.7	800.5
Agriculture	12,647.7	10,845.1
Industry	5,582.2	3,358.6
Workers' housing	267.4	115.0
Tourism	1,439.9	1,103.6
Severely depressed areas	3,051.1	1,990.4
Earthquake-stricken areas in Sicily	98.6	77.5
Emergency operations in areas affected by the earthquake of 23 November 1980	98.5	62.6
"Special projects"	18,222.6	6,309.6
New law on Naples	200.9	127.1
Infrastructures subtotal	61,991.2	38,362.4
Incentives		
Industry: Capital grants	8,990.2	6,577.6
Grants for interest payments	14,445.3	5,404.2
Other sectors: Agriculture	3,170.0	2,447.7
Tourism	147.7	136.1
Crafts and cottage industries	376.3	338.6
Fisheries	369.0	331.6
Technological advance and civil development	1,559.2	1,264.5
Agricultural credit	1,141.1	929.7
Loans for hotels and tourism	1,565.9	1,292.0
CASMEZ loans for "special projects"	219.9	107.3
Shareholdings	553.1	527.9
Loans covered by foreign funds	4,724.2	4,510.3
Loans covered by foreign funds for "special projects"	6.8	4.7
Incentives subtotal	37,268.9	23,852.2
Other commitments	5,002.5	4,997.8
Total	104,262.6	67,212.4

Source: Table 6 of the appendix to *A Thirty-year Review of the Cassa per il Mezzogiorno* (Rome: CASMEZ General Paper, 1983).

PART IV
The European Economic Community's Unbalanced Integration and the Mezzogiorno's Underdevelopment

9
The Consequences of the Mezzogiorno's Underdevelopment

Economic Development without Employment

THE MEZZOGIORNO'S INFERIOR position in the Italian and international economies has produced eight negative consequences: rural exodus, economic deserts, social disintegration, anomalous urbanization, anomalous consumerism, hypertertiarization, emigration and the entrepreneurial Mafia and the Mafia model of capitalist accumulation. These consequences have a common denominator: the Mezzogiorno's underdevelopment manifests itself as economic development without sufficient employment opportunities for its population.[1] Its demographic development has aggravated this in that it has consistently registered a birth rate higher than that of north-central Italy. Moreover, the great improvements in the area's standard of living after World War II, especially in health care, hygiene, and sanitation, have produced, in comparison with north-central Italy, a longer lifespan that has more than offset a higher infant mortality rate.[2] The Mezzogiorno counted 17.7 million inhabitants in 1951, 18.6 million in 1961, 18.9 million in 1971 and 19.9 million in 1981.[3]

Rural Exodus

Italy's participation in the EEC stimulated above all the development of Italian industry because this sector was (and is) the most productive and therefore the most remunerative and attractive to investors. Italy's industrial development greatly reduced agricultural employment because the rural population was attracted to the higher incomes available in the industrial sector.[4] Land reform (law no. 230 of 12 May 1950, law no. 841 of 21 October 1950, and the Sicilian

Regional Government's law no. 104 of 27 December 1950) impeded the Mezzogiorno's agricultural sector from realizing its potential by promoting the mechanization of farms (with equipment manufactured principally in north-central Italy) more than the development of agricultural infrastructures (for example, irrigation systems).[5] The reduction of the population of the Mezzogiorno's rural areas, compared to the rural areas of the northwest and the center/northeast economic systems, was severe and disorderly because the Mezzogiorno's agriculture, in comparison with north-central Italy's, was already less productive and was responsible for the employment and for the underemployment of a relatively greater share of the population (consequences of the Mezzogiorno's inferior position in the Italian economy).

The Mezzogiorno's agriculture was further disadvantaged by the CAP's discrimination against Mediterranean agricultural products. Indeed, Italy has acquiesced in this discrimination because under the adverse conditions created by the EEC's unbalanced integration, the exigencies of international economic competition have induced the northwestern elite to expand its international markets as much as possible at the Mezzogiorno's expense. In this case, the northwestern elite has realized its goal by exchanging Italy's industrial products, manufactured principally in north-central Italy, for Mediterranean agricultural products cultivated outside the Mezzogiorno. The northwestern elite can only hope that the revenue gained from the exportation of Italian industrial products may adequately compensate Italy's agricultural deficits.

The population decline of the Mezzogiorno's rural areas hindered the redistribution of land to the dictates of the land reform. It also created disequilibria both in the geographic distribution of the labor force in the Mezzogiorno and in the spatial development of the Mezzogiorno's agriculture. Some of the Mezzogiorno's areas had an excess of manpower while other areas had an insufficiency,[6] and the Mezzogiorno's agriculture suffered in the severely depopulated internal mountainous areas (now known as the Mezzogiorno's "osso," (or "bone," areas) but flourished with capital-intensive plantations located in the geographically suited coastal areas (now known as the Mezzogiorno's "polpa," (or "lean meat," areas).[7] The reduced employment in the nation's agricultural sector and the consequent reduction of the rural population created greater per capita incomes for those persons who retained employment in the agricultural sector, stimulated rapid agricultural development (in comparison with earlier periods), and induced the urbanization of the population.[8]

Economic Deserts

The policies of incentives and dependent industrialization created inadequate employment opportunities in the Mezzogiorno for the people who left agriculture by locating large, capital-intensive industries in the Mezzogiorno and by intensifying the competition for the control of the Mezzogiorno's internal market between the Mezzogiorno's and north-central Italy's small and medium businesses.[9] Placing these industries in the Mezzogiorno increased per capita incomes by absorbing some unemployment and underemployment and by increasing the cost of labor. The greater per capita incomes in industry and in agriculture made the Mezzogiorno a market more attractive than ever to north-central Italy's businesses, which were located in more dominant economic systems and were therefore already more efficient and productive than the weaker Mezzogiorno businesses. In effect, the policies of incentives and dependent industrialization created in the Mezzogiorno "economic deserts"—that is, areas without or with few small and medium businesses (especially those which could serve as the external economies of large businesses). This occurred because the large, capital-intensive industries placed in the Mezzogiorno destroyed many of its small and medium businesses, and prevented the development of others, by increasing incomes in the area and, therefore, by intensifying the competition for the control of its internal market between the area's small and medium businesses and north-central Italy's more efficient and productive ones.[10]

The Threat of Social Disintegration, The Policy of Social Control

The northwestern elite expends capital unproductively in the Mezzogiorno under the policy of social control so that the reduction of the rural population will not cause the rural area's social disintegration. An important element of this policy is the transfer of monies to southern Italians by means of employment subsidies, emigrants' remittances, unemployment insurance, and social security pensions, all of which substitute for the wages and salaries of missing jobs in the Mezzogiorno, as table 37 shows.

Between 1951 and 1973, the transfer of monies to the agricultural sector from other sectors totaled $27 billion. More than half of this amount was transferred between 1970 and 1973; in 1974 alone the transfers came to $3 billion. The per capita transfers to employees in

Table 37

Income Formation in the Mezzogiorno
(in Percentages)

Incomes	Communes	Area	Population
Autonomous[a]	20.2	28.9	57.6
Dependent on external production[b]	15.5	12.1	6.7
Subsidized[c]	64.3	59.0	35.7
Total	100.0	100.0	100.0

Source: Nicola Maria Boccella, *Il Mezzogiorno sussidiato: Redito e trasferimenti alle famiglie nei comuni meridionali* (The subsidized Mezzogiorno: Produced income and transfers to families in the southern communes) (Milan: Franco Angeli, 1982), chap. 2, esp. 52-53 and 56.

[a] Income produced locally is $\geq$ 90 percent of total income.

[b] Income produced locally is < 90 percent of total income; emigrants' remittances are $\geq$ 5.0 percent of total income.

[c] Income produced locally is < 90 percent of total income; emigrants' remittances are < 5.0 percent of total income.

the agricultural sector increased from $27 in 1951, when the total of these transfers equaled the value of 1 percent of Italy's agricultural product, to $1,612 in 1974. These transfers in 1972 equaled the value of 38 percent of Italy's agricultural product and 2.5 percent of its GNP, and represented twice the value of the investments in its agricultural system. In 1973 they provided two-thirds of the incomes of those employed in agriculture. Of the $27 billion transferred to the agricultural sector between 1951 and 1973, 80 percent ($21.6 billion) was transferred to the Mezzogiorno's agricultural sector.

EEC directive no. 268 of 25 May 1975 perfectly complements the transfer of monies to southern Italians under the policy of social control by providing income supplements paid directly to farmers.[11] The directive attempts to impede the mass depopulation and the social disintegration provoked in the EEC's mountainous and disadvantaged agricultural areas by modernizing and rationalizing the EEC states' agricultural systems under EEC directives nos. 159, 160, and 161 of 7 April 1972.

The Rise and Fall of the "State Bourgeoisie"

The capital expended for the development of the parastate industries in the Mezzogiorno under the incentive and dependent industrialization policies strengthened the "state bourgeoisie." In the late 1960s and early 1970s, the "state bourgeoisie" contested the northwestern elite's political dominance by arrogating to itself the prerogative to manage the Mezzogiorno's development. The "state bourgeoisie" actively promoted the parastate industries' productive diversification with little apparent regard for the desires or the interests of north-central Italy's private oligopolies.[12] For this reason, the northwestern elite disciplined the "state bourgeoisie" by reducing sharply between 1973 and 1978 the quantity of capital invested in the parastate industries located in the Mezzogiorno, as is evident in table 38.

The Mezzogiorno's Anomalous Urbanization

The Mezzogiorno's urbanization is anomalous in that the population urbanized not because its urban areas might have offered a great quantity of remunerative, secure, and stable employment opportunities, but rather because its rural areas no longer offered traditional (although unproductive) agricultural employment. The population urbanized because the risks of a precarious economic future in the city outweighed the certainties of a more precarious economic future in the countryside (except, of course, for the minority that retained employment in the modernizing agricultural sector). In comparison with the employment offered to urban dwellers by north-central Italy, the Mezzogiorno's urban areas have fewer employment opportunities that are equally or more remunerative, secure, and stable.[13]

The Mezzogiorno's Anomalous Consumerism

The Mezzogiorno's consumerism is also abnormal in that the value and volume of the goods and services consumed in the area exceed the value and volume of the goods and services produced there. This situation exists because the political actors that dominate the Mezzogiorno determine the composition of internal demand. They use their political power to ensure the consumption of their products in the area so that the real income produced there may accrue to them as earnings to be used as investment capital. Such consumerism hinders the accumulation and the investment, according to internal

Table 38

Investments in the Mezzogiorno's Industries and Parastate
Industries as a Percentage of Italy's Total, 1951-1981

	Industrial Investments	Industrial Investments in the Parastate Industries	Value Added in Manufacturing
1951	15.7	---	12.4
1952	14.6	---	12.6
1953	17.2	---	12.5
1954	14.3	---	12.8
1955	19.0	---	12.5
1956	17.0	---	12.6
1957	14.7	23.2	12.6
1958	15.1	26.0	12.3
1959	15.8	30.3	12.1
1960	17.6	42.7	11.7
1961	18.3	40.0	11.4
1962	22.0	43.1	11.3
1963	26.2	51.7	11.7
1964	30.5	52.5	12.3
1965	28.1	53.3	13.0
1966	23.7	47.3	13.2
1967	24.4	42.1	13.4
1968	24.5	38.0	13.1
1969	27.5	45.6	13.2
1970	26.3	53.6	13.6
1971	33.4	60.8	13.7
1972	36.7	65.0	13.3
1973	32.4	57.7	13.5
1974	31.2	46.4	11.6
1975	31.1	44.5	14.1
1976	29.2	35.8	14.0
1977	25.7	34.7	13.8
1978	22.1	34.2	14.1
1979	21.9	38.7	14.3
1980	20.0	48.3	14.2
1981	19.2	46.8	14.4

Source: Alfredo Del Monte, "Gli effetti della politica regionale sullo sviluppo industriale del Mezzogiorno" (The effects of regional policy on the Mezzogiorno's industrial development), *Rivista Trimestrale Mezzogiorno d'Europa* (Mezzogiorno d'Europa Quarterly Review; available in English), no. 4 (October/December 1984): 585. Also note that data are from ISTAT and Ministry of State Participations: old series for 1951-69; new series for 1970-81.

Table 39

Composition of Internal Demand in the Mezzogiorno
and in North-Central Italy in 1976
(in Percentages)

Origin of Goods and Services Consumed		Destination of Goods and Services Produced	
in the Mezzogiorno			
Internal production	77.0	Internal consumption	84.0
Imports from North-central Italy	15.0	Exports to North-central Italy	11.0
Imports from abroad	8.0	Exports abroad	5.0
in North-Central Italy			
Internal production	86.7	Internal consumption	85.4
Imports from the Mezzogiorno	3.7	Exports to the Mezzogiorno	5.2
Imports from abroad	9.6	Exports abroad	9.4

Source: Bruno Ferrara, *Nord-Sud, interdipendenza di due economie* (North-South, the interdependence of two economies) (Milan: Cassa per il Mezzogiorno/Franco Angeli, 1976), 89.

exigencies, of the real income produced by the Mezzogiorno by draining it to the economic systems of these political actors. The Mezzogiorno's underdevelopment is more directly functional, in strictly economic terms, to the positive, balanced development of the economic systems of the northwest and the center/northeast than to the positive, balanced development of dominant foreign economic systems (see table 39).

The Mezzogiorno's Hypertertiarization

The Mezzogiorno experiences hypertertiarization—an anomalous growth of the tertiary sector—because this sector, under the policy of social control, absorbs some of the Mezzogiorno's unemployment and underemployment by offering unproductive jobs to substitute for the productive jobs lacking in the area. This hypertertiarization, which originated in Italy's unification under the Kingdom of Sardinia and is a historically constant consequence of the Mezzogiorno's underdevelopment, was more intense before the implementation of the policies of incentives and dependent industrialization than after since these policies have reduced the economic importance of the area's tertiary sector by increasing the industrial sector's importance.

Nonetheless, the area's hypertertiarization remains a note-worthy phenomenon for three reasons. First, in comparison with north-central Italy, employment in the Mezzogiorno's tertiary sector increases at a disproportionately high rate compared to the productivity growth rate in its industrial and agricultural sectors. Second, unlike north-central Italy's tertiary sector, the Mezzogiorno's tertiary sector has not developed productive, marketable ancillary services; therefore, it has not acquired a greater functional complementarity with the industrial sector. Third, the low productivity of the Mezzogiorno's tertiary sector hinders the accumulation of capital for productive investment not only in the Mezzogiorno but in the national economy as well.[14]

Although the Mezzogiorno's tertiary sector may not have acquired a greater functional complementarity with the industrial sector, two initiatives undertaken in the mideighties by the organizations and the investors cited below indicate the development of such a complementarity between the sectors. First, in September 1984, Tecnopolis, a high-technology research city built by the Italian government and the University of Bari, became operative in Valenzano, near Bari (Puglia). Tecnopolis, which links the University of Bari with twenty universities of various Mediterranean-basin countries, carries out research projects financed by businesses and organizations such as FIAT, Olivetti, IBM, Control Data Corporation, the Bank of Italy, and the Intergovernmental Bureau of Informatics and participates in projects with the research organizations of Silicon Valley (United States). Tecnopolis ostensibly exists to foster the Mezzorgiorno's development but can provide only middle-level technological services to the vast majority of the area's businesses because so few of them utilize high-technology services (a consequence of the Mezzogiorno's underdevelopment).[15]

Second, on 6 October 1984, Pitagora (Pythagoras), an economic data bank, began operations in Cosenza (Calabria). Pitagora, linked to the Statistical Office of the European Communities (EUROSTAT), the Organization of Economic Cooperation and Development (OECD), and the International Monetary Fund (IMF), provides information about the Italian economy, other economies, and the international economy to banks and businesses.[16] It remains to be seen whether these initiatives will foster the accumulation and the investment, according to internal exigencies, of the real income produced by the Mezzogiorno or whether these initiatives, undertaken to satisfy external exigencies, will serve the best interests of the economic systems that dominate the Mezzogiorno, as the initiatives to industrialize the area have done.

Emigration from the Mezzogiorno

Emigration is a salient consequence of the Mezzogiorno's underdevelopment: for example, between 1951 and 1971, 4,148,517 southern Italians emigrated, most temporarily, some permanently, to north-central Italy and to other countries. Of this total, 2,051,872 emigrated between 1951 and 1961 and 2,096,645 between 1961 and 1971.[17] Under the policies of incentives and dependent industrialization, the emigration of southern Italians is more functional than ever both to the interests of the northwestern elite and to the positive, balanced development of the economic systems of the northwest and the center/northeast.

There are three reasons why this is so. First, the Mezzogiorno's economic development without employment made the Mezzogiorno's unemployed and underemployed a work force useful primarily to the industrial expansion of the economic systems of the northwest and the center/northeast and secondarily to the industrial expansion of foreign states (mostly those of the EEC).[18] Second, the remittances of the temporary and permanent emigrants (from all of Italy to other countries) are a substantial source of revenue for Italy's balance of payments: for example, between 1970 and 1978, these remittances added $12.8 billion to the national current account.[19] Third, emigration is the "safety valve" of the policy of social control, which is unable to neutralize the negative repercussions of the policies of incentives and dependent industrialization.[20]

Although emigration may be a safety valve, the northwestern elite cannot consider emigration a panacea for the negative repercussions of the policies of incentives and dependent industrialization. Willing or not, it must contend politically with the emigrants, not only those of the Mezzogiorno but of all Italy, and must realize that the prospect of emigration does not always exist. Excessive migration from the Mezzogiorno to north-central Italy saturates that area's industrial sector with workers. It strengthens the trade unions, allied primarily with the Left. It also obliges the northwestern elite either to create unproductive jobs in the tertiary sector and in the public administration or to send the emigrants back to their former regions to accept unproductive jobs or some other form of welfare.

Moreover, in order to reduce their labor costs as much as possible, the entrepreneurs of the EEC states that depend to a significant degree on immigrant labor discriminate against intra-EEC immigrant workers in favor of extra-EEC immigrant workers. This happens because the socio-economic obligations toward the latter are minimal compared to the socio-economic obligations toward the former, whom the host countries must treat as domestic workers according to the EEC's Social Policy. With the passing of time, this discrimination has increased (see table 40).

Between 1951 and 1971, 1,885,149 Italians emigrated abroad, most temporarily, some permanently; of this total 1,319,604 left between 1951 and 1961, while 565,545 left between 1961 and 1971.[21] Between 1972 and 1975, 470,340 Italian emigrated, but in each year their number decreased: 141,852 in 1972; 123,802 in 1973; 112,020 in 1974; and 92,666 in 1975.[22] Emigration is a delicate problem because Italians do not like to leave their country in order to work abroad. A poll conducted by *La Repubblica* (7 February 1984) revealed that 93 percent of all Italians preferred to live in Italy. The countries that the remaining 7 percent would like to settle in are shown in table 41.

The Entrepreneurial Mafia and the Mafia Model of Capitalist Accumulation

The Mafia originated in southern Italy, more specifically in western Sicilia, in southern Calabria, and in the Naples area, between the sixteenth and the nineteenth centuries. It would be difficult if not impossible to narrow the time period even further because historiography on the subject lacks consensus and because historical evidence is inconclusive about the Mafia's development. Nonetheless, it seems appropriate to consider the period between the sixteenth and the nineteenth centuries as the Mafia's gestation period. By the early nineteenth century, the system of political and economic relationships that created and expressed the Mafia had been established.

Three factors combined to engender the Mafia in southern Italy. First, between 1504 and 1713, the Kingdom of the Two Sicilys suffered under the oppressive domination of the Kingdom of Spain, which attempted to sustain itself in its imperial conflicts with the English, French, Austrians, and Turks in part by exploiting southern Italy's resources.[23] During the sixteenth century the Spanish sov-

Table 40

Extra-EEC and Intra-EEC Immigrant Workers, 1957-1970

	Extra-EEC immigrant workers as % of total immigrant workers in the EEC (1)	Intra-EEC[a] immigrant workers as % of total immigrant workers in the EEC (2)	Total % (3) (1)+(2) =(3)	Immigrant workers[a] from the Mezzogiorno as % of: (a)total im. wrkrs. in the EEC; (b)intra-EEC im. wrkrs.	
				(a)	(b)
1957	47.7	52.3	100.0		
1962	57.6	42.4	100.0		
1968	54.0	46.0	100.0	27	59
1970	74.0	26.0	100.0	13	50

Source: Maria Valeria Agostini, *Regioni europee e scambio ineguale: Verso una politica regionale comunitaria?* (The European regions and unequal exchange: Toward a community regional policy?) (Bologna: Il Mulino, 1976), 33.

[a] International migrations only.

ereigns transferred to their viceroys much of the political authority of southern Italy's barons, who nonetheless retained ownership of their fiefs and jurisdiction over them. Although more severe in the parts of northern Italy under Spanish control (1535-1713), Spanish exploitation impoverished southern Italy and undermined the socioeconomic stability of individuals and families, especially those of the lower and lower-middle classes.[24]

Second, agricultural capitalism's genesis in the Kingdom of the Two Sicilys during the latter half of the eighteenth century intensified the socioeconomic insecurity created by Spain's misgovernment. The inflation that accompanied capitalism's genesis ruined baron rentiers with fixed incomes; it favored instead the entrepreneurial tenants who earned a profit by producing agricultural commodities to be exchanged (sold) in local and international markets in order to pay their workers' meager salaries and their landlords' rent. Wealth concentrated in the hands of these entrepreneurial tenents who, in fact, became "new barons" by expropriating and then, in the nineteenth century, privatizing the old landlords' fiefs. The demesne's privatization not only created a free labor market that forced agricultural workers to sell their labor power in order to live; it also created labor relations which offered to these workers no legal recourse against inequities or abuses in their relations with property owners or with the government.[25]

Third, the Neapolitan Bourbons' piloted industrialization policy— understood in the context of the international distribution of power

Table 41

Countries Preferred by Would-be Emigrants

Countries Preferred	% of Italian Population
United Kingdom	1.1
United States	1.1
West Germany	1.1
Scandinavian countries	1.0
France	.7
Japan	.3
Soviet Union/Central Europe	.2
India	.1
Other countries	1.4

Source: Monitorskopea Repubblica Poll, *La Repubblica,* 7 February 1984, 9.

and division of labor of the nineteenth century—further intensified the socioeconomic insecurity produced by Spain's misgovernment and agricultural capitalism's genesis. The international distribution of power conditioned capitalism's development in the Kingdom of the Two Sicilys.

Following the 1816 Restoration, the Neapolitan Bourbons faced contradictory needs. On the one hand, in order to stay in power, the Bourbons had to hold the southern Italian bourgeoisie in check. On the other hand, in order to compete with England, France, Austria, and Spain—countries stronger not only economically but politically and above all militarily—for an advantageous position in the international division of labor, the Bourbons had to foster the development not only of agricultural capitalism but of industrial capitalism as well.

The Bourbons realized that the Kingdom of the Two Sicilys, without industrial development and diversification, would become a de facto colony in the international division of labor, a supplier of agricultural foodstuffs and raw materials to more powerful countries. For this reason, beginning in 1823, the Bourbons implemented a policy of piloted industrialization, coupled with a policy of strong agricultural protectionism. To industrialize the Kingdom of the Two Sicilys, the Bourbons created unequal exchange relations between agriculture and private industry to the latter's favor; they invited foreign industrial capital and even created industry. Unlike northern Italy, where indus-

Table 42

Italian Citizens Emigrating from Their Regions in January 1984

	Population (1)	Emigrants (2)	(2)% / (1)
Italy	55,923,999	4,076,686	7.3
Liguria	1,867,363	112,914	6.0
Lombardia	8,837,656	136,346	1.5
Piemonte	4,451,271	141,087	3.2
Valle d'Aosta	113,720	17,290	15.2
Northwest average	3,817,503	101,909	2.7
Emilia-Romagna	3,935,834	176,811	4.5
Friuli-Venezia Giulia	1,244,406	242,484	19.5
Lazio	4,921,859	169,445	3.4
Marche	1,390,388	119,029	8.6
Toscana	3,566,763	80,528	2.3
Trentino-Alto Adige	866,377	80,343	9.3
Umbria	795,218	74,090	9.3
Veneto	4,277,501	256,726	6.0
Center/northeast average	2,624,793	149,932	5.7
Abruzzo	1,211,323	177,201	14.6
Basilicata	614,596	146,720	23.9
Calabria	2,034,425	525,280	25.8
Campania	5,280,268	337,712	6.4
Molise	329,705	113,691	34.5
Puglia	3,771,329	314,224	8.3
Sardegna	1,552,767	183,200	11.8
Sicilia	4,861,230	671,565	13.8
Mezzogiorno average	2,456,955	308,699	12.6

Source: Gianni Giadresco, "Premiato ed espulso" (Rewarded and expelled), *Rinascita*, no. 4 (27 January 1984): 16-17.

try at this time was an accessory activity of agriculture, in the Kingdom of the Two Sicilys industrial-agricultural relations expressed an inverse relationship, one which anticipated, at least tendentially, mature capitalism.[26]

The Bourbons' attempt to accelerate development in the Kingdom of the Two Sicilys by guiding industrialization required the intensification of agricultural exploitation, the compression of salaries, and the repression of worker associations. Such was the price to be paid so that other countries might not subordinate the kingdom economically. The Bourbons attempted to mitigate the negative socioeconomic repercussions of this policy by lightening the agricultural areas' fiscal burden and by constructing public works there. Nonetheless, southern Italy's lower and lower-middle classes faced precarious socioeconomic conditions without legal remedies for their difficulties.

These three factors created intense insecurity in the Kingdom of the Two Sicilys by producing economic conditions so precarious that individuals and families, especially those belonging to the lower and lower-middle classes, could rise or fall suddenly and rapidly in the social order. This socioeconomic insecurity gave rise to the Mafia. In its original and truest form the Mafia was not an organization but rather a type of behavior and power.

Mafia was the word used for the ethic that one adopted in order to acquire and maintain a secure social position in an insecure social environment. The traditional Mafia philosophy is *omertà*, "the capacity to be a man."[27] According to this belief, life is a "war of all against all," and a true man, the *mafioso*, is one with personal honor acquired by means of individual violence. The mafioso is a man of respect (*uomo di rispetto*), a man able to make himself (feared and) respected (*farsi rispettare*) by being able to avenge affronts and injure enemies by himself.[28] The traditional Mafia ethic affirms aggression by equating honor with superior power: justice is force, not an ideal.[29]

The meaning of *Mafia* and the various terms that denote a similar ethic in different geographic areas reflects the individual's need to attempt to secure his social position in an insecure social environment by resorting to individual violence and personal means. *Mafia* (which applies properly to Sicily) is of uncertain etymology but probably derives from the Arabic word for protection. *'Ndrangheta* (from Calabria) comes from the ancient Greek *andragathia*, a "valorous man," one that is haughty, clever, contemptuous of danger, and without scruples. *Camorra* (used in the Naples area) is also of uncertain etymology but derives either from a word common to the Mediterranean region, *morra* ("pack" or "gang") or from the Spanish word *gamurra* ("extortion payoff").[30]

Omertà has a concomitant meaning: "a conspiracy of silence." In the environment of socioeconomic insecurity that caused the Mafia's origin, people refused to collaborate with the official organs of justice. Often without legal remedies for their difficulties, people considered these organizations, and the states that they represented, the cause of their problems. "Official justice" enjoyed little legitimacy.

According to the traditional Mafia ethic, a mafioso's prestige and honor (power) are commensurate with his ability both to behave like a mafioso (display his behavior with impunity in open violation of the established laws) and to govern (manage the constant and open all-against-all competition for personal honor or power). The mafioso acquires his honor by using violence and maintains it by creating an authority that legitimizes and thus enhances it.

The mafioso creates his authority by astutely combining violence and tactical diplomacy. He uses violence, and the threat of violence, to quell and to deter challenges. He uses diplomacy to delude unsuspecting foes and create the perception that he may be a protector, mediator, counselor, judge, father-figure, and friend of all.

Moreover, according to the traditional Mafia ethic, although wealth may at times accompany the mafioso's honor, wealth and honor are not synonymous. Personal honor, not personal wealth, is supreme.[31]

After Italy's unification, in the social environment created by the Mezzogiorno's underdevelopment, the mafioso's honor and authority gave him substantial political autonomy. In theory, this autonomy should make the mafioso a competitor and therefore an adversary and an enemy of the state. However, Italy has tolerated the Mafia (save the Kingdom of Italy during the Fascist regime, which suppressed it) and has maintained social order by collaborating with it—even officially on numerous occasions. The Mafia has been a convenient and effective mediator of foreign political domination over the Mezzogiorno on the one hand, and of social conflict and cooperation in the Mezzogiorno on the other.[32]

A mafioso, assisted by four or five close associates, manages social conflict and cooperation in a given area of southern Italy by exercising his authority over the population through a "cosca"—that is, a hierarchical network of people linked by family ties and friendships. The cosca is the fundamental Mafia unit that gives the mafioso his identity and in whose context he competes for honor. The mafioso must constantly contend with real and potential challenges from within and without the cosca (for example, from other cosche). He remains the head of the cosca (*capocosca*) for only as long as he remains the person most feared and respected.[33]

In the twentieth century the mafioso's authority, together with the traditional Mafia ethic upon which his authority was based, suffered two severe blows. First, the Fascist regime debilitated his authority and ethic by suppressing his activities and asserting the state's authority.[34] However, American and English occupation forces in World War II resuscitated the mafioso's authority: they released incarcerated mafiosi and placed them in local political offices in the Mezzogiorno so that they might serve as anti-Fascist, anti-Left agents of social control.[35] Nonetheless, at the end of the war, the mafioso's authority was very weak.

Second, Italy's integration in the international economy under a tempered American hegemony undermined the mafioso's already weak authority. It modified Italy's mass social values in such a way as to delegitimize further the traditional Mafia ethic. The American values of materialism and consumerism that accompanied Italy's post-World War II prosperity identified merit and virtue not with individual violence but rather with wealth and success. Between 1945 and 1965, the mafioso's prestige and authority fell progressively into crisis, causing him to become socially ostracized.

Italy asserted its prerogative to monopolize physical violence on its territory. The PCI and the trade unions penetrated into the Mezzogiorno and limited the mafioso's activities. Since southern Italians no longer accorded legitimacy to the traditional Mafia ethic, they therefore no longer admired and feared the mafioso.[36]

As already discussed, during the 1960s the northwestern elite had become increasingly aware that the policies of incentives and dependent industrialization produced contradictory repercussions. Although these policies promised to strengthen the elite's privileged position by intensifying the Mezzogiorno's underdevelopment, they also threatened to undermine its position by exacerbating the Mezzogiorno's disequilibria and provoking social disintegration.

This threat induced the northwestern elite, through the DC, to make the mafioso both a politically inferior mediator of northern Italian, West German, and American political domination over the Mezzogiorno and an agent of social control. To this end, beginning in the mid-1960s, the northwestern elite integrated the Mezzogiorno's mafiosi into the DC and charged them to manage directly, according to the DC's political dictates, the area's credit market, job market for public administration, and distribution of government contracts for construction in the area.[37]

In order to reacquire their lost authority and prestige, the mafiosi reacted to their social exclusion and political subordination in two ways: they created a new Mafia ethic and they adopted the capitalist mode of production.

The new Mafia ethic, which adapted the traditional ethic to the socioeconomic conditions of the post-World War II Mezzogiorno, redefined honor on the basis of the American values of consumerism and materialism and on the basis of the spirit of capitalism or the religion of accumulation. The new ethic equates honor with wealth. Life remains a constant and open all-against-all competition for honor. However, a mafioso's honor is now commensurate with his wealth and individual violence is now a means to the end of capital accumulation.

The mafiosi adopted the capitalist mode of production because it is the most efficient accumulator of wealth and therefore the most efficient "accumulator of honor."[38] In this way the mafiosi transformed themselves into "entrepreneurial mafiosi" who are characterized by ethical irrationality and pragmatic rationality.

Ethical irrationality characterizes the entrepreneurial mafioso because he bases his behavior on two aggressive, animalistic, and predatory concepts: honor is acquired by means of individual violence and honor is defined by the American values of consumerism and materialism, and by the spirit of capitalism or religion of accumulation. This religion's dogma glorifies the accumulation of wealth for its own sake. Pragmatic rationality also characterizes the entrepreneurial mafioso because he rationally attempts to satisfy his irrational, insatiable desire to acquire honor (wealth) by combining the use of violence as a means to the end with the capitalist mode of production—that is, by creating the "Mafia model of capitalist accumulation."[39]

The Mafia model of capitalist accumulation provides the entrepreneurial mafioso with three fundamental advantages over legitimate entrepreneurs. First, the mafioso discourages competition. He overwhelms legitimate entrepreneurs by using or threatening to use violence against them. Second, the mafioso lowers salaries and wages. He reduces labor costs by evading workers' insurance and social security payments and by refusing to give overtime pay. He also takes advantage of the Mezzogiorno's unemployed and underemployed by offering them illegal jobs that pay less than the legal minimum wage. Last, the mafioso disposes of financial resources. He acquires capital from illegal activities, principally from international drug traffic, arms sales, kidnappings, extortion, and the theft of art and jewels. He then overwhelms legitimate entrepreneurs and dominates markets by investing this illicit capital, which need not be reimbursed (with or without interest) to anyone, in "legitimate" Mafia enterprises. These are enterprises that would be completely legitimate were their investment capital not "dirty."[40]

The emergence, during the 1970s, of the Mafia model of capitalist accumulation marks the mafioso's transformation from a political mediator into an entrepreneur whose private vices are not public virtues. The mafia model induces the mafioso to resort to violence, not only in his relationships with other mafiosi but with the rest of society. It also increases the use of violence, because capitalism intensifies the competition for honor among mafiosi by intensifying the competition for wealth. Such an incitement to ever-greater violence puts the mafiosi into constant conflict with the Italian judicial system. It induces him to repudiate the state's prerogative to monopolize physical violence on Italian territory. It also promotes the organizational development of his activities, which allows him to respond better to capitalist competition and therefore to compete better for honor (wealth) with other mafiosi and with the rest of society.[41]

During the 1970s, this organizational development transformed the Mafia from a type of behavior and power without a formal organization into one with a formal organization—the entrepreneurial Mafia, characterized by a factionalized hierarchy of mafiosi in constant conflict with each other in the competition for honor and wealth. Its organizational and financial strength allowed the mafioso to regain his lost political autonomy.[42] This strength allows its model of capitalist accumulation to project itself outward from the Mezzogiorno, to reproduce, and to regenerate elsewhere.[43]

However, the entrepreneurial Mafia's factionalism induces it to lacerate itself and society. Although the mafioso, by equating honor with wealth when he made himself a capitalist, may have adopted the values and the lifestyle of cultures developed outside and imposed on the Mezzogiorno, his traditional values (manipulative friendships, family ties, personal honor acquired by means of individual violence) still form the basis of his identity. No sociopolitical agent has yet constrained him by means of institutional regulation to change his modus operandi, to renounce his traditional values in order to be able to adopt new ones. In essence, the entrepreneurial mafioso is a man of more than one culture.[44] Moreover, the entrepreneurial Mafia is more an agent of social disintegration (because it is violent and destructive) than an agent of economic development (because it is capitalist and productive).[45]

The 1980s saw the entrepreneurial Mafia divided into two major competing factions: the Nuova Famiglia (New Family), governed by Michele Zaza, and the Nuova Famiglia Organizzata (Organized New Family), governed by Raffaele Cutolo. In the early 1980s these factions engaged in bloody conflict because Cutolo attempted, unsuccessfully, to wrest control of the entrepreneurial Mafia's lucrative international drug traffic from Zaza, the ally of the American Mafia, the Cosa Nostra (Our Concern).[46] As stated earlier, the cosca, which traditionally counted between fifteen and twenty people but now, because of extended families numbers between seventy and eighty adult males, remains the fundamental Mafia unit.[47]

Systematic relationships exist between Italy's politicians and the Mafia's leaders.[48] At the third level,[49] the politicians involved belong mostly to the DC, some to the PSI, a few to other parties, and none to the PCI, which is uninvolved on the third level.[50] These politicians agree to protect from legal prosecution as much as possible, and so far with great efficacy, those mafiosi who agree to supply votes for elections by organizing consensus through favoritism and intimidation.[51]

The politicians involved enter into alliances with the Mafia not to enrich themselves but rather to acquire, maintain, or increase their power. The money they take is used to defray the ever-increasing costs of electoral campaigns.[52]

In the Mezzogiorno, the Mafia assumes ever greater control over employment in the public administration and over the distribution of the state's subsidies and pensions by penetrating the state apparatus. In some areas, the Mafia has become the political elite class.[53] Moreover, north-central Italy's private oligopolies often nourish the Mafia by offering subcontracts to the mafiosi because they use their three competitive advantages over legitimate entrepreneurs to render services at lower cost. The oligopolies conspire with the Mafia to artificially raise the costs of public works projects in order to defraud the state.[54]

Compared to the other political parties, the PCI undertakes the most effective political action against the Mafia. Pio La Torre, the parliamentary deputy and the PCI's Sicilian regional secretary (assassinated by the Mafia in Palermo on 25 April 1982), introduced Italy's most progressive anti-Mafia bill. It became law no. 416/416 bis of 13 September 1982, known more commonly as the Rognoni-La Torre Law. For the first time examining magistrates had the authority to investigate systematically the accounts of suspected mafiosi and Mafia-style organizations (*organizzazioni di stampo mafioso*). These are organizations that subordinate their associates and require their tacit complicity in the commission of crimes through intimidation.[55]

On 2 November 1984 the EEC for the first time addressed the Mafia problem. Pancrazio De Pasquale, the president of the EEC's Regional Policy Commission and PCI member, proposed that the European Parliament adopt a resolution inviting the EEC Commission to investigate the Mafia's involvement in the management of the EEC's funds for Sicily. On 14 February 1985 the parliament adopted the resolution.[56]

However, the EEC still lacks authority to undertake substantive

Table 43

Mafia Extortion in Italy, 1983

	Number of Businesses (1)	Number of[a] Businesses Extorted (2)	$\frac{(2)}{(1)}$%	Mafia's[b] Assassinations and Attempts in 1983
Italy	1,436,742	146,153	10.2	256
Liguria	34,916	349	1.0	---
Lombardia	217,646	10,882	5.0	7
Piemonte	115,651	5,782	5.0	4
Valle d'Aosta	4,197	21	0.5	---
Northwest average	93,103	4,259	4.6	3
Emilia-Romagna	124,617	1,246	1.0	---
Friuli-Venezia Giulia	34,916	349	1.0	---
Lazio	111,595	8,928	8.0	23
Marche	42,179	422	1.0	1
Toscana	102,749	514	.5	4
Trentino-Alto Adige	33,568	1	.003	2
Umbria	19,719	39	.3	1
Veneto	126,628	3,160	2.5	---
Center/northeast average	74,496	1,832	2.5	4
Abruzzo	33,827	338	1.0	2
Basilicata	13,610	68	.5	4
Calabria	47,188	17,931	38.0	57
Campania	110,540	45,760	41.4	61
Molise	7,920	---	---	---
Puglia	87,591	7,008	8.0	21
Sardegna	39,878	798	2.0	8
Sicilia	105,846	42,338	40.0	59
Mezzogiorno average	55,800	14,280	25.6	27

Source: *La Repubblica*, 23 March 1984, 12.

[a]Confcommercio estimate based on the 10 percent sample of its members who answered its questionnaire. Confcommercio (General Confederation of Italian Commerce and Tourism) has 800,000 members.

[b]Ministry of the Interior data.

political action against the Mafia. In 1983 West Germany and Denmark, in a defense of national sovereignty, blocked the adoption of norms that would have given the EEC authority to oversee the management of disbursed EEC funds by conducting direct, surprise inspections.[57]

The Mafia threatens more to undermine than to strengthen the northwestern elite's dominant position in Italy because the Mafia model of capitalist accumulation threatens to make the entrepreneurial Mafia more an agent of social disintegration in Italy than an agent of social control in the Mezzogiorno.[58] The pernicious consequences of the Mafia's activities for Italian society are increasingly manifest. For example, in 1984 the Mafia recycled its illicit finance capital through six thousand businesses under its control,[59] extorted an average annual LIT 1,000 billion from about 10 percent of Italy's legitimate entrepreneurs,[60] and commited violent crimes (see table 43). Such consequences create political disaffections that the Left champions.

Should the political costs of the Mafia as an agent of social disintegration in Italy outweigh its political benefits as an agent of social control in the Mezzogiorno, the domestic needs of political legitimation would oblige the northwestern elite to attempt to subordinate the Mafia politically or even to eliminate it and substitute a more suitable agent of social control. In the 1960s, the northwestern elite, through the DC, saved the Mezzogiorno's mafiosi from social emargination because the "state bourgeoisie," together with social security pensions, subsidized incomes, public works projects, and a system of political patronage and clientelism seemed insufficient to keep the Mezzogiorno under political and economic control. Although the entrepreneurial Mafia may now be more costly politically than ever before, the northwestern elite does not yet consider itself able to manage the Mezzogiorno's underdevelopment and therefore to govern Italy without the entrepreneurial Mafia.

10
The State of Affairs and Future Prospects

Exacerbated Disequilibria

BY 1988 THE EEC HAD NOT promoted the balanced, harmonious development prescribed by Article 2 of the Treaty of Rome for all member states. It had promoted instead the positive, balanced development of the economic systems of the politically dominant member states at the expense of the politically subordinate ones. This happened because the politically dominant states, and not the legal dictates of the Treaty of Rome, determined the EEC's development.

Between 1957 and 1985 Italy's participation in an EEC dominated politically by West Germany and France under a tempered American hegemony increased the Italian economy's involvement in the process of capital accumulation among the EEC states principally to the advantage and benefit of the West German and French economies. As the data in Appendix B (Statistical Appendix to chapter 9) reveal, in comparison with the EEC average, Italy registered a lower per capita income, a lower growth rate, a higher inflation rate, and a higher unemployment rate. In this period the disparities between Italy and the EEC average with regard to these socioeconomic indicators widened over time to Italy's disadvantage.

The EEC's unbalanced integration induced the northwestern elite to protect its privileged position in Italy by minimizing the negative consequences of the country's participation in the EEC for the economic system of the northwest. To this end, the northwestern elite intensified the Mezzogiorno's underdevelopment. It increased the Mezzogiorno's involvement in the process of capital accumulation in the Italian economy to the advantage and benefit of the economic system of the northwest by implementing the policies of incentives and dependent industrialization.

Under these policies, the Mezzogiorno's development depends not upon the accumulation and the investment, according to internal exigencies, of the real income produced by the Mezzogiorno but rather upon the infusion of external resources, the capital-intensive Italian and foreign investments that cause the Mezzogiorno's economic development without employment. As the data in Appendix B show, in comparison with the economic systems of the northwest and the center/northeast, the Mezzogiorno receives a smaller share of Italy's Common Regional Fund (created ostensibly to attenuate the disequilibria between the Mezzogiorno and the rest of Italy) and registers a higher unemployment rate, greater value added and greater employment in agriculture, lesser value added and lesser employment in industry, a lower per capita income, and a lower consumption of goods and services per family. Moreover, these disparities between the Mezzogiorno and the rest of Italy increase over time to the Mezzogiorno's disadvantage.

The countries that dominate Italy—the United States, West Germany, and France—are not adverse to the Mezzogiorno's underdevelopment because an Italy with an underdeveloped Mezzogiorno is a less threatening economic and political rival than one with a balanced economy. Economically it is a less productive and therefore weaker competitor. Politically the dominant nations can offer, through financial, diplomatic, and covert means, to help the Italian ruling class to legitimize its position and therefore to retain power, provided that it does not assert interests contrary to theirs. Moreover, these countries can threaten to punish the Italian ruling class with the same means should it behave in a way unacceptable to them.[1]

Initiatives for Italy's Greater Autonomy

In order to reduce the influence of the countries that dominate Italy, the Italian power elite must increase Italy's autonomy in the international system. This would allow the Italian ruling class to deal with the exigencies of international economic competition and the domestic needs of political legitimation in ways more advantageous to itself. Moreover, increased autonomy could give the Italian economy a more beneficial function in the international division of labor. To give Italy greater autonomy, the Italian Establishment, beginning in the 1970s, has undertaken three initiatives: the productive development of the Italian work force, the Italian economy's "active internationalization," and the development of a southern EEC bloc.

During the 1970s and 1980s Italian entrepreneurs have partially responded to the pressures of international economic competition under the adverse conditions created by the EEC's unbalanced inte-

Table 44

Productivity and the Cost of Labor per Unit, by Country
(1975=100)

	Productivity in 1984	% of Change	Cost of Labor per Unit Produced in 1984	% of Change
France	151.6	51.6	204.0	104.0
Italy	158.8	58.8	299.7	199.7
Japan	157.3	57.3	107.2	7.2
United Kingdom	131.7	31.7	228.7	128.7
United States	127.2	27.2	151.0	51.0
West Germany	133.0	33.0	125.2	25.2

Source: *La Repubblica*, 6 July 1985, 2: results of a study issued in July 1985 by the Centro di Statistica Aziendale (Center for Business Statistics) and the Cassa di Risparmio di Firenze (Savings Bank of Florence).

gration and to the domestic pressures of Italy's trade unions for higher wages and for greater employment by greatly increasing productivity, as the data in table 44 show.

The Italian economy's internationalization has traditionally been more passive than active: its subsidiary role in the upper ranks of the international division of labor is a function determined by Italy's participation in an EEC dominated politically by West Germany and France under a tempered American hegemony. As the data presented in chapter 7 reveal, foreign investors strongly influence the Italian economy's development by investing huge amounts of capital. In comparison with Italian entrepreneurs, for example, American, British, and West German investors influence other economies more: the United States, the United Kingdom, and West Germany invest, respectively, thirty-four, ten, and five times more capital abroad than does Italy.[2]

Until recently, a few large industrial groups were responsible for 75 percent of Italian investments abroad, of which 61 percent were concentrated in rubber and electric machines. Moreover, 50 percent of Italian investments abroad were located in "developing countries"—41 percent in Latin America alone.[3]

During the 1970s, Italian entrepreneurs began to respond to the

Italian economy's "passive internationalization" by accelerating its "active internationalization," which means that they increased Italian investments abroad and diversified these investments territorially and sectorally. Between 1974 and 1981, the turnover of Italian companies operating in Italy grew by an average of 19 percent per year while the turnover of Italian companies operating abroad grew by an annual average of 26 percent. In this period Italian investments in advanced industrial countries increased by 24.7 percent; moreover, the investments made by small and medium businesses, compared to large ones, increased by 4 percent. In 1981 Italian investments abroad amounted to LIT 4,500 billion; in that year, companies that operated abroad with the participation of Italian capital invoiced more than LIT 30,000 billion, equal then to about half the value of Italian exports.[4]

Between 1981 and 1986 the Italian economy's active internationalization accelerated further. At the end of 1985, for every LIT 100 invoiced by Italian industry, LIT 12 were invoiced by the foreign branches of Italian multinational corporations.[5] In 1985 330 Italian investors participated in 680 foreign companies, which invoiced LIT 33,000 billion and employed 232,000 people.[6]

The Italian economy's greater labor productivity and active internationalization have produced promising results. In 1986 the Italian economy became the fifth largest in the world: Italy's gross national product and per capita income exceeded the United Kingdom's and approached France's.[7]

The adherence of Greece, Portugal, and Spain, all producers of great quantities of Mediterranean agricultural products, to the Treaty of Rome could shift the balance of power within the EEC from northern Europe toward the Mediterranean area. Should Italy and the other Mediterranean states of the EEC cooperate politically, they could succeed in asserting their interests in the EEC, in ending the political and economic dominance of West Germany and France, in restructuring the CAP, and in ending the CAP's discrimination against Mediterranean agricultural products.

However, should Italy and the other Mediterranean countries fail to cooperate, there could be an economic war among the EEC's weak, which, besides preserving the dominance of West Germany and France, would in all probability most damage the Mezzogiorno's agriculture. It would be unable to sustain the collective competition of Greece, Portugal, and Spain, especially if the northwestern elite or another future Italian ruling class should forsake even more the Mezzogiorno's agriculture in order to exchange Italian industrial products from the north for greater quantities of Greek, Portuguese, and Spanish agricultural products.[8]

Initial indications seem to augur well for the development of a southern EEC bloc based on a Rome-Madrid axis designed to offset the Bonn-Paris axis that traditionally dominates the EEC. On 20 January 1986 at Taormina, near Catania (Sicily), and on 23 January 1987 at Palma di Maiorca (Spain), Italian and Spanish political delegations, led by each country's prime minister, held summit meetings that established the political foundations of Italo-Spanish collaboration with regard to scientific research and the production of manufactured goods and armaments. The delegations also agreed on the following issues: terrorism with the end of greater collaboration in measures adopted for security; defense policy with the goal of international arms reductions; political and economic relations with Central America, South America, and the Middle East with the plan of promoting European interests there; political and economic relations with the United States with the end of increasing the EEC's autonomy; the strengthening of EEC institutions and regional development initiatives with the goal of attenuating regional disequilibria; and the CAP's reform with the end of terminating discrimination against Mediterranean agricultural products.[9]

Toward an Uncertain Future

It remains to be seen whether or not the Italian economy's greater productivity and active internationalization will give it a more advantageous function in the international division of labor. It also remains to be seen whether the Italian political elite will be able to develop, together with the other Mediterranean states of the EEC, especially Spain, a southern bloc capable of shifting the balance of power within the EEC from northern Europe toward the Mediterranean area. These seem to be the most promising and realistic prospects for greater autonomy at the Italian Establishment's disposal.

It also remains to be seen what Italy's greater autonomy, if realized, will mean for the Mezzogiorno. This much is certain: without greater political autonomy and a more balanced territorial development of the national economy, Italy will remain subordinate politically and economically to the United States, West Germany, and France and the Mezzogiorno will remain underdeveloped.

Appendixes

Appendix A
Statistical Appendix to Chapter 6, "The European Economic Community and the Italian Lira"
(tables 45–46)

Table 45

Percent Contribution of EEC Currencies
to the Value of the EUA/ECU, May 1975–May 1984

	5/30/75	10/30/75	1/30/76	5/26/76	10/29/76
DM	27.1	27.2	27.6	29.1	31.0
FF	21.8	22.1	22.2	22.3	20.7
L	15.7	15.4	15.5	14.3	12.8
HFL	9.1	9.1	9.3	9.5	10.2
LIT	13.4	13.6	12.6	11.8	11.4
FB	8.0	8.0	7.9	8.3	8.8
DKR	3.1	3.1	3.1	3.2	3.3
IRL	1.3	1.3	1.5	1.2	1.1
FLUX	.3	.3	.3	.3	.3

	1/28/77	5/27/77	10/28/77	1/26/78	5/30/78
DM	30.7	31.1	31.6	31.9	32.1
FF	20.8	20.6	20.5	19.8	20.4
L	13.6	13.5	13.6	14.0	13.2
HFL	10.1	10.3	10.2	10.3	10.4
LIT	11.1	10.9	10.7	10.2	10.3
FB	8.8	9.0	9.0	9.1	9.1
DKR	3.3	3.2	3.1	3.1	3.1
IRL	1.2	1.2	1.2	1.2	1.1
FLUX	.3	.3	.3	.4	.4

	10/30/78	1/29/79	5/30/79	10/30/79	1/31/80
DM	33.1	33.0	32.9	33.4	33.2
FF	20.0	20.0	19.7	19.8	19.7
L	12.8	13.1	13.9	13.4	14.0
HFL	10.6	10.6	10.4	10.4	10.4
LIT	9.6	9.6	9.7	9.5	9.4
FB	9.3	9.3	9.0	9.1	9.0
DKR	3.1	3.1	3.0	3.0	2.8
IRL	1.1	1.1	1.1	1.1	1.1
FLUX	.4	.4	.4	.4	.4

DM = West German mark HFL = Dutch florin DKR = Danish crown
FF = French franc LIT = Italian lira IRL = Irish pound
L = British pound FB = Belgian franc FLUX = Luxembourg franc

Table 45—*Continued*

	5/30/80	10/30/80	1/30/81	5/27/81	10/28/81
DM	32.9	32.3	31.8	32.5	33.9
FF	19.6	19.5	19.2	19.1	18.8
L	14.6	15.9	17.2	16.8	15.1
HFL	10.3	10.3	10.1	10.1	10.6
LIT	9.2	9.0	8.8	8.6	8.4
FB	9.1	8.9	8.8	8.8	8.1
DKR	2.8	2.8	2.7	2.7	2.8
IRL	1.1	1.1	1.1	1.1	1.1
FLUX	.4	.3	.3	.3	.3

	1/28/82	5/27/82	10/29/82	1/28/83	5/30/83
DM	33.8	34.7	35.2	36.1	36.3
FF	18.5	18.5	17.3	17.7	16.8
L	15.8	15.6	16.2	14.4	15.7
HFL	10.6	10.8	11.2	11.3	11.2
LIT	8.3	8.3	8.1	8.2	8.0
FB	7.9	7.4	7.8	7.9	8.0
DKR	2.7	2.7	2.6	2.7	2.7
IRL	1.1	1.1	1.1	1.1	1.1
FLUX	.3	.3	.3	.3	.3

	10/28/83	1/30/84	5/29/84
DM	36.7	36.7	37.0
FF	16.7	16.7	16.7
L	15.3	15.5	15.0
HFL	11.3	11.3	11.4
LIT	7.9	7.9	7.9
FB	7.9	7.8	7.9
DKR	2.7	2.7	2.7
IRL	1.0	1.0	1.0
FLUX	.3	.3	.3

DM = West German mark   HFL = Dutch florin   DKR = Danish crown
FF = French franc   LIT = Italian lira   IRL = Irish pound
L = British pound   FB = Belgian franc   FLUX = Luxembourg franc

Table 45--*Continued*

Note: Since percentages have been rounded off to the nearest tenth, their totals do not always correspond exactly to 100.0 percent, which is the precise composite value of the EUA/ECU. Calculations are based on the exchange rate between the EUA/ECU and the currencies of the EEC-member states on the indicated dates in relation to the coefficient determining each currency's contribution to the value of the EUA/ECU. The currency's coefficient as the percentage of the exchange rate between that currency and the EUA/ECU is the percent contribution of that currency to the value of the EUA/ECU. The currencies of the EEC states contribute to the value of the EUA/ECU according to the following coefficients:

DM	.828	FB	3.66
FF	1.15	DKR	.217
L	.0885	IRL	.00759
HFL	.286	FLUX	.14
LIT	109.0		

The source for the coefficients is *Venticinque anni 1958-1983* (Twenty-five years 1958-1983) (Luxembourg: Banca Europea per gli Investimenti, 1983), 6. The exchange rate between the EUA/ECU and the currencies of the EEC states is published every weekday in the *Official Journal of the European Communities*.

Appendixes 145

Table 46

Contribution of EEC Currencies to Value of ECU,
September 1984–May 1985
(in Percentages)

	9/18/84	10/20/84	1/30/85	5/30/85
DM	32.1	32.2	32.3	32.0
FF	19.0	19.2	19.3	19.2
L	14.9	14.5	14.1	15.3
HFL	10.1	10.2	10.2	10.1
LIT	10.2	10.1	10.2	9.8
FB	8.1	8.2	8.2	8.2
DKR	2.7	2.7	2.8	2.7
IRL	1.2	1.2	1.2	1.2
FLUX	.3	.3	.3	.3
DR	1.3	1.3	1.3	1.2

DM = West German mark
FF = French franc
L = British pound
HFL= Dutch florin
DR = Greek drachma
LIT = Italian lira
FB = Belgian franc
DKR = Danish crown
IRL = Irish pound
FLUX= Luxembourg franc

Note: In September 1984 the finance ministers of the EEC-member states (except Italy, which was represented by its treasury minister) modified the percent contribution of the currencies of the EEC states to the value of the ECU. Beginnning 18 September 1984, the currencies of these states now contribute to the value of the ECU according to the following coefficients:

```
       DM   .719         FB    3.71
       FF   1.31         DKR   .219
       L    .0878        IRL   .00871
       HFL  .256         FLUX  .14
       LIT  140.0        DR    1.15
```

The source for the coefficients is *La Repubblica*, 18 September 1984,

Appendix B
Statistical Appendix to Chapter 9, "The Consequences of the Mezzogiorno's Underdevelopment"
(tables 47–76)

Appendixes

Table 47

Key Economic Indicators:
EEC Averages, 1955-1983

	1960	1961	1964	1969	1971
1. Agriculture					
As % of employment	16.2	15.4	13.0	10.6	9.5
As % of GNP	7.3	6.9	6.3	5.4	4.6
Value added (ECU)	18,009	18,549	22,039	28,308	30,081
Average farm size (in hectares)	10.6			11.9[a]	13.4
Average man-land ratio				1.5[b]	1.73
2. Industry					
As % of employment	40.6	41.0	41.7	41.3	41.0
As % of GNP	45.9	45.9	45.6	44.1	43.5
Value added (ECU)	112,723	122,693	159,819	230,132	285,481
3. Tertiary sector					
As % of employment	29.4	29.7	30.6	32.5	33.3
As % of GNP	36.6	36.8	37.2	38.6	39.3
Value added (ECU)	89,742	98,442	130,444	201,375	257,945
4. Public administration					
As % of employment	13.7	13.8	14.7	15.7	16.2
As % of GNP	10.6	10.7	11.1	11.7	12.3
Value added (ECU)	26,078	28,666	38,999	61,050	80,893
5. Unemployment rate			1.5[c]		2.0[d]
6. Per capita income (ECU)	992	1,067	1,354	1,949	2,387
7. Per capita public spending (ECU)				888[e]	993

[a] 1966-67, 10.1
[b] for 1966-67
[c] for 1960-65
[d] for 1966-70
[e] for 1970

Continued on next page

Table 47—*Continued*

	1974	1979	1981	1982
1. Agriculture				
As % of employment	8.2	7.2	6.9	6.8
As % of GNP	4.1	3.6	3.3	3.5
Value added (ECU)	38,485	61,249	69,191	79,069
Average farm size (in hectares)	14.5[f]	15.3[g]	15.4[h]	
Average man-land ratio	1.69[f]	1.62[g]		
2. Industry				
As % of employment	39.9	37.1	35.8	35.0
As % of GNP	42.5	40.7	39.2	38.6
Value added (ECU)	405,927	689,648	823,440	883,889
3. Tertiary sector				
As % of employment	34.5	36.9	37.8	38.3
As % of GNP	39.9	41.7	42.7	43.0
Value added (ECU)	381,052	706,419	897,099	983,994
4. Public administration				
As % of employment	17.4	18.8	19.5	19.9
As % of GNP	13.3	13.8	14.6	14.6
Value added (ECU)	126,587	233,474	307,340	333,086
5. Unemployment rate	2.9[i]	5.5	7.6	9.2[j]
6. Per capita income (ECU)	3,358	5,904	7,152	7,758
7. Per capita public spending (ECU)	1,548	2,974	3,917	

[f] for 1975
[g] for 1977
[h] for 1980
[i] 1973, 2.5
[j] 1983, 10.3

Continued on next page

Table 47--*Continued*

	1955-59	1960-64	1965-69	1970-74	1975-79	1980-83
8. Inflation rate	0.98	1.36	1.48	4.84	9.28	15.03
		1960-64	1964-69	1969-74	1974-79	1979-82
9. Growth rate of GNP		9.3	8.3	12.8	12.2	10.6
10. Growth rate of agriculture as part of GNP		5.2	5.1	6.9	9.2	8.9
11. Growth rate of industry as part of GNP		9.1	7.6	12.0	11.2	8.6
12. Growth rate of tertiary sector as part of GNP		9.8	9.1	13.6	13.1	12.1
13. Growth rate of public administration as part of GNP		10.6	9.4	15.7	13.0	12.6

Note: Mr. Wolfgang Knuppel of EUROSTAT, Luxembourg, with Prot. no. 012426 of 30 October 1984, provided the data for Table 47.

Table 48

Sectoral Distribution of Gross Value
Added at Market Prices in 1970
(in MIA LIT)

	Agriculture	Industry	Tertiary	Public Admin.	Total
Italy	5,122.0	26,968.0	31,257.0	7,053.0	61,701.0
Liguria	128.2	1,037.6	1,752.9	285.7	2,832.2
Lombardia	497.5	7,310.5	5,681.9	860.0	13,073.3
Piemonte	334.0	3,568.8	2,742.3	462.9	6,473.6
Valle d'Aosta	5.3	68.6	97.1	21.1	167.5
Northwest average	241.25	2,996.38	2,568.55	407.43	5,636.65
Emilia-Romagna	627.6	2,181.0	2,323.1	487.6	4,988.8
Friuli-Venezia Giulia	84.5	568.7	847.7	249.4	1,461.9
Lazio	308.1	1,816.0	3,914.4	1,097.0	5,818.9
Marche	158.3	556.0	715.6	170.6	1,410.3
Toscana	261.4	1,888.3	2,250.9	460.0	4,287.3
Trentino-Alto Adige	77.1	345.2	503.7	150.1	901.4
Umbria	75.4	347.3	391.6	99.1	798.2
Veneto	477.5	2,144.8	2,158.4	492.6	4,682.1
Center/northeast average	258.74	1,232.16	1,638.18	400.80	3,043.61
Abruzzo	142.7	354.1	480.7	142.6	960.2
Basilicata	67.6	171.5	187.0	64.3	420.8
Calabria	165.2	470.9	679.4	199.5	1,294.9
Campania	492.8	1,473.1	2,162.2	550.6	4,058.0
Molise	41.3	68.6	109.8	37.9	217.4
Puglia	480.8	987.0	1,407.1	392.7	2,822.4
Sardegna	168.3	470.5	713.2	225.3	1,322.2
Sicilia	528.4	1,129.5	2,137.9	604.0	3,709.6
Mezzogiorno average	260.89	949.35	984.66	277.11	1,850.69

Note: Data provided by Ms. Jenny Hopkins of EUROSTAT's Regional and Financial Statistics Department, with Prot. no. 016030 of 30 April 1985.

Table 49

Sectoral Distribution of Gross Value
Added at Market Prices in 1970
(in Percentages)

	Agriculture	Industry	Tertiary	Public Admin.
Italy	8.0	44.0	51.0	11.0
Liguria	5.0	37.0	62.0	10.0
Lombardia	4.0	56.0	43.0	7.0
Piemonte	5.0	55.0	42.0	7.0
Valle d'Aosta	3.0	41.0	58.0	13.0
Northwest average	4.0	47.0	51.0	9.0
Emilia-Romagna	13.0	44.0	47.0	10.0
Friuli-Venezia Giulia	6.0	39.0	58.0	17.0
Lazio	5.0	31.0	67.0	19.0
Marche	11.0	40.0	51.0	12.0
Toscana	6.0	44.0	53.0	11.0
Trentino-Alto Adige	9.0	38.0	56.0	17.0
Umbria	9.0	44.0	49.0	12.0
Veneto	10.0	46.0	46.0	11.0
Center/northeast ave.	9.0	41.0	53.0	14.0
Abruzzo	15.0	37.0	50.0	15.0
Basilicata	16.0	41.0	44.0	15.0
Calabria	13.0	36.0	52.0	15.0
Campania	12.0	36.0	53.0	14.0
Molise	19.0	32.0	51.0	17.0
Puglia	17.0	35.0	50.0	14.0
Sardegna	13.0	36.0	54.0	17.0
Sicilia	14.0	30.0	58.0	16.0
Mezzogiorno average	15.0	35.0	52.0	15.0

Source: See note to table 48.

Table 50

Sectoral Distribution of Gross Value
Added at Market Prices in 1974
(in MIA LIT)

	Agriculture	Industry	Tertiary	Public Admin.	Total
Italy	8,096.0	48,173.0	55,326.0	13,237.0	107,434.0
Liguria	180.0	1,831.0	2,868.8	515.0	4,665.3
Lombardia	691.8	13,086.9	10,028.0	1,622.1	22,762.1
Piemonte	490.6	6,190.8	4,701.3	866.7	10,980.9
Valle d'Aosta	8.0	133.6	201.7	38.2	335.5
Northwest average	342.6	5,310.6	4,450.0	760.5	9,686.0
Emilia-Romagna	946.8	4,151.0	4,278.1	929.2	9,021.2
Friuli-Venezia Giulia	108.2	1,137.3	1,482.9	432.9	2,636.0
Lazio	486.7	3,086.5	6,703.3	1,813.7	9,660.1
Marche	225.1	1,021.5	1,288.3	345.0	2,460.8
Toscana	402.5	3,340.1	3,911.9	919.7	7,371.9
Trentino-Alto Adige	102.2	676.6	929.6	277.5	1,670.9
Umbria	121.9	626.9	713.8	205.0	1,420.2
Veneto	741.1	3,816.4	4,007.4	965.9	8,318.8
Center/northeast ave.	391.8	2,232.0	2,914.4	736.1	5,320.0
Abruzzo	243.8	649.7	909.1	276.2	1,757.6
Basilicata	127.2	310.5	351.4	136.3	775.2
Calabria	305.1	762.4	1,291.7	449.5	2,309.4
Campania	815.6	2,840.1	3,866.6	1,045.3	6,988.1
Molise	57.6	139.0	201.0	72.0	391.3
Puglia	815.7	1,892.4	2,593.0	805.6	5,153.3
Sardegna	255.2	813.6	1,269.6	410.9	2,263.9
Sicilia	952.9	2,026.7	3,728.5	1,110.3	6,491.5
Mezzogiorno average	446.6	1,179.3	1,776.4	538.3	3,266.3

Source: See note to table 48.

Table 51

Sectoral Distribution of Gross Value
Added at Market Prices in 1974
(in Percentages)

	Agriculture	Industry	Tertiary	Public Admin.
Italy	8.0	45.0	51.0	12.0
Liguria	4.0	39.0	61.0	11.0
Lombardia	3.0	57.0	44.0	7.0
Piemonte	4.0	56.0	43.0	8.0
Valle d'Aosta	2.0	48.0	52.0	9.0
Northwest average	3.0	48.0	52.0	9.0
Emilia-Romagna	10.0	46.0	47.0	10.0
Friuli-Venezia	14.0	43.0	56.0	16.0
Lazio	15.0	32.0	69.0	19.0
Marche	9.0	42.0	52.0	14.0
Toscana	5.0	45.0	53.0	12.0
Trentino-Alto Adige	7.0	40.0	56.0	17.0
Umbria	9.0	44.0	50.0	14.0
Veneto	9.0	46.0	48.0	12.0
Center/northeast ave.	7.0	42.0	54.0	14.0
Abruzzo	14.0	37.0	52.0	16.0
Basilicata	16.0	40.0	45.0	18.0
Calabria	13.0	33.0	56.0	19.0
Campania	12.0	35.0	55.0	15.0
Molise	15.0	36.0	51.0	18.0
Puglia	16.0	37.0	50.0	16.0
Sardegna	11.0	36.0	56.0	18.0
Sicilia	15.0	31.0	57.0	17.0
Mezzogiorno average	14.0	36.0	53.0	17.0

Source: See note to table 48.

Table 52

Sectoral Distribution of Gross Value
Added at Market Prices in 1979
(in MIA LIT)

	Agriculture	Industry	Tertiary	Public Admin.	Total
Italy	18,610.0	115,571.0	139,574.0	34,476.0	262,179.0
Liguria	321.8	3,699.8	7,056.2	1,345.0	10,568.8
Lombardia	1,730.3	30,260.2	25,173.0	4,187.5	54,153.7
Piemonte	1,258.5	14,335.9	11,737.1	2,264.7	26,259.1
Valle d'Aosta	21.5	280.4	467.8	90.1	752.4
Northwest average	833.0	12,144.1	11,108.5	1,971.8	22,933.5
Emilia-Romagna	2,429.8	10,239.7	11,076.8	2,422.8	22,719.3
Friuli-Venezia Giulia	303.0	2,696.8	3,572.1	936.8	6,298.1
Lazio	1,043.9	7,215.8	16,989.8	5,048.7	23,449.7
Marche	565.4	2,782.0	3,299.2	896.5	6,417.0
Toscana	906.0	8,575.2	9,835.4	2,355.2	18,540.4
Trentino-Alto Adige	363.3	1,817.9	2,451.0	646.5	4,416.9
Umbria	292.4	1,594.6	1,862.4	524.9	3,605.5
Veneto	1,765.1	9,561.0	10,193.8	2,311.7	20,822.4
Center/northeast ave.	958.6	5,560.4	7,410.1	1,892.9	13,283.7
Abruzzo	560.6	1,752.2	2,349.3	737.7	4,540.4
Basilicata	305.3	878.6	908.2	344.7	2,049.3
Calabria	825.3	1,660.5	3,238.2	1,138.7	5,606.5
Campania	1,668.8	6,052.1	9,868.0	2,952.0	17,157.0
Molise	143.4	407.0	543.3	195.8	1,067.2
Puglia	1,588.7	4,738.3	6,577.9	2,163.9	12,524.7
Sardegna	522.7	2,132.3	3,163.5	1,097.6	5,638.0
Sicilia	1,994.2	4,890.7	9,211.0	2,815.2	15,592.6
Mezzogiorno average	951.1	2,814.0	4,482.4	1,430.7	8,022.0

Source: See note to table 48.

Appendixes

Table 53

Sectoral Distribution of Gross Value
Added at Market Prices in 1979
(in Percentages)

	Agriculture	Industry	Tertiary	Public Admin.
Italy	7.0	44.0	53.0	13.0
Liguria	3.0	35.0	67.0	13.0
Lombardia	3.0	56.0	46.0	8.0
Piemonte	5.0	55.0	45.0	9.0
Valle d'Aosta	3.0	37.0	62.0	12.0
Northwest average	4.0	46.0	55.0	11.0
Emilia-Romagna	11.0	45.0	49.0	11.0
Friuli-Venezia Giulia	5.0	43.0	57.0	15.0
Lazio	4.0	31.0	72.0	22.0
Marche	9.0	43.0	51.0	14.0
Toscana	5.0	46.0	53.0	13.0
Trentino-Alto Adige	8.0	41.0	55.0	15.0
Umbria	8.0	44.0	52.0	15.0
Veneto	8.0	46.0	49.0	11.0
Center/northeast ave.	7.0	42.0	55.0	15.0
Abruzzo	12.0	39.0	52.0	16.0
Basilicata	15.0	43.0	44.0	17.0
Calabria	15.0	30.0	58.0	20.0
Campania	10.0	35.0	58.0	17.0
Molise	13.0	38.0	51.0	18.0
Puglia	13.0	37.0	53.0	17.0
Sardegna	9.0	38.0	56.0	19.0
Sicilia	13.0	31.0	59.0	18.0
Mezzogiorno average	13.0	37.0	54.0	18.0

Source: See note to table 48.

Table 54

Sectoral Distribution of Gross Value
Added at Market Prices in 1981
(in MIA LIT)

	Agriculture	Industry	Tertiary	Public Admin.	Total
Italy	23,924.0	165,292.0	218,114.0	57,330.0	388,989.0
Liguria	432.5	4,976.6	10,617.0	2,191.8	15,354.8
Lombardia	2,064.9	43,166.6	39,402.5	7,132.8	79,731.4
Piemonte	1,571.0	19,383.3	18,210.2	3,759.8	37,540.4
Valle d'Aosta	28.4	397.4	703.5	152.2	1,105.0
Northwest average	1,024.2	16,981.0	17,233.3	3,309.2	33,432.9
Emilia-Romagna	3,105.0	15,445.9	17,325.6	3,980.6	34,143.1
Friuli-Venezia Giulia	360.0	4,033.5	5,731.0	1,592.9	9,626.4
Lazio	1,502.5	10,518.7	25,821.4	8,044.1	35,284.7
Marche	738.9	4,126.4	5,335.4	1,603.8	9,813.3
Toscana	1,114.8	12,037.8	15,538.4	3,903.1	27,383.3
Trentino-Alto Adige	423.5	2,515.7	4,005.1	1,139.3	6,573.7
Umbria	395.0	2,299.1	3,017.7	957.7	5,480.6
Veneto	2,104.4	13,907.9	16,170.8	3,911.3	31,031.2
Center/northeast ave.	1,218.0	8,110.6	11,618.2	3,141.6	19,917.0
Abruzzo	722.4	2,571.6	3,794.7	1,307.7	6,885.1
Basilicata	352.3	1,209.9	1,445.6	614.7	2,932.6
Calabria	1,076.1	2,701.1	5,167.0	1,974.3	8,753.1
Campania	2,199.9	8,827.5	15,475.6	4,927.8	25,808.8
Molise	184.0	590.6	897.7	362.4	1,624.4
Puglia	2,391.9	6,661.8	10,239.8	3,479.8	18,674.1
Sardegna	614.7	2,625.8	4,845.1	1,752.0	7,843.2
Sicilia	2,541.8	7,294.8	14,369.9	4,544.9	23,399.8
Mezzogiorno average	1,260.4	4,060.4	7,029.4	2,370.5	11,990.1

Source: See note to table 48.

Table 55

Sectoral Distribution of Gross Value
Added at Market Prices in 1981
(in Percentages)

	Agriculture	Industry	Tertiary	Public Admin.
Italy	6.0	42.0	56.0	15.0
Liguria	3.0	32.0	69.0	14.0
Lombardia	3.0	54.0	49.0	9.0
Piemonte	4.0	52.0	49.0	10.0
Valle d'Aosta	3.0	36.0	64.0	14.0
Northwest average	3.0	44.0	58.0	12.0
Emilia-Romagna	9.0	45.0	51.0	12.0
Friuli-Venezia Giulia	4.0	42.0	60.0	17.0
Lazio	4.0	30.0	73.0	23.0
Marche	4.0	42.0	54.0	16.0
Toscana	4.0	44.0	57.0	14.0
Trentino-Alto Adige	6.0	38.0	61.0	17.0
Umbria	7.0	42.0	55.0	17.0
Veneto	7.0	45.0	52.0	13.0
Center/northeast ave.	6.0	41.0	58.0	16.0
Abruzzo	10.0	37.0	55.0	19.0
Basilicata	12.0	41.0	49.0	21.0
Calabria	12.0	31.0	59.0	23.0
Campania	9.0	34.0	60.0	19.0
Molise	11.0	36.0	55.0	22.0
Puglia	13.0	36.0	55.0	19.0
Sardegna	8.0	33.0	62.0	22.0
Sicilia	11.0	31.0	61.0	19.0
Mezzogiorno average	11.0	35.0	57.0	21.0

Source: See note to table 48.

Table 56

Growth Rate of Gross Value Added at Market Prices,
1970-1974, by Sector
(1970=1.00)

	Agriculture	Industry	Tertiary	Public Admin.	Total GDP
Italy	1.58	1.79	1.77	1.88	1.74
Liguria	1.40	1.76	1.64	1.80	1.65
Lombardia	1.39	1.79	1.76	1.89	1.74
Piemonte	1.47	1.73	1.71	1.87	1.70
Valle d'Aosta	1.51	1.95	2.08	1.81	2.00
Northwest average	1.44	1.81	1.80	1.84	1.77
Emilia-Romagna	1.51	1.90	1.84	1.91	1.81
Friuli-Venezia Giulia	1.28	2.00	1.75	1.74	1.80
Lazio	1.58	1.70	1.71	1.65	1.66
Marche	1.42	1.80	1.80	2.02	1.74
Toscana	1.54	1.77	1.74	2.00	1.72
Trentino-Alto Adige	1.56	1.96	1.85	1.85	1.85
Umbria	1.62	1.81	1.82	2.07	1.78
Veneto	1.55	1.78	1.86	1.96	1.78
Center/northeast ave.	1.51	1.84	1.80	1.90	1.77
Abruzzo	1.71	1.83	1.89	1.94	1.83
Basilicata	1.88	1.81	1.88	2.12	1.84
Calabria	1.85	1.62	1.90	2.25	1.78
Campania	1.66	1.68	1.79	1.90	1.72
Molise	1.39	2.03	1.83	1.90	1.80
Puglia	1.70	1.92	1.84	2.05	1.83
Sardegna	1.52	1.73	1.78	1.82	1.71
Sicilia	1.80	1.79	1.74	1.84	1.75
Mezzogiorno average	1.69	1.80	1.83	1.98	1.78

Source: See note to table 48.

Appendixes

Table 57

Growth Rate of Gross Value Added at Market Prices,
1974-1979, by Sector
(1970=1.00)

	Agriculture	Industry	Tertiary	Public Admin.	Total GDP
Italy	2.30	2.40	2.52	2.60	2.44
Liguria	1.79	2.02	2.46	2.61	2.27
Lombardia	2.50	2.31	2.51	2.58	2.38
Piemonte	2.57	2.32	2.50	2.61	2.39
Valle d'Aosta	2.69	2.10	2.32	2.36	2.24
Northwest average	2.39	2.19	2.45	2.54	2.32
Emilia-Romagna	2.57	2.47	2.59	2.61	2.52
Friuli-Venezia Giulia	2.80	2.37	2.41	2.16	2.39
Lazio	2.14	2.34	2.53	2.78	2.43
Marche	2.51	2.72	2.56	2.60	2.61
Toscana	2.25	2.57	2.51	2.56	2.51
Trentino-Alto Adige	3.02	2.69	2.64	2.33	2.64
Umbria	2.40	2.54	2.61	2.56	2.54
Veneto	2.38	2.51	2.54	2.39	2.50
Center/northeast ave.	2.51	2.53	2.55	2.50	2.52
Abruzzo	2.30	2.70	2.58	2.67	2.58
Basilicata	2.40	2.83	2.58	2.53	2.64
Calabria	2.71	2.18	2.51	2.53	2.43
Campania	2.05	2.44	2.55	2.82	2.46
Molise	2.49	2.93	2.70	2.72	2.73
Puglia	1.95	2.50	2.54	2.69	2.43
Sardegna	2.05	2.62	2.49	2.67	2.49
Sicilia	2.09	2.41	2.47	2.54	2.40
Mezzogiorno average	2.26	2.58	2.55	2.65	2.52

Source: See note to table 48.

Table 58

Growth Rate of Gross Value Added at Market Prices,
1979-1981, by Sector
(1970=1.00)

	Agriculture	Industry	Tertiary	Public Admin.	Total GDP
Italy	1.29	1.43	1.56	1.66	1.48
Liguria	1.34	1.35	1.50	1.63	1.45
Lombardia	1.19	1.43	1.57	1.70	1.47
Piemonte	1.25	1.35	1.55	1.66	1.43
Valle d'Aosta	1.32	1.42	1.50	1.69	1.47
Northwest average	1.28	1.39	1.53	1.67	1.46
Emilia-Romagna	1.28	1.51	1.56	1.64	1.50
Friuli-Venezia Giulia	1.19	1.50	1.60	1.70	1.53
Lazio	1.44	1.46	1.52	1.59	1.50
Marche	1.31	1.48	1.62	1.79	1.53
Toscana	1.23	1.40	1.58	1.66	1.48
Trentino-Alto Adige	1.17	1.38	1.63	1.76	1.49
Umbria	1.35	1.44	1.62	1.82	1.52
Veneto	1.19	1.45	1.59	1.69	1.49
Center/northeast ave.	1.27	1.45	1.59	1.71	1.51
Abruzzo	1.29	1.47	1.62	1.77	1.52
Basilicata	1.15	1.38	1.59	1.78	1.43
Calabria	1.30	1.63	1.60	1.73	1.57
Campania	1.32	1.46	1.57	1.67	1.50
Molise	1.28	1.45	1.65	1.85	1.52
Puglia	1.51	1.41	1.56	1.61	1.49
Sardegna	1.18	1.23	1.53	1.60	1.39
Sicilia	1.27	1.49	1.56	1.61	1.50
Mezzogiorno average	1.29	1.44	1.59	1.70	1.49

Source: See note to table 48.

Appendixes

Table 59

Sectoral Distribution of Employment, 1970
(in Thousands)

	Agriculture	Industry	Tertiary	Public Admin.	Total
Italy	3,605.0	7,693.0	8,443.3	2,805.5	19,741.3
Liguria	57.6	221.5	415.5	112.0	694.6
Lombardia	198.3	1,874.1	1,354.4	342.4	3,426.8
Piemonte	248.7	910.7	681.5	185.9	1,840.9
Valle d'Aosta	5.9	17.5	22.1	7.9	45.5
Northwest average	127.6	756.0	618.4	162.1	1,502.0
Emilia-Romagna	340.8	617.0	671.9	192.2	1,629.7
Friuli-Venezia Giulia	58.7	184.4	260.8	114.5	503.9
Lazio	181.2	440.0	1,018.3	418.9	1,639.5
Marche	165.2	195.1	197.3	70.0	557.6
Toscana	185.9	566.2	586.0	184.1	1,338.1
Trentino-Alto Adige	53.2	100.1	173.5	65.7	326.8
Umbria	71.2	106.4	113.5	42.5	291.1
Veneto	248.9	673.2	625.2	203.3	1,547.3
Center/northeast ave.	163.1	360.3	455.8	161.4	979.3
Abruzzo	129.9	131.2	152.0	55.6	413.1
Basilicata	79.5	69.0	62.6	25.3	211.1
Calabria	204.3	188.6	212.4	79.7	605.3
Campania	411.7	519.0	637.2	230.6	1,567.9
Molise	56.0	27.7	35.7	14.6	119.4
Puglia	420.3	317.7	427.1	155.4	1,165.1
Sardegna	109.1	121.8	212.8	87.7	443.7
Sicilia	378.6	411.8	583.5	217.2	1,373.9
Mezzogiorno average	223.7	223.4	290.4	108.3	737.4

Source: See note to table 48.

Table 60

Sectoral Distribution of Employment, 1970
(in Percentages)

	Agriculture	Industry	Tertiary	Public Admin.
Italy	18.0	39.0	43.0	14.0
Liguria	8.0	32.0	60.0	16.0
Lombardia	6.0	55.0	40.0	10.0
Piemonte	14.0	49.0	37.0	10.0
Valle d'Aosta	13.0	38.0	49.0	17.0
Northwest average	10.0	44.0	47.0	13.0
Emilia-Romagna	21.0	38.0	41.0	12.0
Friuli-Venezia Giulia	12.0	37.0	52.0	23.0
Lazio	11.0	27.0	62.0	26.0
Marche	30.0	35.0	35.0	13.0
Toscana	14.0	42.0	44.0	14.0
Trentino-Alto Adige	16.0	31.0	53.0	20.0
Umbria	24.0	37.0	39.0	15.0
Veneto	16.0	44.0	40.0	13.0
Center/northeast ave.	18.0	31.0	46.0	17.0
Abruzzo	31.0	32.0	37.0	13.0
Basilicata	38.0	33.0	30.0	12.0
Calabria	34.0	31.0	35.0	13.0
Campania	26.0	33.0	41.0	15.0
Molise	47.0	23.0	30.0	12.0
Puglia	36.0	27.0	37.0	13.0
Sardegna	25.0	27.0	48.0	20.0
Sicilia	28.0	30.0	42.0	16.0
Mezzogiorno average	33.0	30.0	38.0	14.0

Source: See note to table 48.

Table 61

Sectoral Distribution of Employment, 1974
(in Thousands)

	Agriculture	Industry	Tertiary	Public Admin.	Total
Italy	3,174.0	7,585.8	9,187.2	3,218.3	19,947.0
Liguria	53.8	211.9	439.6	129.9	705.3
Lombardia	162.3	1,842.9	1,478.3	402.0	3,483.5
Piemonte	217.5	903.3	773.4	239.5	1,894.2
Valle d'Aosta	6.9	18.5	23.5	8.6	48.9
Northwest average	110.1	744.2	678.7	195.0	1,533.0
Emilia-Romagna	299.7	601.0	739.0	231.5	1,639.7
Friuli-Venezia Giulia	38.8	179.7	272.8	118.1	491.3
Lazio	153.6	452.5	1,074.9	425.7	1,681.0
Marche	123.5	202.0	218.7	82.9	544.2
Toscana	135.8	553.0	642.8	221.5	1,331.6
Trentino-Alto Adige	54.8	105.1	186.9	71.0	346.8
Umbria	52.8	112.1	123.8	49.7	288.7
Veneto	215.7	649.2	685.4	234.4	1,550.3
Center/northeast ave.	134.3	356.8	493.0	179.4	984.2
Abruzzo	114.5	137.5	165.6	65.4	417.6
Basilicata	80.4	66.6	70.6	32.1	217.6
Calabria	170.8	163.5	241.0	103.9	575.3
Campania	352.4	508.3	691.6	260.8	1,552.3
Molise	50.4	30.7	38.2	16.5	119.3
Puglia	419.1	338.2	474.3	187.7	1,231.6
Sardegna	100.6	122.6	223.1	98.4	446.3
Sicilia	370.6	387.2	623.7	238.7	1,381.5
Mezzogiorno average	207.4	219.3	316.0	125.4	742.7

Source: See note to table 48.

Table 62

Sectoral Distribution of Employment, 1974
(in Percentages)

	Agriculture	Industry	Tertiary	Public Admin.
Italy	16.0	38.0	46.0	16.0
Liguria	8.0	30.0	62.0	18.0
Lombardia	5.0	53.0	42.0	12.0
Piemonte	11.0	48.0	41.0	13.0
Valle d'Aosta	14.0	38.0	48.0	18.0
Northwest average	10.0	42.0	48.0	15.0
Emilia-Romagna	18.0	37.0	45.0	14.0
Friuli-Venezia Giulia	8.0	37.0	56.0	24.0
Lazio	9.0	27.0	64.0	25.0
Marche	23.0	37.0	40.0	15.0
Toscana	10.0	42.0	48.0	17.0
Trentino-Alto Adige	16.0	30.0	54.0	20.0
Umbria	18.0	39.0	43.0	17.0
Veneto	14.0	42.0	44.0	15.0
Center/northeast ave.	15.0	36.0	49.0	18.0
Abruzzo	27.0	33.0	40.0	16.0
Basilicata	37.0	31.0	32.0	15.0
Calabria	30.0	28.0	42.0	18.0
Campania	23.0	33.0	45.0	17.0
Molise	42.0	26.0	32.0	14.0
Puglia	34.0	27.0	39.0	15.0
Sardegna	23.0	27.0	50.0	22.0
Sicilia	27.0	28.0	45.0	17.0
Mezzogiorno average	30.0	29.0	41.0	17.0

Source: See note to table 48.

Table 63

Sectoral Distribution of Employment, 1979
(in Thousands)

	Agriculture	Industry	Tertiary	Public Admin.	Total
Italy	2,840.0	7,532.0	10,225.0	3,587.0	20,597.0
Liguria	43.6	208.4	471.0	140.6	723.0
Lombardia	145.5	1,782.2	1,653.4	460.2	3,581.1
Piemonte	170.4	883.2	845.0	267.2	1,898.6
Valle d'Aosta	5.1	19.5	27.1	8.9	51.7
Northwest average	91.2	723.3	749.1	219.2	1,563.6
Emilia-Romagna	248.4	599.2	814.9	252.7	1,662.5
Friuli-Venezia Giulia	31.5	184.7	284.5	119.9	500.7
Lazio	132.6	454.4	1,205.7	482.0	1,792.7
Marche	97.1	205.2	239.4	91.7	541.7
Toscana	137.9	549.6	701.8	240.9	1,389.3
Trentino-Alto Adige	47.2	106.9	207.5	74.9	361.6
Umbria	38.8	116.1	139.4	56.2	294.3
Veneto	180.8	639.5	751.1	248.1	1,571.4
Center/northeast ave.	114.3	357.0	543.0	195.8	1,014.3
Abruzzo	104.6	135.3	188.1	72.3	428.0
Basilicata	76.8	67.5	80.2	34.6	224.5
Calabria	178.5	159.7	269.9	114.7	608.1
Campania	332.4	520.0	797.5	304.6	1,649.9
Molise	47.4	30.8	44.1	19.4	122.3
Puglia	394.3	353.8	542.3	213.9	1,290.4
Sardegna	92.1	128.4	255.3	112.7	475.8
Sicilia	335.0	387.6	706.8	271.5	1,429.4
Mezzogiorno average	195.1	222.9	360.5	143.0	778.6

Source: See note to table 48.

Table 64

Sectoral Distribution of Employment, 1979
(in Percentages)

	Agriculture	Industry	Tertiary	Public Admin.
Italy	14.0	37.0	50.0	17.0
Liguria	6.0	29.0	65.0	19.0
Lombardia	4.0	50.0	46.0	13.0
Piemonte	9.0	47.0	45.0	14.0
Valle d'Aosta	10.0	38.0	52.0	17.0
Northwest average	7.0	41.0	52.0	16.0
Emilia-Romagna	15.0	36.0	49.0	15.0
Friuli-Venezia Giulia	6.0	37.0	57.0	24.0
Lazio	7.0	25.0	67.0	27.0
Marche	18.0	38.0	44.0	17.0
Toscana	10.0	40.0	51.0	17.0
Trentino-Alto Adige	13.0	30.0	57.0	21.0
Umbria	13.0	39.0	47.0	19.0
Veneto	12.0	41.0	48.0	16.0
Center/northeast ave.	12.0	36.0	53.0	20.0
Abruzzo	24.0	32.0	44.0	17.0
Basilicata	34.0	30.0	36.0	15.0
Calabria	29.0	26.0	44.0	19.0
Campania	20.0	32.0	48.0	18.0
Molise	39.0	25.0	36.0	16.0
Puglia	31.0	27.0	42.0	17.0
Sardegna	19.0	27.0	54.0	24.0
Sicilia	23.0	27.0	49.0	19.0
Mezzogiorno average	27.0	28.0	44.0	18.0

Source: See note to table 48.

Table 65

Sectoral Distribution of Employment, 1981
(in Thousands)

	Agriculture	Industry	Tertiary	Public Admin.	Total
Italy	2,655.0	7,532.0	10,573.2	3,512.0	20,760.2
Liguria	45.0	205.1	484.6	138.2	734..7
Lombardia	136.7	1,756.0	1,725.7	468.6	3,618.4
Piemonte	167.6	861.1	862.0	258.5	1,890.7
Valle d'Aosta	5.6	19.6	28.9	8.5	54.1
Northwest average	88.7	710.5	775.3	218.5	1,574.5
Emilia-Romagna	227.3	606.4	825.8	244.4	1,659.5
Friuli-Venezia Giulia	31.3	183.4	266.3	94.1	481.0
Lazio	125.8	451.0	1,235.8	456.8	1,812.6
Marche	102.3	208.4	247.0	94.6	557.7
Toscana	133.4	549.7	726.1	237.0	1,409.2
Trentino-Alto Adige	47.5	105.5	218.3	65.5	371.3
Umbria	37.4	117.5	148.7	59.4	303.6
Veneto	170.0	639.3	777.0	233.7	1,586.3
Center/northeast ave.	109.4	357.7	555.6	185.7	1,022.7
Abruzzo	82.9	140.0	202.4	76.0	425.3
Basilicata	64.9	71.9	85.5	37.8	222.3
Calabria	146.7	162.3	284.9	119.8	593.9
Campania	297.2	532.2	840.3	306.2	1,669.7
Molise	43.3	31.4	47.6	21.4	122.3
Puglia	383.1	359.8	559.5	204.2	1,302.4
Sardegna	95.0	130.3	265.4	110.7	490.7
Sicilia	312.0	401.1	741.4	276.6	1,454.5
Mezzogiorno average	178.1	228.6	378.4	144.1	785.1

Source: See note to table 48.

Table 66

Sectoral Distribution of Employment, 1981
(in Percentages)

	Agriculture	Industry	Tertiary	Public Admin.
Italy	13.0	36.0	51.0	17.0
Liguria	6.0	28.0	66.0	19.0
Lombardia	4.0	49.0	48.0	13.0
Piemonte	9.0	46.0	46.0	14.0
Valle d'Aosta	10.0	36.0	53.0	16.0
Northwest average	7.0	40.0	53.0	16.0
Emilia-Romagna	14.0	37.0	50.0	15.0
Friuli-Venezia Giulia	7.0	38.0	55.0	20.0
Lazio	7.0	25.0	68.0	25.0
Marche	18.0	37.0	44.0	17.0
Toscana	9.0	39.0	52.0	17.0
Trentino-Alto Adige	13.0	28.0	59.0	18.0
Umbria	12.0	39.0	49.0	20.0
Veneto	11.0	40.0	49.0	15.0
Center/northeast ave.	11.0	35.0	53.0	18.0
Abruzzo	19.0	33.0	48.0	18.0
Basilicata	29.0	32.0	38.0	17.0
Calabria	25.0	27.0	48.0	20.0
Campania	18.0	32.0	50.0	18.0
Molise	35.0	26.0	39.0	17.0
Puglia	29.0	28.0	43.0	16.0
Sardegna	19.0	27.0	54.0	23.0
Sicilia	21.0	28.0	51.0	19.0
Mezzogiorno average	24.0	29.0	46.0	19.0

Source: See note to table 48.

Table 67

Distribution of Per Capita Income
among Italy's Twenty Regions
(EEC Average=100)

	1971	1974	1979	1981
Italy	74.2	68.5	63.2	68.8
Liguria	97.0	88.2	78.4	84.4
Lombardia	98.8	91.8	82.8	89.7
Piemonte	91.8	85.6	79.1	83.7
Valle d'Aosta	99.4	105.3	90.4	98.6
Northwest average	96.8	92.7	82.7	89.2
Emilia-Romagna	84.6	81.3	78.1	86.3
Friuli-Venezia Giulia	77.7	75.2	69.1	78.0
Lazio	80.7	70.7	64.3	70.7
Marche	67.4	63.0	62.1	69.5
Toscana	80.5	73.5	70.4	76.5
Trentino-Alto Adige	70.6	68.7	69.0	75.3
Umbria	66.3	63.6	61.1	68.0
Veneto	74.9	69.4	65.4	71.5
Center/northeast ave.	75.3	70.7	67.4	75.5
Abruzzo	55.4	52.1	51.0	56.6
Basilicata	47.5	44.9	45.5	48.1
Calabria	43.5	40.5	37.3	42.5
Campania	53.2	47.4	43.2	47.3
Molise	44.5	42.3	44.2	49.5
Puglia	52.8	49.4	44.5	48.3
Sardegna	59.8	52.5	48.5	49.3
Sicilia	53.3	48.1	43.5	47.8
Mezzogiorno average	51.3	47.2	44.7	48.7

Source: Data provided by Ms. Jenny Hopkins of EUROSTAT's Regional and Financial Statistics Department, with Prot. no. 014175 of 1 February 1985.

Table 68

Distribution of Average Monthly Income per Family
and Per Capita among Italy's Twenty Regions
(in Thousands of LIT)

	1982		1983		1984	
	Family Income	Per Cap Income	Family Income	Per Cap Income	Family Income	Per Cap Income
Italy	1,264	419	1,458	483	1,641	544
Liguria	1,176	475	1,329	537	1,472	594
Lombardia	1,499	526	1,769	620	1,966	689
Piemonte	1,240	469	1,454	550	1,610	609
Valle d'Aosta	1,243	471	1,390	526	1,606	607
Northwest average	1,377	503	1,614	589	1,792	654
Emilia-Romagna	1,380	494	1,641	587	1,805	646
Friuli-Venezia Giulia	1,294	479	1,491	551	1,677	620
Trentino-Alto Adige	1,350	442	1,542	504	1,773	580
Veneto	1,440	464	1,577	507	1,803	581
Northeast average	1,390	475	1,589	542	1,786	610
Lazio	1,236	410	1,383	458	1,676	558
Marche	1,388	447	1,646	497	1,769	569
Toscana	1,253	435	1,423	494	1,696	589
Umbria	1,114	369	1,340	443	1,516	501
Center average	1,252	420	1,414	474	1,653	564
Abruzzo	1,144	372	1,354	440	1,466	476
Basilicata	967	303	1,178	368	1,395	437
Calabria	1,192	364	1,297	397	1,342	410
Campania	1,083	314	1,373	398	1,492	433
Molise	919	310	1,113	374	1,177	397
Puglia	1,069	320	1,176	353	1,367	410
Sardegna	1,044	305	1,225	357	1,437	419
Sicilia	1,118	335	1,229	368	1,346	403
Mezzogiorno average	1,095	328	1,268	380	1,401	420

Source: La Repubblica, 25 July 1985, 28.

Table 69

Unemployment Rate in Italy

1974	1979	1981	1982
4.8[a]	7.5	8.8	10.5[b]

Source: Official Italian data; see also note to table 47.
[a]1973, 4.9
[b]1983, 11.9

Table 70

Inflation Rate in Italy

1955–59	1960–64	1965–69	1970–74	1975–79	1980–83
0.54	1.72	1.04	5.42	15.58	32.15

Source: See note to table 47.

Table 71

EEC-Harmonized Unemployment Rates for Italy[a]
April 1983 and April 1984

	April 1983			April 1984		
	Unempl. Rate (%)	No. of Unempl. (thous)	Active Pop/ Labor Force (thous)	Unempl. Rate (%)	No. of Unempl. (thous)	Active Pop/ Labor Force (thous)
Italy	8.6	1,929.6	22,540.2	9.6	2,161.3	22,540.2
Liguria	5.9	35.0	595.7	9.5	56.4	595.7
Lombardia	5.8	220.0	3,793.0	6.4	242.1	3,793.0
Piemonte	7.3	144.2	1,975.3	8.0	158.7	1,975.3
Valle d'Aosta	3.6	1.8	48.8	5.8	2.8	48.8
Northwest average	5.7	100.3	1,603.2	7.4	115.0	1,603.2
Emilia-Romagna	6.7	117.8	1,751.5	8.7	152.2	1,751.5
Friuli-Venezia Giulia	7.7	37.6	488.6	8.0	39.3	488.6
Lazio	7.8	154.6	1,988.6	9.0	178.8	1,988.6
Marche	6.0	37.5	629.5	7.2	45.6	629.5
Toscana	8.4	123.7	1,476.4	8.4	124.2	1,476.4
Trentino-Alto Adige	4.7	17.2	366.1	5.8	21.2	366.1
Umbria	8.4	27.3	325.5	11.0	35.7	325.5
Veneto	7.4	133.9	1,819.5	8.1	146.5	1,819.5
Center/northeast ave.	7.1	81.2	1,105.7	8.3	92.9	1,105.7
Abruzzo	7.7	38.5	498.6	7.9	39.5	498.6
Basilicata	11.8	27.2	230.8	10.7	24.8	230.8
Calabria	13.3	95.5	720.3	14.2	102.4	720.3
Campania	13.0	266.3	2,043.4	14.1	287.4	2,043.4
Molise	10.0	11.9	119.9	7.7	9.2	119.9
Puglia	10.6	151.5	1,428.2	11.2	160.4	1,428.2
Sardegna	16.0	90.3	563.7	18.0	101.7	563.7
Sicilia	11.8	197.7	1,676.6	13.9	232.3	1,676.6
Mezzogiorno average	11.8	109.9	910.2	12.2	119.7	910.2

Source: See note to table 48.

[a] These data differ from official Italian data.

Table 72

Family Consumption of Goods and Services, 1970-1980
(in Billions of LIT)

	Italy	North-central Italy	Mezzogiorno	Mezzo. as % of Italy	Mezzo. as % of North-central Italy
1970	39,057.0	28,708.8	10,348.2	26.5	36.0
1971	42,397.0	31,180.5	11,216.5	26.5	36.0
1972	46,639.0	34,324.7	12,314.3	26.4	35.9
1973	55,623.0	40,525.7	15,097.3	27.1	37.3
1974	69,008.0	50,419.1	18,588.9	26.9	36.9
1975	79,906.0	58,442.9	21,463.1	26.9	36.7
1976	97,511.0	71,540.2	25,970.8	26.6	36.3
1977	117,005.0	85,875.4	31,129.6	26.6	36.2
1978	135,691.0	99,610.3	36,080.7	26.6	36.2
1979	163,881.0	120,038.2	43,842.8	26.8	36.5
1980	206,561.0	151,650.0	54,911.0	26.6	36.2
Avg.	95,752.6	70,210.5	25,542.1	26.7	36.4

Source: See note to table 48 (ISTAT data).

Table 73

Distribution of Resources of the Common Regional Fund
among Italy's Fifteen Ordinary Regions
(in MIA LIT)

	Abruzzo	Basilicata	Calabria	Campania	Emilia-Romagna	Lazio	Liguria	Lombardia	Marche	Molise	Piemonte	Puglia	Toscana	Umbria	Veneto
1972	12,986	8,372	24,748	46,797	30,799	32,367	12,709	50,467	11,221	3,815	31,980	37,210	25,591	7,486	28,889
1973	19,368	12,516	38,693	75,911	47,257	44,552	19,309	78,974	17,190	6,055	49,398	60,047	39,344	11,393	44,540
1974	18,831	13,022	40,632	85,396	44,426	46,137	20,018	82,067	19,444	6,298	51,170	58,694	40,945	11,859	46,412
1975	19,478	13,466	39,782	89,272	45,278	47,046	20,355	83,303	18,125	6,978	52,105	56,443	37,192	12,181	47,459
1976	22,055	15,069	44,353	99,861	52,069	61,554	23,235	108,814	18,948	7,810	60,190	69,002	43,295	13,860	54,720
1977	35,896	26,089	71,852	150,471	81,770	88,578	34,836	157,235	34,911	13,254	92,461	105,371	70,795	23,081	83,096
1978	47,418	34,463	94,916	198,772	108,018	117,011	46,018	207,706	46,117	17,509	122,141	139,194	93,520	30,489	109,769
1979	52,172	37,918	104,432	218,698	118,847	128,741	50,632	228,528	51,053	19,264	136,897	153,152	102,896	33,546	120,773
1980	73,999	53,784	148,124	310,197	168,620	182,604	71,815	324,257	72,389	27,324	193,980	217,226	145,945	47,581	171,302
1981	94,708	68,834	189,576	397,005	215,817	233,705	91,912	415,021	92,721	34,970	248,865	278,019	186,787	60,896	219,240
1982	104,735	72,266	208,939	371,331	264,937	307,965	108,362	433,820	111,424	37,786	261,709	293,105	225,022	84,595	250,540
1983	95,721	76,632	230,937	440,788	293,028	339,731	121,431	485,203	115,884	41,866	293,976	325,989	249,228	93,616	278,750
1984	127,714	86,316	252,526	488,198	320,355	369,423	132,843	505,934	132,155	45,966	323,440	359,032	273,551	101,927	306,174

Source: Dott.ssa Roberta Faggian of the Documentation Service, Public Spending Monitoring Office, the Veneto Regional Council, on 3 January 1985 provided the author with annual ministerial decrees from which the data are taken.

Table 74

Distribution of Resources of the Common Regional Fund
among Italy's Three Economic Systems, Ordinary Regions Only

	Northwest[a]		Center/Northeast[b]		Mezzogiorno[c]	
	Avg. Allocation in LIT (Mill's) Per Region	% of Fund's Resources	Avg. Allocation in LIT (Mill's) Per Region	% of Fund's Resources	Avg. Allocation in LIT (Mill's) Per Region	% of Fund's Resources
1972	31,719	41.3	22,726	29.6	22,352	29.1
1973	49,227	41.5	34,046	28.7	35,431	29.9
1974	51,085	41.5	34,870	28.3	37,145	30.2
1975	51,921	41.9	34,546	27.9	37,569	30.3
1976	64,079	43.3	40,741	27.6	43,025	29.1
1977	94,844	42.0	63,705	28.2	67,155	29.8
1978	125,288	42.0	84,154	28.2	88,712	29.8
1979	138,685	42.2	92,642	28.2	97,606	29.7
1980	196,684	42.2	131,406	28.2	138,442	29.7
1981	251,932	42.2	168,194	28.2	177,185	29.7
1982	267,963	40.8	207,413	31.6	181,360	27.6
1983	300,203	41.1	228,372	31.3	201,988	27.7
1984	320,739	40.2	250,597	31.4	226,625	28.4
1972–84	149,566	41.4	107,185	29.7	104,199	28.9

Source: This table is an elaboration of data in table 73.

[a] Liguria, Lombardia, Piemonte

[b] Emilia-Romagna, Lazio, Marche, Toscana, Umbria, Veneto

[c] Abruzzo, Basilicata, Calabria, Campania, Molise, Puglia

Table 75

Accounts of Italy's Regional Institutions of Government,
1977 and 1979
(in Billions of LIT)

	1977		1979	
	Total Revenue	Total Expenditure	Total Revenue	Total Expenditure
Italy	15,619.0	20,398.0	30,713.0	33,896.0
Liguria	490.6	749.0	1,146.9	1,333.4
Lombardia	2,252.3	3,107.7	4,040.7	4,950.2
Piemonte	1,128.7	1,439.0	2,201.1	2,421.4
Valle d'Aosta	78.8	102.3	125.1	154.3
Northwest average	987.6	1,349.5	1,878.5	2,214.8
Emilia-Romagna	1,099.5	1,592.1	2,219.7	2,733.0
Friuli-Venezia Giulia	635.0	631.9	1,202.8	1,104.7
Lazio	1,237.0	2,277.0	2,888.4	3,790.4
Marche	341.4	570.7	725.6	875.9
Toscana	946.8	1,300.8	1,804.1	2,282.1
Trentino-Alto Adige	669.4	505.5	865.6	884.3
Umbria	193.6	265.2	430.6	488.8
Veneto	1,160.6	1,356.1	2,069.9	2,286.5
Center/northeast ave.	785.4	1,062.4	1,525.8	1,805.7
Abruzzo	324.8	396.8	615.6	633.0
Basilicata	182.3	211.3	368.1	369.3
Calabria	506.5	646.4	1,170.5	951.9
Campania	1,042.7	1,600.7	2,619.2	2,638.4
Molise	92.1	98.4	202.9	156.0
Puglia	898.7	1,160.6	1,782.3	1,752.8
Sardegna	669.4	636.3	1,054.6	973.9
Sicilia	1,668.8	1,750.2	3,179.3	3,115.7
Mezzogiorno average	673.2	812.6	1,374.1	1,323.9

Source: See note to table 48.

Appendixes

Table 76

Accounts of Italy's Regional Institutions of Government:
Total Expenditure as Percentage of Total Revenue,
1977 and 1979

	1977	1979
Italy	130.6	110.4
Liguria	152.7	116.3
Lombardia	138.0	122.5
Piemonte	127.5	110.0
Valle d'Aosta	129.8	123.3
Northwest average	137.0	118.0
Emilia-Romagna	144.8	123.1
Friuli-Venezia Giulia	99.5	91.8
Lazio	184.1	131.2
Marche	167.2	120.7
Toscana	137.4	126.5
Trentino-Alto Adige	75.6	102.2
Umbria	137.0	113.5
Veneto	116.8	110.5
Center/northeast ave.	132.8	114.9
Abruzzo	122.2	102.8
Basilicata	115.9	100.3
Calabria	127.6	81.3
Campania	153.5	100.7
Molise	106.8	76.9
Puglia	129.1	98.3
Sardegna	95.1	92.3
Sicilia	104.9	98.0
Mezzogiorno average	119.4	93.8

Source: This table is an elaboration of data from table 75.

Notes

Chapter 1. For a Political Conceptualization of History and Underdevelopment

1. See, for example, Anthony A. Brewer, *Marxist Theories of Imperialism: A Critical Survey* (London: Routledge and Kegan Paul, 1980).

2. General literature attests to the predominance of the development/underdevelopment dichotomy as the basis for the conceptualization of underdevelopment: for example, part 3 of Brewer, *Marxist Theories,* is entitled "Modern Marxist Theories of Development and Underdevelopment"; one of Ronald H. Chilcote's books is entitled *Theories of Development and Underdevelopment* (Boulder, Colo.: Westview Press, 1984).

3. Orthodox Marxists and liberals have this idea despite placing it in different perspectives: for liberals, capitalist development as an end in itself will ultimately heal humanity's divisions; for orthodox Marxists, capitalism's historic mission is to bring humanity to the threshold of socialism.

4. For a profound discussion of the theoretical implications of this statement, see the excellent work by Chantal Mouffe, ed., *Gramsci and Marxist Theory* (London: Routledge and Kegan Paul, 1979).

5. See definitions of development, for example, in Celso Furtado, *Teorie dello sviluppo economico* (Theories of economic development) (Bari: Laterza, 1972); Fernando Enrique Cardoso and Enzo Faletto, *Dependency and Development in Latin America* (Berkeley and Los Angeles: University of California Press, 1979); Arnaldo Bagnasco, *Tre Italie: La problematica territoriale dello sviluppo italiano* (Three Italys: The territorial problematic of Italian development) (Bologna: Il Mulino, 1977); and Luciano Ferrari Bravo and Alessandro Serafini, *Stato e sottosviluppo: Il caso del Mezzogiorno italiano* (The state and underdevelopment: The case of Italy's Mezzogiorno) (Milan: Feltrinelli, 1972).

6. See Robert O. Keohane and Joseph S. Nye, *Power and Interdependence: World Politics in Transition* (Boston: Little, Brown, 1977). Various definitions of integration occur, for example, in Peter Robson, *The Economics of International Integration* (London: George Allen and Unwin, 1980); and John Pinder, "Positive and Negative Integration: Some Problems of Economic Union in the EEC," *The World Today,* March 1968, 88–110.

Different categories of integration are found in Stuart Holland, *Le regioni e lo sviluppo economico europeo* (The regions and European economic development) (Bari: Laterza, 1977); Pinder, "Positive and Negative Integration"; Ali Mohammed El-Agraa, ed., *The Economics of the European Community* (New York: St. Martins Press, 1980); and Jacques Pelkmans, "Economic Theories of Integration Revisited," *Journal of Common Market Studies* 18 (June 1980): 333–54. Especially interesting is Pelkmans's argument that, strictly speaking, a common market cannot exist.

7. The consummate analysis of power and therefore of politics is Niccolò Ma-

chiavelli, *Il principe* (The prince; first printed in 1532.) One of the best English-language translations is that of Peter Bondanella and Mark Musa, eds., *The Portable Machiavelli* (New York: Penguin Books, 1979), 77–166.

8. See Marina von Neumann Whitman, "International and Interregional Payments Adjustment: A Synthetic View," Princeton Studies in International Finance, no. 19 (Princeton: Princeton University, Department of Economics, 1967).

9. Many observations about the diversification of demand and internal production appear in Ragnar Nurkse, *La formazione del capitale nei paesi sottosviluppati* (Capital formation in underdeveloped countries) (Turin: Giulio Einaudi, 1965); and Furtado, *Teorie dello sviluppo economico*.

10. Other definitions of underdevelopment occur, for example, in Antonio Mutti and Irene Poli, *Sottosviluppo e meridione* (Underdevelopment and the Italian south) (Milan: Mazzotta, 1975); Lucio Libertini, *Integrazione capitalistica e sottosviluppo: I nuovi termini della questione meridionale* (Capitalistic integration and underdevelopment: The new terms of the southern question) (Bari: Laterza, 1968); Ferrari Bravo, and Serafini, *Stato e sottosviluppo;* Cardoso and Faletto, *Dependency and Development in Latin America;* and Furtado, *Teorie dello sviluppo economico*.

11. Excellent studies of dependence are provided by Theotonio Dos Santos, "The Structure of Dependence," in *Readings in U.S. Imperialism,* ed K. T. Fahn and Donald C. Hodges (Boston: Porter Sargent, Publisher, 1971); Umberto Di Giorgi and Roberto Moscati, "The Role of the State in the Uneven Spatial Development of Italy: The Case of the Mezzogiorno," *Review of Radical Political Economics* 12 (Fall 1980): 50; and Gabriel Palma, "Dependency: A Formal Theory of Underdevelopment or Methodology for the Analysis of Concrete Situations of Underdevelopment?" *World Development* 6 (1978): 881.

Peter Evans discusses the concept of dependence in *Dependent Development: The Alliance of Multinational, State, and Local Capital in Brazil* (Princeton: Princeton University Press, 1979), chaps. 1 and 2. For a profound conceptual discussion of center-periphery relations, see Jean Gottman, ed., *Centre and Periphery: Spatial Variation in Politics* (Beverly Hills, Calif.: Sage Publications, 1980). Excellent studies of dependent accumulation appear in Riccardo Parboni, *The Dollar and Its Rivals* (London: Verso, 1981); and Giancarlo Martinengo and Piercarlo Padoan, *Lo SME e il dollaro: Interdipendenza e gerarchia nei rapporti tra aree valutarie* (The European monetary system and the dollar: Interdependence and hierarchy in the relationships between currency areas) (Rome: Edizioni Scientifiche Italiane, 1983).

12. *Real income* refers to the quantity of goods and services produced by an economic system and made available to be purchased or utilized with money income. See Milton H. Spencer, *Contemporary Economics* (New York: Worth Publishers, 1971), 133.

13. The idea that insufficient capitalistic exploitation produces underdevelopment is advanced, for example, by Geoffrey Kay, *Sviluppo e sottosviluppo: Un'analisi marxista* (Development and underdevelopment: A Marxist analysis) (Milan: Feltrinelli, 1976).

14. An unorthodox if not revolutionary interpretation of the origins of the Mezzogiorno's underdevelopment, based on this idea, is provided by Edmondo Maria Capecelatro and Antonio Carlo, *Contro la "questione meridionale"* (Against the "southern question") (Rome: Samonà e Savelli, 1972); and Edmondo Maria Capecelatro and Antonio Carlo, eds., *Per la critica del sottosviluppo meridionale: Antologia di scritti* (For a critique of southern Italy's underdevelopment: An anthology of writings) (Florence: La Nuova Italia, 1973).

15. See Paolo Sylos Labini, *Il sottosviluppo e l'economia contemporanea* (Underdevelopment and the contemporary economy) (Bari: Laterza, 1983), 42.

Chapter 2. Italy from the Mezzogiorno's Origin to American Hegemony

1. The Kingdom of Italy (18 February 1861–2 June 1946) expressed the integration of the political authority of the following sovereign political actors: the Kingdom of Sardinia (1720–1861), the Kingdom of the Two Sicilys (1059–1860), the Grand Duchy of Toscana (1567–1860), the Duchy of Modena (1452–1860), and the Duchy of Parma (1545–1860).

2. See the perceptive study by Capecelatro and Carlo, *Contro la "questione meridionale,"* and Capecelatro and Carlo, eds., *Per la critica del sottosviluppo meridionale*. See also the excellent study by Luigi de Rosa, *La rivoluzione industriale in Italia e il Mezzogiorno* (The industrial revolution in Italy and the Mezzogiorno) (Bari: Laterza, 1973). Taken with a grain of salt, George H. Hildebrand, *Growth and Structure in the Economy of Modern Italy* (Cambridge: Harvard University Press, 1965), offers additional information.

3. See Capecelatro and Carlo, *Contro la "questione meridionale,"* and Capecelatro and Carlo, eds., *Per la critica del sottosviluppo meridionale*.

4. Italy has seven economic regions, according to Lloyd Saville (*Regional Economic Development in Italy* [Durham, N.C.: Duke University Press, 1967]), and three according to the more realistic study by Bagnasco (*Tre Italie*).

5. The economic system of the northwest occupies 61,746 square kilometers, or about 20.5 percent of Italian territory, within the jurisdiction of four subnational administrative regions: Liguria, Lombardy, Piedmont, and Valle d'Aosta.

6. The economic system of the center/northeast occupies 111,444 square kilometers, or about 37 percent of Italian territory, within the jurisdiction of eight subnational administrative regions: Emilia-Romagna, Friuli-Venezia Giulia, Latium (the northern two-thirds), the Marches, Trentino-Alto Adige, Tuscany, Umbria, and Veneto.

7. The Mezzogiorno, southern Italy's economic system, occupies 128,010 square kilometers, or about 42.5 percent of Italian territory, within the jurisdiction of nine subnational administrative regions. Eight of the nine are wholly within the Mezzogiorno: Abruzzo, Basilicata (also known as Lucania), Calabria, Campania, Molise, Puglia, Sardinia, and Sicily. Only the southern third of the remaining region, Latium, is part of the Mezzogiorno.

8. The literature on this point is vast. Comprehensive analysis is offered, for example, by Capecelatro and Carlo, *Contro la "questione meridionale"*; Bagnasco, *Tre Italie*; and Alfredo Del Monte and Adriano Giannola, *Il Mezzogiorno nell'economia italiana* (The Mezzogiorno in the Italian economy) (Bologna: Il Mulino, 1978).

9. Given the prevalent cultural interpretations of the economic information available at that time concerning the Mezzogiorno's economic history, even Antonio Gramsci (1891–1937) was one of the many who believed that capitalism had never developed sufficiently in the Italian South to overthrow feudalism. Indeed, this belief still seems prevalent today. Gramsci considered the agreement between the northwestern elite and the Mezzogiorno's landlord class to be the *blocco storico* (historic bloc) that impeded the spread of capitalism from northern Italy to the Mezzogiorno. Gramsci assesses quite correctly the *blocco storico*'s negative effects on the Italian South after Italy's unification. However, the point is that the *blocco storico* did not impede the spread of capitalism to a precapitalist area but transformed the organic development of capitalism in the Italian South, underway long before Italy's unification, into the Mezzogiorno's underdevelopment. See Antonio Gramsci, *La questione meridionale* (The southern question) (1926; reprint, Rome: Editori Riuniti, 1974).

10. A detailed analysis of the Mezzogiorno's subordination and impoverishment is found in Capecelatro and Carlo, *Contro la "questione meridionale."*

11. An excessive infusion of ideology mars the otherwise interesting and provocative argument presented by Gabriele Fergola, *Il Mezzogiorno: Problema nazionale* (The Mezzogiorno: National problem) (Rome: IRSE, 1976).

12. See, for example, Paul Corner, "Fascist Agrarian Policy and the Italian Economy in the Interwar Years," in *Gramsci and Italy's Passive Revolution*, ed. John A. Davis (London: Croom Helm, 1979).

13. See the excellent study by Roland Sarti, *Fascism and the Industrial Leadership in Italy 1919–1940: A Study in the Expansion of Private Power under Fascism* (Berkeley and Los Angeles: University of California Press, 1971).

14. See Martin Clark, *Antonio Gramsci and the Revolution That Failed* (New Haven, Conn.: Yale University Press, 1977).

15. See Sarti, *Fascism and the Industrial Leadership in Italy*, and Del Monte and Giannola, *Il Mezzogiorno nell'economia italiana*.

16. See Palmiro Togliatti, *Lectures on Fascism* (New York: International Publishers, 1976); C. J. Lowe and F. Marzari, *Italian Foreign Policy 1870–1940* (London: Routledge and Kegan Paul, 1975); Sarti, *Fascism and the Industrial Leadership in Italy*; Elisabeth Wiskemann, *Fascism in Italy: Its Development and Influence* (London: Macmillan & Co., 1969); idem, *Europe of the Dictators 1919–1945* (Ithaca, N.Y.: Cornell University Press, 1966); Salvatore La Francesca, *La politica economica del fascismo* (Fascism's economic policy) (Bari: Laterza, 1972); Gianni Toniolo, *L'economia dell'Italia fascista* (Fascist Italy's economy) (Bari: Laterza, 1980); and Corner, "Fascist Agrarian Policy." Useful for statistics and institutional descriptions but void of substantive analysis is William G. Welk, *Fascist Economic Policy: An Analysis of Italy's Economic Experiment* (Cambridge: Harvard University Press, 1938).

17. See Percy A. Allum, "Thirty Years of Southern Policy in Italy," *Political Quarterly* 52 (July/September 1981): 314.

18. See, for example, ibid. and Norman Kogan, "The Italian Communist Party: The Modern Prince at the Crossroads," in *Eurocommunism and Detente*, ed. Rudolf L. Tokes (New York: New York University Press, 1978).

19. See Kogan, "The Italian Communist Party."

20. See Paul Y. Hammond, *The Cold War Years: American Foreign Policy Since 1945* (New York: Harcourt, Brace and World, 1969).

21. See Giuseppe Mammarella, *Italy After Fascism: A Political History 1943–1965* (Notre Dame, Ind.: University of Notre Dame Press, 1966); and Simon Serfaty and Lawrence Gray, eds., *The Italian Communist Party: Yesterday, Today and Tomorrow* (Westport, Conn.: Greenwood Press, 1980.)

22. See Allum, "Thirty Years"; Serfaty and Gray, *The Italian Communist Party*; Kogan, "The Italian Communist Party"; and Mammerella, *Italy After Fascism*.

Chapter 3. The Mezzogiorno after World War II: Underdevelopment Renewed

1. See Allum, "Thirty Years," 314; Corner, "Fascist Agrarian Policy"; Del Monte and Giannola, *Il Mezzogiorno nell'economia italiana*.

2. See Del Monte and Giannola, *Il Mezzogiorno nell'economia italiana*, and Piero Barucci, *Ricostruzione, pianificazione, Mezzogiorno: La politica economica in Italia dal 1943 al 1955* (Reconstruction, planning, Mezzogiorno: Economic policy in Italy from 1943 to 1955) (Bologna: Il Mulino, 1978).

3. See Giacomo Schettini, "Il partito della Cassa" (The Cassa's plight), *Rinascita*, no. 33 (25 August 1984): 5; and Del Monte and Giannola, *Il Mezzogiorno nell'economia italiana*.

4. See Del Monte and Giannola, *Il Mezzogiorno nell'economia italiana*, and Fergola, *Il Mezzogiorno*.

5. See Mammarella, *Italy After Fascism;* Del Monte and Giannola, *Il Mezzogiorno nell'economia italiana;* and Istituto Nazionale di Sociologia Rurale (INSOR), *La riforma fondiaria: trent'anni dopo* (Land reform: Thirty years later) (Milan: Franco Angeli/INSOR, 1979).

6. See Di Giorgi and Moscati, "The Role of the State in the Uneven Spatial Development of Italy," 50; Allum, "Thirty Years"; and Del Monte and Giannola, *Il Mezzogiorno nell'economia italiana*.

7. See INSOR, *La riforma fondiaria;* Mammarella, *Italy After Fascism;* Del Monte and Giannola, *Il Mezzogiorno nell'economia italiana;* and Alan B. Mountjoy, *The Mezzogiorno* (London: Oxford University Press, 1973).

These are the eight reform districts. The Law for the Sila and the Sicilian Law took their names from the reform districts to which they were applied. The Summary Law produced the enabling decrees of February and April 1951 for the six following reform districts: (1) the Maremma zone of Latium and Tuscany and Abruzzo's Fucino zone; (2) Romagna's Po Delta; (3) Basilicata, Molise, and Puglia; (4) Sardinia; (5) Calabria's Caulonia zone; and (6) the Volturno zone on the border between Campania and Latium, together with Campania's Sele zone.

8. See INSOR, *La riforma fondiaria;* Mammarella, *Italy After Fascism;* and Mountjoy, *The Mezzogiorno*.

9. See Mountjoy, *The Mezzogiorno;* Hildebrand, *Growth and Structure;* and Del Monte and Giannola, *Il Mezzogiorno nell'economia italiana*.

10. See Joseph A. Martellaro, *Economic Development in Southern Italy 1950–1960* (Washington, D.C.: Catholic University of America Press, 1965).

11. See Del Monte and Giannola, *Il Mezzogiorno nell'economia italiana*, chap. 6.

12. See Joseph La Palombara, *Italy: The Politics of Planning* (Syracuse, N.Y.: Syracuse University Press, 1966), chap. 3; Percy A. Allum, *Italy—Republic without Government?* (New York: W. W. Norton, 1973), chap. 7; Mammarella, *Italy After Fascism;* Del Monte and Giannola, *Il Mezzogiorno nell'economia italiana*, chap. 6; and Martellaro, *Economic Development in Southern Italy*, intro.

13. With regard to the policy of direct industrialization, see, for example, Del Monte and Giannola, *Il Mezzogiorno nell'economia italiana*, chap. 9; Bagnasco, *Tre Italie;* Gisele Podbielski, *Venticinque anni di intervento straordinario nel Mezzogiorno* (Twenty-five years of extraordinary intervention in the Mezzogiorno) (Rome: Giuffrè/SVIMEZ, 1978); and Antonello Paba, "I poli di sviluppo: Un Riesame" (Development poles: Another look"), *Quaderni dell'economia sarda*, nos. 3–4 (September/December 1976): 111–26.

With regard to the incentives policy, see Andrea Saba, *La politica di incentivazione degli investimenti industriali in Italia e in Europa* (Incentives policy for industrial investments in Italy and in Europe) (Rome: Ateneo, 1967), and Mario Canino, "I nuovi incentivi per il Mezzogiorno" (New incentives for the Mezzogiorno), *Rassegna economica*, no. 3 (May/June 1976): 703–29.

14. See Martellaro, *Economic Development in Southern Italy*, chap. 1.

15. See Hildebrand, *Growth and Structure*, 66.

16. See Mammarella, *Italy After Fascism*, 225–26.

17. See Maurizio Benetti, Mauro Ferrara, and Corrado Medori, *Il capitale straniero nel Mezzogiorno* (Foreign capital in the Mezzogiorno) (Rome: Coines, 1975), 60–67.

18. See Augusto Graziani and Enrico Pugliese, eds., *Investimenti e disoccupazione nel Mezzogiorno* (Investments and unemployment in the Mezzogiorno) (Bologna: Il Mulino, 1979), 17.
19. See Benetti, Ferrara, and Medori, *Il capitale straniero nel Mezzogiorno*, 60–67.
20. See Del Monte and Giannola, *Il Mezzogiorno nell'economia italiana*, chap. 6.
21. Ibid.
22. Ibid., 204.
23. See the brilliant study by Luca Meldolesi, *Disoccupazione ed esercito industriale di riserva in Italia* (Unemployment and the industrial reserve army in Italy) (Bari: Laterza, 1972).
24. See Benetti, Ferrari, and Medori, *Il capitale straniero nel Mezzogiorno*.
25. See Del Monte and Giannola, *Il Mezzogiorno nell'economia italiana*, 207.

Chapter 4. Italy and Western Europe's Integration under American Hegemony

1. The European Economic Community is an intergovernmental organization founded upon the Treaty of Rome of 25 March 1957. The treaty entered into effect on 1 January 1958 with six adherents: Belgium, France, Italy, Luxembourg, the Netherlands, and West Germany. On 1 January 1973, Denmark, Ireland, and the United Kingdom joined the EEC, as did Greece on 1 January 1981 and Portugal and Spain on 1 January 1986. Greenland, a Danish region, seceded from the EEC on 1 February 1985.
2. See Claudia Morviducci, *Il Parlamento italiano e le comunità europee* (The Italian Parliament and the European communities) (Milan: Giuffré, 1979).
3. See Umberto Leanza, *Legislazione per il Mezzogiorno e Mercato Comune Europeo* (Legislation for the Mezzogiorno and the European Common Market) (Rome: Giuffré, 1963).
4. The constitution distinguishes between "ordinary regions" and "special regions," which have greater legislative autonomy. There are fifteen ordinary regions: Abruzzo, Basilicata (known also as Lucania), Calabria, Campania, Emilia-Romagna, Latium, Liguria, Lombardy, the Marches, Molise, Piedmont, Puglia, Tuscany, Umbria, and Veneto. The five remaining regions are special because their historical relationships with the Italian state reflect an awareness of regional identity that manifests itself in a strong desire for regional political autonomy. This awareness of regional identity derives from the particular linguistic and cultural conditions that prevail in Friuli-Venezia Giulia (with its Slav minority), Trentino-Alto Adige (with its Austro-German minority), Valle d'Aosta (with its French minority), and from the particular political and cultural conditions that prevail in Sardinia and Sicily.

My synthesis of the juridical relationships between the Italian state and its institutions of regional government is based primarily on Allum, *Italy—Republic without Government?* chap. 9; Carl Marzani, *The Promise of Eurocommunism* (Westport, Conn.: Lawrence Hill, 1980), esp. chap. 8; and Elisabeth Wiskemann, *Italy Since 1945* (London: Macmillan & Co., 1971), esp. chap. 1. The Consolato Generale d'Italia in Boston graciously provided me useful information with correspondence no. 3116 of 30 May 1984.

5. On 2 August 1984 the Italian Parliament put the CASMEZ into liquidation. The event ostensibly marked the beginning of a period in which the Italian government would presumably reconsider the ways in which the state could intervene in the Mezzogiorno. See *La Repubblica*, 4 August 1984, 3.

For additional information about the CASMEZ, see Del Monte and Giannola, *Il Mezzorgiorno nell'economia italiana;* Allum, *Italy—Republic without Government?*; Cassa per il Mezzogiorno, *A Thirty-year Review of the Cassa per il Mezzogiorno* (Rome: CASMEZ General Paper, 1983); Cassa per il Mezzogiorno, *How the Cassa per il Mezzogiorno Is Organized* (Rome: CASMEZ Enclosure to the General Report, 1983); Giorgio Gugliormella, *La stima degli effetti della spesa pubblica nelle prospettive di modifiche strutturali di lungo termine* (An evaluation of the effects of public spending on the prospects for long-term structural modifications), paper presented at the FORMEZ Study Encounter, "La pubblica amministrazione nel Mezzogiorno di fronte all'analisi costi-benefici" (A cost-benefit analysis of the public administration in the Mezzogiorno), Naples, 26 October 1983; La Palombara, *Italy;* Mountjoy, *The Mezzogiorno;* and Gisele Podbielski, *Italy: Development and Crisis in the Post-war Economy* (Oxford: Clarendon Press, 1974).

6. See Maria Valeria Agostini, *Regioni europee e scambio ineguale: Verso una politica regionale comunitaria?* (The European regions and unequal exchange: Toward a community regional policy?) (Bologna: Il Mulino, 1976), 28. See also Gianni Bonvicini and Joseph Sassoon, *Prospettive dell'integrazione economica europea* (Prospects for European economic integration) (Turin: Fondazione Giovanni Angelli, 1977); idem; *Governare l'economia europea: Divergenze e processi integrativi* (Governing the European economy: Divergences and integrative processes) (Turin: Fondazione Giovanni Agnelli, 1978); and J. Zijlstra and B. Goudzwaard, *Politica economica e problemi della concorrenza nella CEE e negli stati membri* (Economic policy and problems of competition in the EEC and in the member states) (Brussels: CEE, 1966).

7. A sophisticated analysis of the effect of the distribution of power among states on their monetary exchanges is found in Martinengo and Padoan, *Lo SME e il dollaro.*

8. The international division of labor refers to the territorial distribution of productive facilities in the international economy according to the value of the goods and services produced. This distribution conforms generally to the distribution of power in the international system. The politically dominant states control the accumulation and investment of capital in the international economy by reserving for themselves the production of the most remunerative goods and services, to be exchanged for goods and services of lesser value produced elsewhere.

9. OECD statistics for 1984 showed the following distribution of per capita income (in US dollars) among OECD countries: Switzerland, $15,096; USA, $13,994; Norway, $13,317; Canada, $13,125; Sweden, $13,095; Denmark, $10,950; West Germany, $10,708; Finland, $9,829; and Australia, $9,729. At that time, Italy ranked eighteenth with a per capita income of $6,249. Ahead of Italy ranked, for example, England ($7,970) and New Zealand ($6,931). However, it should be noted that these figures, by not reflecting the internal buying power of the corresponding value of the various national currencies, did not accurately indicate the real wealth of the average person in each country. See p. 1 of "Affari e Finanza" (business and finance weekly insert), no. 7 in *La Repubblica*, 23/24 December 1984.

The Italian economy emerged from World War II damaged but not devastated: at the end of 1946, the economy's GNP was 61 percent of its prewar level, compared with England's near 100 percent, the Netherlands' 74 percent, France's 50 percent, and Germany's 30 percent. On this point, see Barucci, *Ricostruzione, pianificazione, Mezzogiorno.*

Although the German economy may have emerged devastated from World War II, West Germany's GNP in 1984 was 2.2 times greater than Italy's. See *La Repubblica*, 2 January 1985, 35.

10. See El-Agraa, *Economics of the European Community,* chap. 7.

11. Information on the CAP's effect on the international economy can be gleaned from many sources; among them are Timothy M. Shaw, "EEC-ACP Interactions and Images as Redefinitions of Eur-africa: Exemplary, Exclusive and/or Exploitative?" *Journal of Common Market Studies* 18 (December 1980): 135; Stanley Andrews, *Agriculture and the Common Market* (Ames: Iowa State University Press, 1973); W. J. Legg and E. F. Szczepanik, "EEC Food Policies for the 1990s," *Futures* 10 (August 1978): 342; Gary P. Sampson and Alexander J. Yeats, "An Evaluation of the Common Agricultural Policy as a Barrier Facing Agricultural Exports to the European Economic Community," *American Journal of Agricultural Economics* 59 (February 1977): 99; John Marsh and Christopher Ritson, *Agricultural Policy and the Common Market*, European series no. 16 (London: Chatham House-PEP, 1971); Werner J. Feld, "Implementation of the European Community's Common Agricultural Policy: Expectations, Fears, Failures," *International Organization* 33 (Summer 1979): 335; M. D. M. Franklin, "The Common Agricultural Policy—1974," *Journal of Agricultural Economics* 26 (January 1975): 139; A. L. Lougheed, "The Common Agricultural Policy and International Trade," *National Westminster Bank Quarterly Review* (November 1971): 22; Michael B. Dolan and James A. Caporaso, "The External Relations of the European Community," *Annals of the American Academy of Political and Social Science* 440 (November 1978): 135; and Emanuele Macaluso, "The Agricultural Policy of the EEC," *World Marxist Review* 20 (March 1977): 110.

12. See Helen Wallace, William Wallace, and Carole Webb, eds., *Policy Making in the European Community*, 2d ed. (Chichester: John Wiley and Sons, 1983), 177.

13. See Leanza, *Legislazione per il Mezzogiorno e Mercato Comune Europeo*, 7.

14. See Del Monte and Giannola, *Il Mezzogiorno nell'economia italiana*, esp. chap. 9.

Chapter 5. The European Economic Community and Italy's Commercial Exchange

1. See Vera Cao-Pinna, ed., *Le esportazioni italiane: Prospettive al 1970* (Italian exports: Prospects to 1970) (Turin: Boringhieri, 1965) 17; and Libertini, *Integrazione capitalistica e sottosviluppo*, 19 and 217.

2. See Cao-Pinna, *Le esportazioni italiane*.

3. See Robert M. Stern, *Il commercio estero italiano e la sua influenza sullo sviluppo economico nazionale* (Italian foreign trade and its influence on national economic development) (Milan: Etas Kompass, 1968), 32.

4. See Libertini, *Integrazione capitalistica e sottosviluppo*, 217.

5. See Cao-Pinna, *Le esportazioni italiane*, 17 and 68.

6. Elvio Dal Bosco and Florina Pierelli, "Evoluzione della struttura del commercio estero dei paesi membri della CEE" (The evolution of the foreign trade structure of the EEC member countries), in *Contributi alla ricerca economica/Servizio studi della Banca d'Italia* (Contributions to economic research/Research Service of the Bank of Italy), no. 3 (Rome: Bank of Italy, 1973), 211–43.

7. Cao-Pinna, *Le esportazioni italiane*, 28.

8. Donald C. Templeman, *The Italian Economy* (New York: Praeger, 1981), chap. 7.

9. Cao-Pinna, *Le esportazioni italiane*, 17.

10. Templeman, *The Italian Economy*, chap. 7.

11. Ibid.

12. See *La Repubblica*, 2 July 1985, 34.

Chapter 6. The European Economic Community and the Italian Lira

1. Excellent studies of currencies are provided by Martinengo and Padoan, *Lo SME e il dollaro;* Parboni, *The Dollar and Its Rivals;* and John Kenneth Galbraith, *Money: Whence It Came, Where It Went* (Boston: Houghton Mifflin, 1975).

2. See Parboni, *The Dollar and Its Rivals,* esp. chap. 1.

3. Ibid., esp. chap. 4. The Japanese yen is the other de facto reserve currency in the international economy because the Japanese economy's place and function in the international economy are similar to those of West Germany. See p. 1 of "Affari e Finanza" (business and finance weekly insert), *La Repubblica,* 27/28 January 1985.

4. An excellent discussion of seigniorage is provided by Parboni, *The Dollar and Its Rivals,* chap. 1.

5. Ibid., chaps. 1–3. See also Keohane and Nye, *Power and Interdependence,* chaps. 4–6.

6. See Parboni, *The Dollar and Its Rivals,* chap. 5.

7. Ibid. France renounced the Basle Accord in January 1974 (and definitively in March 1976, after having recommitted itself in July 1975); Sweden renounced it in August 1977. After August 1977, Norway, West Germany, and the minor EEC states alone honored the Basle Accord.

8. Ibid.

9. See Keohane and Nye, *Power and Interdependence,* chaps. 4–6.

10. Discussions of the European Monetary System are provided by Parboni, *The Dollar and Its Rivals,* chap. 5; Robert Triffin, "The European Monetary System," in *Integration and Unequal Development: The Experience of the EEC,* ed. Dudley Seers and Constantine Vaitsos (New York: St Martin's Press, 1980); Ugo Borsari, "Da L'Aja a Brema: Per una storia del sistema monetario europeo" (From the Hague to Bremen: For a history of the European Monetary System), *Civitas,* no. 1 (1979); Gavyn Davies, "The EMS Wriggles Less Than the Snake but It May Be No Healthier," *Euromoney,* July 1982, 170; Claudio Signorile, *Il nuovo Mezzogiorno e l'economia nazionale* (The new Mezzogiorno and the national economy) (Bari: Laterza, 1982), chap. 3; Cosmo Giacomo Sallustio Salvemini, *Gli squilibri regionali nella Comunità Economica Europea e insufficienza dello SME* (Regional inequalities in the European Economic Community and the Insufficiency of the European Monetary System) (Milan: Giuffrè, 1979); and Horst Ungerer, Owen Evans, and Peter Nyberg, *The European Monetary System: The Experience 1979–1982,* Occasional Paper No. 19 (Washington, D.C.: International Monetary Fund, 1983).

For discussions of European monetary integration, see Documentazione Europea, *Unione economica e monetaria europea* (European economic and monetary union) (Luxembourg: Office of Official Publications of the European Communities, 1981); and El-Agraa, *The Economics of the European Community,* chaps. 9–10.

11. See p. 1 of "Affari e Finanza" (business and finance weekly insert), *La Repubblica,* 9/10 December 1984.

12. See *La Repubblica,* 17 May 1984, 31; and 26 July 1984, 27.

13. Ibid., 8 March 1984, 27.

14. Ibid., 13 December 1983, 33.

15. See Parboni, *The Dollar and Its Rivals,* chap. 5.

16. See *La Repubblica,* 6 March 1984, 35; 10 November 1984, 30; 11 December 1984, 31; 14 February 1985, 2; 26 March 1985, 33; 27 March 1985, 33.

On 13 April 1985, in Palermo, the finance ministers of the EEC states (except Italy, represented by its treasury minister) strengthened the EMS and the ECU by reaching a limited agreement based on three points: (1) the central banks of the EEC states were now authorized to utilize part of their ECUs (held as reserves) to maintain the parity within the EMS of their respective national currencies relative to the other EEC currencies; (2) official ECUs would now earn interest based on market rates, not on an adjusted average of the official rediscount rates of the central banks of the EEC states; and (3) the central banks of non-EEC states could now hold official ECUs as reserves. See *La Repubblica*, 14/15 April 1985, 29.

17. See Bonvicini and Sassoon, *Governare l'economia europea*, 53–54.

Chapter 7. The European Economic Community and Foreign Capital in Italy and in the Mezzogiorno

1. See Istituto per l'Assistenza allo sviluppo Meridionale, *Iniziative industriali a partecipazione estera nel Mezzogiorno* (Industrial initiatives with the participation of foreign capital in the Mezzogiorno) (Rome: IASM, 1981).
2. See Benetti, Ferrara, and Medori, *Il capitale straniero nel Mezzogiorno*, 104; and Sergio Gemma, *La normativa per gli investimenti esteri e le agevolazioni nel Mezzogiorno* (The legislation for foreign investments and for facilitations in the Mezzogiorno) (Rome: IASM, n.d.).
3. See Benetti, Ferrara, and Medori, *Il capitale straniero nel Mezzogiorno*; and Douglas F. Lamont and Robert Purtshert, *Managing Foreign Investment in Southern Italy: U.S. Businesses in Developing Areas of the EEC* (New York: Praeger, 1973), 94.
4. See Benetti, Ferrara, and Medori, *Il capitale straniero nel Mezzogiorno*.
5. See *La Repubblica*, 28 March 1985, 30.
6. Ibid., 4/5 March 1984, 30.
7. Ibid., 5 June 1985, 34; 8 August 1984, 30; and 30 January 1985, 28.
8. Ibid., 25 July 1984, 32.
9. Ibid., 7 August 1984, 34.
10. Ibid., 5 September 1984, 35.
11. Ibid., 29 March 1985, 32; and 30 March 1985, 34.
12. Ibid., 2 April 1985, 34.
13. Ibid., "Affari e Finanza" (business and finance weekly insert), 14/15 April 1985, 1.
14. Ibid., 26 April 1984, 29.
15. Ibid.
16. Ibid., 22 December 1983, 27–28.
17. Ibid., 24 October 1984, 36.
18. Ibid., "Affari e Finanza" (business and finance weekly insert), 3/4 March 1985, 2.
19. Ibid., 8 January 1985, 33.
20. See IASM, *Iniziative industriali a partecipazione estera nel Mezzogiorno*, 11 and 13.
21. See Benetti, Ferrara, and Medori, *Il capitale straniero nel Mezzogiorno*.
22. See European Commission, *The Seventeenth General Report of the European Communities* (Luxembourg: Office of Official Publications of the European Communities, 1979), section 7.
23. Ibid.
24. See Salverino De Vito, "Il Mezzogiorno e la Comunità Europea" (The Mezzogiorno and the European community), *Rivista Trimestrale Mezzogiorno d'Europa*

(Mezzogiorno d'Europa Quarterly Review; also available in English), no. 4 (October/December, 1984): 481.

25. See *CGIL-CISL-UIL sulla politica agricola comunitaria* (CGIL-CISL-UIL on the Common Agricultural Policy) (Rome: Edizioni SEUSi, 1972), 46. For additional information on the Common Agricultural Policy see Michele De Benedictis, "Contraddizioni e conflitti di interesse nella politica agricola comune" (Contradictions and conflicts of interest in the Common Agricultural Policy), *La questione agraria*, no. 1 (1981); and Michele De Benedictis and F. De Filippis, "La revisione della PAC: Illusioni e realtà" (The revision of the CAP: Illusions and realities), *Cooperazione in agricoltura*, no. 1 (1982).

26. See Vincenzo Guizzi, *Comunità europea e sviluppo del Mezzogiorno* (The European community and the Mezzogiorno's development) (Milan: Giuffrè, 1978), 108.

27. See Rosemary Galli and Saverio Torcasio, *La partecipazione italiana alla politica agricola comunitaria* (Italy's participation in the Common Agricultural Policy) (Bologna: Il Mulino, 1976), 247.

28. See *La Repubblica*, 3 April 1984, 35.

29. Ibid., 10 May 1985, 33.

30. This seems the only way to state coherently the EIB's declaration that it does not operate to earn a profit yet cannot operate in deficit.

31. Data relating to the EIB's operations in Italy and in the Mezzogiorno are from Banca Europea per gli Investimenti, *Venticinque anni 1958–1983*, 10–32. It should be noted that although ECU 15,974.4 million plus ECU 9,634.3 million may equal ECU 25,608.7 million, the EIB's investments in the EEC total ECU 22,487.9 million because the investments duplicated by more than one project equal ECU 3,120.8 million, to be subtracted from the apparent total.

32. Ibid. The ECU 7,710.4 million invested to finance regional development projects in Italy equals 48.27 percent of the EIB's total investment of this type in the EEC, while the ECU 2,194.2 million equals 22.76 percent of the EIB's total investments to finance projects of interest to the EEC.

Chapter 8. The European Economic Community and the Northwestern Elite's Investment in the Mezzogiorno's Underdevelopment

1. See Del Monte and Giannola, *Il Mezzogiorno nell'economia italiana*, chaps. 7–10.

2. Ibid.

3. Ibid., chap. 11.

4. See Benetti, Ferrara, and Medori, *Il capitale straniero nel Mezzogiorno*, 62, 60, and 61.

5. See Del Monte and Giannola, *Il Mezzogiorno nell'economia italiana*, 204.

6. Ibid., 181.

7. My elaboration of data extracted from Leanza, *Legislazione per il Mezzogiorno e mercato comune europeo*, and Gigi Padovani, *L'Europa a due velocità (Europe at two speeds)* (Turin: Stampatori, 1979).

8. See Del Monte and Giannola, *Il Mezzogiorno nell'economia italiana*, chap. 9.

9. In actuality it was the first program since the Vanoni Plan of 1954. See Podbielski, *Venticinque anni di intervento straordinario nel Mezzogiorno*, 52–53.

10. See Del Monte and Giannola, *Il Mezzogiorno nell'economia italiana*, chap. 9.

Notes 189

11. See Bagnasco, *Tre Italie*, 59.
12. See Del Monte and Giannola, *Il Mezzogiorno nell'economia italiana*, 181.
13. Ibid., chap. 7.
14. See Benetti, Ferrara, and Medori, *Il capitale straniero nel Mezzogiorno*, 62.
15. See Del Monte and Giannola, *Il Mezzogiorno nell'economia italiana*, 207.
16. See Benetti, Ferrara, and Medori, *Il capitale straniero nel Mezzogiorno*, 62.
17. See Del Monte and Giannola, *Il Mezzogiorno nell'economia italiana*, chap. 9.
18. Ibid.
19. Ibid.
20. Ibid., 181.
21. Ibid., 207.
22. Ibid., 204.
23. See Graziani and Pugliese, *Investimenti e disoccupazione nel Mezzogiorno*, 17.
24. See Signorile, *Il nuovo Mezzogiorno e l'economia nazionale*, 68.
25. Ibid., 83.
26. See *La Repubblica*, 4 August 1984, and 5/6 August 1984, 3.
27. Ibid., 11 September 1984, 35; and 18 October 1984, 28.
28. Ibid., 4/5 November 1984, 33; 18/19 November 1984, 2; 13 April 1985, 8; and 17 April 1985, 2.
29. Ibid., 5 July 1984, 30.

Chapter 9. The Consequences of the Mezzogiorno's Underdevelopment

1. See Del Monte and Giannola, *Il Mezzogiorno nell'economia italiana*, chap. 11. Interesting observations about the relationships between the lack of employment opportunities in the Mezzogiorno and the Mafia's activities are provided by Simonetta Bisi, "La criminalità nell'Italia meridionale con particolare riferimento alle organizzazioni di stampo mafioso" (Criminality in southern Italy with particular reference to Mafia-style organizations), in *La questione meridionale*, vol. 16, monograph 95, of *I problemi di Ulisse* (Florence: Sansoni Editore Nuova, 1983); 127–35.
2. See de Rosa, *La rivoluzione industriale in Italia e il Mezzogiorno*, 181–84.
3. See Klaus Rother, "L'attuale sviluppo demografico nel Mezzogiorno" (The current demographic development in the Mezzogiorno), *Rivista Trimestrale Mezzogiorno d'Europa* (Mezzogiorno d'Europa Quarterly Review), no. 4 (October/December 1984): 538.
4. See Del Monte and Giannola, *Il Mezzogiorno nell'economia italiana*, chaps. 7–8.
5. Ibid. chap. 7.
6. Ibid.
7. See Manlio Rossi-Doria, "Limiti e prospettive della transformazione agraria del Mezzogiorno" (The limits of and the prospects for the Mezzogiorno's agrarian transformation), *La questione meridionale*, vol. 16, monograph 95, of *I problemi di Ulisse* (Florence: Sansoni Editore Nuova, 1983), 62–70; Anna Nappa, ed., *Il Mezzogiorno e la politica mediterranea della CEE* (The Mezzogiorno and the EEC's Mediterranean policy) (Naples: FORMEZ, 1978); and Alessandro Corsi, "L'esodo agricolo dagli anni '50 agli anni '70 in Italia e nel Mezzogiorno" (The agricultural exodus from the fifties to the seventies in Italy and in the Mezzogiorno), *Rassegna economica*, no. 3 (May/June 1977): 721.
8. See Del Monte and Giannola, *Il Mezzogiorno nell'economia italiana*, chap. 7.
9. See Augusto Graziani, Alfredo Del Monte, Domenico Piccolo et al., *Incentivi e*

investimenti industriali nel Mezzogiorno (Incentives and industrial investments in the Mezzogiorno) (Milan: Franco Angeli, 1973); Graziani and Pugliese, *Investimenti e disoccupazione nel Mezzogiorno;* Augusto Graziani, ed., *L'economia italiana dal 1945 a oggi* (The Italian economy from 1945 to today) (Bologna: Il Mulino, 1979); and Agostini, *Regioni europee e scambio ineguale.*

10. See Del Monte and Giannola, *Il Mezzogiorno nell'economia italiana,* chaps. 7–8.

11. For more information on the transfer of monies to the Italian economy's agricultural sector see M. Gardner Clark, *Agricultural Social Security and Rural Exodus in Italy,* Western Societies Program Occasional Paper No. 7 (Ithaca, N.Y.: Cornell University Western Societies Program, Center for International Studies, 1977).

12. See Del Monte and Giannola, *Il Mezzogiorno nell'economia italiana,* chap. 10.

13. For more information on the Mezzogiorno's urbanization see Del Monte and Giannola, *Il Mezzogiorno nell'economia italiana,* chap. 7; Pasquale Villani, "Le Città meridionali" (The southern cities), *La questione meridionale,* vol. 16, monograph 95, of *I problemi di Ulisse* (Florence: Sansoni Editore Nuova, 1983), 71–76; Signorile, *Il nuovo Mezzogiorno e l'economia nazionale,* chap. 2; and Salvatore Cafiero, "Una politica delle città per il superamento dei divari (An urban policy for overcoming the differences), in *Il Mezzogiorno nell'Europa a dodici* (The Mezzogiorno in the Europe of Twelve) (Rome: SVIMEZ, 1979), 225–59.

14. For more information on the Mezzogiorno's hypertertiarization see Del Monte and Giannola, *Il Mezzogiorno nell'economia italiana,* chap. 11, and Signorile, *Il nuovo Mezzogiorno e l'economia nazionale,* chap. 2.

15. See *La Repubblica,* 21 February 1984, 38; 27 July 1984, 29; and 11 December 1984, 35.

16. Ibid., 6 October 1984, 35.

17. See Del Monte and Giannola, *Il Mezzogiorno nell'economia italiana,* 199.

18. See Meldolesi, *Disoccupazione ed esercito industriale di riserva in Italia.*

19. See Templeman, *The Italian Economy,* 193.

20. See, for example, Fergola, *Il Mezzogiorno: Problema nazionale,* chap. 2; and Gianni Giadresco, "Premiato ed espulso" (Rewarded and expelled), *Rinascita* no. 4 (27 January 1984): 16–17.

21. See Del Monte and Giannola, *Il Mezzogiorno nell'economia italiana,* 199.

22. See Luigi de Rosa, "L'emigrazione" (Emigration), *La questione meridionale,* vol. 16, monograph 95, in *I problemi di Ulisse* (Florence: Sansoni Editore Nuova, 1983), 77.

23. See Alfonso Manaresi, *Storia medioevale* (Medieval history) (Milan: Trevisini, 1936), chap. 21; Alfonso Manaresi, *Storia moderna* (Modern history) (Milan: Trevisini, 1936), chaps. 4 and 9; and Ulderico Nisticò, *Storia delle Calabrie* (History of the Calabrias) (Cosenza: Walter Brenner Editore, 1984), pt. 4, chap. 11.

The mark of the Kingdom of Spain's oppressive political domination over the Kingdom of the Two Sicilys is inveterate in southern Italy's culture. The Italian name for Spain, *Spagna,* is the root of a verb common to the Calabrese and Sicilian dialects, *spagnarsi,* to be afraid. Evidently, in the hearts and minds of southern Italians, Spain connoted fear.

One of the most interesting cases of the Kingdom of Spain's oppressive political domination over the Kingdom of the Two Sicilys concerns the celebrated Calabrese philosopher Tommaso Campanella (1568–1639), a Dominican friar imprisoned and tortured by the Catholic church for doctrinal heresy and by the Kingdom of Spain, through the Kingdom of the Two Sicilys, for political sedition. Campanella wrote more than one hundred books, of which the most famous is a utopia entitled *Civitas solis* (the city of the sun), written in 1602 and first published in 1623. For more information on Tommaso Campanella's life and works, see Adriano Seroni's "Introduzione" in *La città del sole* (The city of the sun) (Milan: Giangiacomo Feltrinelli Editore, 1979); Daniel J. Donno's introduction in Campanella, *La città del sole: Dialogo poetico/The City of the Sun: A Poetical Dialogue*, Biblioteca Italiana bilingual edition (Berkeley and Los Angeles: University of California Press, 1981); and Luigi Firpo, *Il supplizio di Tommaso Campanella: Narrazioni, documenti, verbali delle torture* (The ordeal of Tommaso Campanella: Narrations, documents, transcripts of the tortures), Collana Omikron no. 20 (Rome: Salerno Editrice, 1985).

Under the Treaty of Utrecht (1713), the Kingdom of Spain ceded its Italian possessions to the Austro-Hungarian Empire. Under the Treaty of Rastadt (1714), the Bourbons replaced the Hapsburgs on the Spanish throne and Piemonte acquired Sicily, reunited with the rest of the Kingdom of the Two Sicilies under Austrian Hapsburg rule according to the Treaty of the Hague (1720). According to the Treaty of Vienna (1738), reaffirmed by the Treaty of Aquisgrana (1748), the Kingdom of the Two Sicilys gained formal independence under the Neapolitan branch of the House of Bourbon, which ruled until 1860 (the year of Italy's unification), save for a few months in 1799 (the short-lived Parthenopean Republic) and from 1806 to 1815 (the Kingdom of Naples under Napoleonic tutelage, when only Sicily remained in Neapolitan Bourbon hands).

24. An old—and historically accurate—Italian saying expresses Spanish oppression in various parts of Italy: "Gli Spagnoli in Sicilia rosicchiavano, a Napoli mangiavano, a Milano divoravano" (In Sicily the Spanish gnawed, in Naples they ate, in Milan they devoured). On this point see Manaresi, *Storia moderna*, chap. 9, esp. 168–72.

25. In the Kingdom of the Two Sicilys, the legal system established with the 1816 Bourbon Restoration expressed juridically the agricultural capitalism that had overthrown feudalism in the 1700s. Private property and a free labor market—the signs of de facto bourgeois rule and now juridical realities—underlay the Bourbon monarchy. The Austro-Hungarian Empire intervened militarily to suppress the 1820 bourgeois revolution in southern Italy. When Austrian Hapsburg military support was absent, as in the 1848 revolution (because the Kingdom of the Two Sicilys supported the Kingdom of Sardinia in its attempt to put an end to Austrian power in Italy), the Neapolitan Bourbons remained in power with difficulty. See Capecelatro and Carlo, "Le tappe dello sviluppo capitalistico al Sud e i pensatori borghesi" (The stages of capitalistic development in southern Italy and bourgeois thinkers), *Per la critica del sottosviluppo meridionale;* and Nisticò, *Storia delle Calabrie*, pt. 5, chaps. 4–5.

26. For more detailed information on the Neapolitan Bourbons' piloted industrialization policy, see Capecelatro and Carlo, "Le tappe dello sviluppo capitalistico al Sud."

27. The word *omertà* is derived from the Sicilian *omu* (Latin *homo*, Italian *uomo*), meaning "man."

28. An enlightening study of the Mafia is provided by Pino Arlacchi, *La mafia imprenditrice: L'etica mafiosa e lo spirito del capitalismo* (The entrepreneurial Mafia: The Mafia ethic and the spirit of capitalism) (Bologna: Il Mulino, 1983).

29. Ibid.

30. See the excellent study by Sergio Turone, *Partiti e mafia dalla P2 alla droga* (The political parties and the Mafia from the P2 Masonic Lodge Scandal to drugs) (Bari: Laterza, 1985), chap. 1.

31. See Arlacchi, *La mafia imprenditrice*.

32. Detailed information on many of the instances of Italy's official collaboration with the Mafia is provided by Adriano Baglivo, *Camorra S.p.A.* (Camorra, Inc.) (Milan: Rizzoli, 1983); and Turone, *Partiti e mafia dalla P2 alla droga*.

33. See Arlacchi, *La mafia imprenditrice*.
34. See, for example, Fergola, *Il Mezzogiorno*, chap. 7, and Arlacchi, *La mafia imprenditrice*, chaps. 1–3.
35. See David W. Ellwood, *L'alleato nemico: La politica dell'occupazione anglo-americana in Italia 1943–1946* (The allied enemy: Anglo-American occupation policy in Italy 1943–1946) (Milan: Feltrinelli, 1977), esp. pt. 2, chap. 2; and Fergola, *Il Mezzogiorno*, chap. 7.
36. See Arlacchi, *La mafia imprenditrice*, chap. 3.
37. Ibid.
38. Ibid., chaps. 3–8.
39. Ibid.
40. Ibid., chap. 4.
41. Ibid.
42. Ibid., chap. 7.
43. See Bruno Gravagnolo's interview of Pino Arlacchi, "Come combattere il Welfare mafioso" (How to fight Mafia-style welfare), *Rinascita*, no. 19 (11 May 1984): 23–25.
44. See Arlacchi, *La mafia imprenditrice*, chap. 5.
45. Ibid., chap. 6.
46. See Baglivo, *Camorra S.p.A.*, chaps. 1, 5, and 6.
47. See Arlacchi, *La mafia imprenditrice*, chap. 5.
48. See Turone, *Partiti e mafia dalla P2 alla droga*.
49. According to Turone, the "first level" refers to the relationships between the executors of "Mafia policy" and civil society; the "second level" refers to the relationships between the formulators of "Mafia policy" (that is, the Mafia's leaders) and its executors; and the third level refers to the relationships between the corrupt members of Italy's political class and the Mafia's leaders.
50. See Turone, *Partiti e mafia dalla P2 alla droga*.
51. Ibid.
52. Ibid.
53. See Arlacchi, *La mafia imprenditrice*, chap. 7.
54. Ibid.
55. The Rognoni–La Torre Law, by authorizing examining magistrates to investigate systematically the accounts of suspected mafiosi and "Mafia-style organizations," has allowed these magistrates to reach the "second level" with noteworthy success and to arrive even at the threshold of the "third level." On this point see Turone, *Partiti e mafia dalla P2 alla droga*.
56. See *La Repubblica*, 3 November 1984, 15; 9 February 1985, 12.
57. Ibid., 27/28 January 1985, 11.
58. See Arlacchi, *La mafia imprenditrice*, chaps. 6 and 7, and Gravagnolo interview, "Come combattere il Welfare Mafioso."
59. See *La Repubblica*, 27 March 1984, 12.
60. Ibid., 23 March 1984, 12.

Chapter 10. The State of Affairs and Future Prospects

1. See the brilliant study by Giuseppe De Lutiis, *Storia dei servizi segreti in Italia* (The history of the Secret Services in Italy) (Rome: Editori Riuniti, 1984); Diana Johnstone, "Integrating Europe to Disintegrate the Left," in *The Politics of Eurocommunism: Socialism in Transition*, ed. Carl Boggs and David Plotke (Boston: South End Press, 1980); and Paul Joseph, "American Policy and the Italian Left," in ibid.

2. See *La Repubblica*, 18 December 1985, 38. For more information on Italian investments abroad see the comprehensive analysis by Nicola Acocella, ed., *Le multinazionali italiane* (Italian multinational corporations) (Bologna: Il Mulino, 1985).
3. Acocella, *Le multinazionali italiane*.
4. Ibid.
5. Ibid.
6. See *La Repubblica*, 20 January 1987, 39.
7. Ibid., 11 February 1987, 12; 12 February 1987, 12; and the "Affari e Finanza" section of *La Repubblica*, 13 February 1987, 1–3.
8. See Nappa, *Il Mezzogiorno e la politica mediterranea della CEE;* Signorile, *Il nuovo Mezzogiorno e l'economia nazionale;* and Collana Documenti SVIMEZ, *Il Mezzogiorno nell'Europa a dodici*.
9. See *La Repubblica*, 21 January 1986, 11; 23 January 1987, 12; 24 January 1987, 10; and 25/26 January 1987, 12.

Select Bibliography

Abadinsky, Howard. *Organized Crime*. 2d ed. Chicago: Nelson Hall, 1985.

Acocella, Nicola, ed. *Le multinazionali italiane* (Italian multinational corporations). Bologna: Il Mulino, 1985.

Agostini, Maria Valeria. *Regioni europee e scambio ineguale: Verso una politica regionale comunitaria?* (The European regions and unequal exchange: Toward a community regional policy?). Bologna: Il Mulino, 1976.

Agostini, Maria Valeria, and Agnello Rossi. *La programmazione delle regioni italiane e i piani di sviluppo regionale della CEE* (The programing of Italy's regions and the EEC's regional development plans). Rome: AICCE, 1979.

Allum, Percy, A. *Italy—Republic without Government?* New York; W. W. Norton, 1973.

———. "Thirty Years of Southern Policy in Italy." *Political Quarterly* 52 (July–September 1981): 314.

Amendola, Mario, and Paolo Baratta. *Investimenti industriali e sviluppo dualistico* (Industrial investments and dualistic development). Rome: Guiffrè/SVIMEZ, 1978.

Amin, Samir. *Accumulation on a World Scale*. New York: Monthly Review Press, 1974.

———.*Imperialism and Unequal Development*. New York: Monthly Review Press, 1977.

Andrews, Stanley. *Agriculture and the Common Market*. Ames: Iowa State University Press, 1973.

Antoniozzi, Dario. *Il cammino verso l'Europa* (The road toward Europe). Rome: Del Carretto, 1979.

Arlacchi, Pino. *La Mafia imprenditrice: L'etica mafiosa e lo spirito del capitalismo* (The entrepreneurial Mafia: The Mafia ethic and the spirit of capitalism). Bologna: Il Mulino, 1983.

———. Interview by Bruno Gravagnolo. "Come combattere il welfare mafioso" (How to fight Mafia-style welfare). *Rinascita* 19 (11 May 1984): 23–25.

Baglivo, Adriano. *Camorra S.p.A.* (Camorra, Inc.) Milan: Rizzoli, 1983.

Bagnasco, Arnaldo. *Tre Italie: La problematica territoriale dello sviluppo italiano* (Three Italys: The territorial problematic of Italian development). Bologna: Il Mulino, 1977.

Bairoch, Paul. *Rivoluzione industriale e sottosviluppo* (The Industrial Revolution and underdevelopment). Turin: Guilio Einaudi, 1967.

Balassa, Bela. "Trade Creation and Trade Diversion in the Common Market: An Appraisal of the Evidence." *Manchester School of Economic and Social Studies* 12 (June 1974): 93–135.

Banca Europea per gli Investimenti. *Venticinque anni 1958–1983* (Twenty-five years 1958–1983). Luxembourg: Banca Europea per gli Investimenti, 1983.

Barucci, Piero. *Ricostruzione, pianificazione, Mezzogiorno: La politica economica in Italia dal 1943 al 1955 (Reconstruction, planning, Mezzogirono: Economic policy in Italy from 1943 to 1955)*. Bologna: Il Mulino, 1978.

Beltrame, Carlo. "*Intorno alle 'regioni problema' d'Europa*" (Concerning Europe's "problem regions"). *Rivista di studi politici internazionali*, no. 1 (January/March 1976): 103–7.

Benetti, Maurizio; Mauro Ferrara; and Corrado Medori. *Il capitale straniero nel Mezzogiorno* (Foreign capital in the Mezzogiorno). Rome: Coines, 1975.

Berman, Harold J. *Law and Revolution: The Formation of the Western Legal Tradition.* Cambridge: Harvard University Press, 1983.

Bernini Carri, Carlo, *Il mercato comune agricolo* (The agricultural common market). Florence: La Nuova Italia Editrice, 1979.

Bisi, Simonetta. "La criminalità nell'Italia meridionale con particolare riferimento alle organizzazioni di stampo mafioso" (Criminality in southern Italy with particular reference to Mafia-style organizations). *La questione meridionale*, vol. 16, monograph 95, of *I problemi di Ulisse* (The problems of Ulysses), 127–35. Florence: Sansoni Editore Nuova, 1983.

Boccella, Nicola Maria. *Il Mezzogiorno sussidiato: Reddito prodotto e trasferimenti alle famiglie nei comuni meridionali* (The subsidized Mezzogiorno: Produced income and transfers to families in the southern communes). Milan: Franco Angeli, 1982.

Bonvicini, Gianni, and Joseph Sassoon. *Prospettive dell'integrazione economica europea* (Prospects for European economic integration). Turin: Fondazione Giovanni Agnelli, 1977.

————,eds. *Governare l'economia europea: Divergenze e processi integrativi* (Governing the European economy: Divergences and integrative processes). Turin: Fondazione Giovanni Agnelli, 1978.

Borsari, Ugo. "Da L'Aja a Brema: Per una storia del sistema monetario europeo" (From the Hague to Bremen: For a history of the European Monetary System). *Civitas*, no. 1 (1979).

Brewer, Anthony A. *Marxist Theories of Imperialism: A Critical Survey.* London: Routledge and Kegan Pual, 1980.

Cafiero, Salvatore. *Le migrazioni meridionali* (The southern migrations). Rome: SVIMEZ/Guiffrè, 1964.

————. "Una politica delle città per il superamento dei divari" (An urban policy for overcoming the differences). In *Il Mezzogirono nell'Europa a dodici*, 225–59. Rome: SVIMEZ, 1979.

Campanella, Tommaso. *La città del sole* (The city of the sun; written originally in Latin, 1602, as *Civitas solis;* first published in 1623). Milan: Giangiacomo Feltrinelli Editore, 1979.

Canino, Mario. "I nuovi incentivi per il Mezzogiorno" (New incentives for the Mezzogiorno). *Rassegna economica*, no. 3 (May/June 1976): 703–29.

Cao-Pinna, Vera, ed. *Le esportazioni italiane: Prospettive al 1970* (Italian exports: Prospects to 1970). Turin: Boringhieri, 1965.

Capecelatro, Edmondo Maria, and Antonio Carlo. *Contro la "questione meridionale"* (Against the "southern question"). Rome: Savonà and Savelli, 1972.

————, eds. *Per la critica del sottosviluppo meridionale: Antologia di scritti* (For the critique of southern Italy's underdevelopment: An anthology of writings). Florence: La Nuova Italia, 1973.

Capecelatro, Edmondo Maria, and Antonio Carlo. *I nuovi termini della "questione meridionale"* (The new terms of the "southern question"). Rome: Savelli, 1974.

Cardoso, Fernando Enrique, and Enzo Faletto. *Dependency and Development in Latin America.* Berkeley and Los Angeles: University of California Press, 1979.

Cassa per il Mezzogiorno (CASMEZ). *How the Cassa per il Mezzogiorno Is Organized.* Rome: CASMEZ Enclosure to the General Report, 1983.

―――. *A Thirty-year Review of the Cassa per il Mezzogiorno.* Rome: CASMEZ General Paper, 1983.

CGIL-CISL-UIL sulla politica agricola comunitaria (CGIL-CISL-UIL on the Common Agricultural Policy). Rome: Edizioni SEUSi, 1972.

Chiaromonte, Gerardo; Pietro Ingrao; and Emanuele Macaluso. *Agricoltura, Mercato Comune e Regioni* (Agriculture, the Common Market, and the regions). Rome: Editori Riuniti, 1973.

Chilcote, Ronald H. *Theories of Development and Underdevelopment.* Boulder, Colo.: Westview Press, 1984.

Ciocca, Pierluigi; Renato Filosa; and Guido M. Rey. "Integrazione e sviluppo dell'economia italiana nell'ultimo ventennio: Un riesame critico" (Integration and the Italian economy's development in the last twenty years: A critical reexamination). In *Contributi alla ricera economica/Servizio studi della Banca d'Italia* (Contributions to economic research/Research Service of the Bank of Italy), 57–135. Rome: Banca d'Italia, 1973.

Clark, Martin. *Antonio Gramsci and the Revolution That Failed.* New Haven, Conn.: Yale University Press, 1977.

Clark, M. Gardner. *Agricultural Social Security and Rural Exodus in Italy.* Western Societies Program Occasional Paper No. 7. Ithaca, N.Y.: Cornell University Western Societies Program, Center for International Studies, 1977.

Cocks, Peter. "Toward a Marxist Theory of European Integration." *International Organization* 34 (Winter 1980): 1.

Collana Documenti SVIMEZ. *La comunità europea allargata e il problema dei divari regionali* (The enlarged European community and the problem of regional disequilibria). Rome: SVIMEZ, 1979.

―――. *Il mezzogiorno nell'Europa a dodici* (The Mezzogiorno in the Europe of Twelve). Rome: SVIMEZ, 1979.

Colombo, Giuseppe. "Il settore agricolo meridionale nel processo di integrazione economica europea" (Southern Italy's agricultural sector in the process of European economic integration). *Rivista di economia agraria*, no. 2 (June 1974): 413–22.

Condorelli, Luigi, and Gerolamo Strozzi. "L'agricoltura fra Comunità Europea, Stato e Regioni" (Agriculture between the European community, the state, and the regions). In Collana *Agricoltura e regioni*, no. 7. Bologna: Il Mulino, 1973.

Confederazione Nazionale dei Coltivatori Diretti. *Politica Agricola comune e Mediterraneo: Documenti* (The Common Agricultural Policy and the Mediterranean: Documents). Rome, 1977.

Corner, Paul. "Fascist Agrarian Policy and the Italian Economy in the Interwar Years." In *Gramsci and Italy's Passive Revolution*, edited by John A. Davis. London: Croom Helm, 1979.

Corsi, Alessandro. "L'esodo agricolo dagli anni '50 agli anni '70 in Italia e nel Mezzogiorno" (Agricultural exodus from the fifties to the seventies in Italy and in the Mezzogiorno). *Rassegna economica*, no. 3 (May/June 1977): 721–53.

Croce, Benedetto. *Politics and Morals* (Published originally in Italian as *Etica e politica*). New York: Philosophical Library, 1945.

Dal Bosco, Elvio. "Le due rive dell'Elba" (The two banks of the Elbe). *Rinascita*, no. 37 (22 September 1984): 28–30.

Dal Bosco, Elvio, and Florina Pierelli. "Evoluzione della struttura del commercio estero dei paesi membri della CEE" (The evolution of the foreign trade structure of the EEC member countries). In *Contributi alla ricerca economica/Servizio studi della Banca d'Italia* (Contributions to economic research/Research service of the Bank of Italy), 211–43. Rome: Banca d'Italia, 1973.

Davies, Gavyn. "The EMS Wriggles Less Than the Snake but It May Be No Healthier." *Euromoney*, July 1982, 170–75.

De Benedictis, Michele. "Contraddizioni e conflitti di interesse nella politica agricola comune" (Contradictions and conflicts of interest in the Common Agricultural Policy). *La questione agraria*, no. 1 (1981).

De Benedictis, Michele, and F. De Filippis. "La revisione della PAC: Illusioni e realtà" (The revision of the CAP: Illusions and realities). *Cooperazione in agricoltura*, no. 1 (1982).

Del Monte, Alfredo. "Gli effetti della politica regionale sullo sviluppo industriale del Mezzogiorno" (The effects of regional policy on the Mezzogiorno's industrial development). *Rivista Trimestrale Mezzogiorno d'Europa* (Mezzogiorno d'Europa Quarterly Review; also available in English), no. 4 (October/December 1984): 583.

———. *Politica regionale e sviluppo economico* (Regional policy and economic development). Milan: Franco Angeli, 1977.

Del Monte, Alfredo, and Adriano Giannola. *Il Mezzogiorno nell'economia italiana* (The Mezzogiorno in the Italian economy). Bologna: Il Mulino, 1978.

De Lutiis, Giuseppe. *Storia dei servizi segreti in Italia* (The history of the Secret Services in Italy). Rome: Editori Riuniti, 1984.

De Meo, Giuseppe, and Giovanni Grittani. "La politica agricola comunitaria e l'agricoltura meridionale" (The Community Agricultural Policy and southern Italy's agriculture). *Rivista di economia agraria*, no. 2 (June 1974): 247–60.

de Rosa, Luigi. "L'emigrazione" (Emigration). *La questione meridionale*, vol. 16, monograph 95, in *I problemi di Ulisse* (The problems of Ulysses); 77–86. Florence: Sansoni Editore Nuova, 1983.

———. *La rivoluzione industriale in Italia e il Mezzogiorno* (The Industrial Revolution in Italy and the Mezzogiorno). Bari: Laterza, 1973.

De Vito, Salverino. "Il Mezzogiorno e la Comunità Europea" (The Mezzogiorno and the European community). *Rivista Trimestrale Mezzogiorno d'Europa* (Mezzogiorno d'Europa Quarterly Review; also available in English), no. 4 (October/December 1984): 481.

Di Giorgi, Umberto, and Roberto Moscati, "The Role of the State in the Uneven Spatial Development of Italy: The Case of the Mezzogiorno." *Review of Radical Political Economics* 12 (Fall 1980): 50.

Documentazione Europa. *La comunità e le sue regioni* (The community and its regions). Luxembourg: Office of Official Publications of the European Communities, 1980.

———. *Destinazione Europa: Cronologia della Comunità Europea* (Destination Europe: Chronology of the European community). Luxembourg: Office of Official Publications of the European Communities, 1980.

———. *La politica sociale della Comunità Europea* (The social policy of the European community). Luxembourg: Office of Official Publications of the European Communities, 1981.

———. *Unione economica e monetaria europea* (European economic and monetary union). Luxembourg: Office of Official Publications of the European Communities, 1981.

Dolan, Michael B., and James A. Caporaso. "The External Relations of the European Community." *Annals of the American Academy of Political and Social Sciences* 440 (November 1978): 135.

Dolan, Michael B., and Brian W. Tomlin. "First World—Third World Linkages: External Relations and Economic Development." *International Organization* 34 (Winter 1980): 41.

Donno, Daniel J. Introduction to *La città del sole: Dialogo poetico / The City of the Sun: A Poetical Dialogue* by Tommaso Campanella. Berkeley and Los Angeles: University of California Press, 1981.

Donolo, Carlo, and Riccardo Scartezzini. "Sviluppo ineguale e marginalità: Elementi per l'analisi sociale del meridione" (Unequal development and marginality: Elements for the social analysis of the Italian south). *International Review of Community Development*, nos. 27–28 (Summer 1972): 37–62.

Dos Santos, Theotonio. "The Structure of Dependence." In *Readings in U.S. Imperialism*, edited by K. T. Fahn and Donald C. Hodges. Boston: Porter Sargent, Publisher, 1971.

Ducci, Antonio. "Situazione vinicola e regolamentazione CEE" (The wine situation and EEC regulations). *Bari economica*, nos. 7–8 (July/August 1975): 35–40.

Ducci, Roberto, and Bino Olivi. *L'Europa incompiuta* (Europe unfinished). Padua: CEDAM, 1970.

El-Agraa, Ali Mohammed, ed. *The Economics of the European Community*. New York: St. Martin's Press, 1980.

El-Agraa, Ali Mohammed, and Anthony John Jones. *Theory of Customs Unions*. Oxford: Philip Allan, 1981.

Ellwood, David W. *L'alleato nemico: La politica dell'occupazione anglo-americana in Italia 1943–1946* (The allied enemy: Anglo-American occupation policy in Italy 1943–1946; published originally in English as *Allied Occupation Policy in Italy 1943–1946*). Milan: Feltrinelli, 1977.

European Commission. *The Community Today*. Luxembourg: Office of Official Publications of the European Communities, 1979.

———. *The Official Journal of the European Communities, Notices and Information*, various issues.

———. *The Seventeenth General Report of the European Communities*. Luxembourg: Office of Official Publications of the European Communities, 1979.

Evans, Peter. *Dependent Development: The Alliance of Multinational, State, and Local Capital in Brazil*. Princeton: Princeton University Press, 1979.

Fabiani, Guido. "Aspetti strutturali e di tendenza nell'agricoltura italiana 1960–1970" (Structural aspects and tendencies in Italian agriculture 1960–1970). *Critica marxista*, no. 6 (November/December 1974): 55.

Fabiani, Guido, and Marcello Gorgoni. "Un'analisi delle strutture dell'agricoltura italiana" (An analysis of the structures of Italian agriculture). *Rivista di economia agraria*, no. 6 (November/December 1973): 65.

Fadda, Sebastiano. "Sulla necessità di un riorientamento dell'intervento straordinario nel Mezzogiorno" (On the necessity of a reorientation of the extraordinary intervention in the Mezzogiorno). *Il Mulino*, no. 270 (July/August 1980): 649.

Falcone, Franca. "Effetti dell'integrazione economica europea sulla struttura delle esportazioni italiane" (The effects of European economic integration on the structure of Italian exports). *Rassegna economica*, no. 5 (September/October 1975): 1139–66.

Fanfani, Roberto. "L'agricoltura nei paesi della CEE nel periodo 1963–1974: Evoluzione strutturale e produttiva" (Agriculture in the EEC countries in the 1963–1974 period: Structural and productive evolution). *Rivista di economia agraria*, no. 3 September 1976): 489–521.

Fantini, Oddone. *L 'integrazione economica europea e il mercato comune* (European economic integration and the Common Market). 3d ed. Padua: CEDAM, 1959.

Feld, Werner J. "Implementation of the European Community's Common Agricultural Policy: Expectations, Fears, Failures." *International Organization* 33 (Summer 1979): 335.

Fergola, Gabriele. *Il Mezzogiorno: Problema nazionale* (The Mezzogiorno: National problem). Rome: IRSE, 1976.

Ferrara, Bruno. *Nord—Sud, interdipendenza di due economie* (North—South: The interdependence of two economies). Milan: CASMEZ/Franco Angeli, 1976.

Ferrari Bravo, Luciano, and Alessandro Serafini. *Stato e sottosviluppo: Il caso del Mezzogiorno italiano* (The state and underdevelopment: The case of the Italian Mezzogiorno). Milan: Feltrinelli, 1972.

Firpo, Luigi. *Il supplizio di Tommaso Campanella: Narrazioni, documenti, verbali delle torture* (The ordeal of Tommaso Campanella: Narrations, documents, transcripts of the tortures), Collana Omikron, no. 20. Rome: Salerno Editrice, 1985.

Franklin, M. D. M. "The Common Agricultural Policy—1974." *Journal of Agricultural Economics* 26 (January 1975): 139.

Furtado, Celso. *Teorie dello sviluppo economico* (Theories of economic development; published originally in French). Bari: Laterza, 1972.

Galbraith, John Kenneth. *Money: Whence It Came, Where It Went*. Boston: Houghton Mifflin, 1975.

Galli, Rosemary, and Saverio Torcasio. *La partecipazione italiana alla politica agraria comunitaria* (Italy's participation in the Common Agricultural Policy). Bologna: Il Mulino, 1976.

Gemma, Sergio. *La normativa per gli investimenti esteri e le agevolazioni nel Mezzogiorno* (The legislation for foreign investments and for facilitations in the Mezzogiorno). Rome: IASM, n.d.

Giadresco, Gianni. "Premiato ed espulso" (Rewarded and expelled). *Rinascita*, no. 4 (27 January 1984): 16–17.

Giolitti, Antonio. "Le dimensioni nuove della politica regionale europea" (The new dimensions of European regional policy). *Comuni d'Europa*, no. 2 (February 1979): 3–4.

Gorgoni, Marcello. "Agrumicoltura italiana e mercato estero" (Italian citrus fruit production and the foreign market). *Rassegna economica*, no. 3 (May/June 1973): 757–77.

Gottman, Jean, ed. *Centre and Periphery: Spatial Variation in Politics*. Beverly Hills, Calif.: Sage Publications, 1980.

Gramsci, Antonio. *La questione meridionale* (The southern question). 1926. Reprint. Rome: Editori Riuniti, 1974.

Graziani, Augusto. "Dualismo e sviluppo economico" (Dualism and economic development). *Rassegna economica*, no. 2 (May–August 1963): 332–48.

———, ed. *L'economia italiana dal 1945 a oggi* (The Italian economy from 1945 to today). Bologna: Il Mulino, 1979.

Graziani, Augusto; Alfredo Del Monte; and Domenico Piccolo et al. *Incentivi e investimenti industriali nel Mezzogiorno* (Incentives and industrial investments in the Mezzogiorno). Milan: Franco Angeli, 1973.

Graziani, Augusto, and Enrico Pugliese, eds. *Investimenti e disoccupazione nel Mezzogiorno* (Investments and unemployment in the Mezzogiorno). Bologna: Il Mulino, 1979.

Gugliormella, Giorgio. *La stima degli effetti della spesa pubblica nelle prospettive di modifiche strutturali di lungo termine* (An evaluation of the effects of public spending on the prospects for long-term structural modifications). Paper presented at the FORMEZ Study Encounter, "La pubblica amministrazione nel Mezzogiorno di fronte all'analisi costi-benefici" (A cost-benefit analysis of the public administration in the Mezzogiorno), Naples, 26 October 1983.

Guizzi, Enzo. "Il ruolo dello Stato e le Regioni nei confronti della Comunità Europa" (The role of the state and the regions as regards the European Community). *Bari economica*, nos. 7–8 (July/August 1975): 41–42.

Guizzi, Vincenzo. *Comunità europea e sviluppo del Mezzogiorno* (The European Community and the Mezzogiorno's development). Milan: Guiffrè, 1978.

Halperin, Morton H.; Jerry J. Berman; and Robert L. Borosage et al. *The Lawless State: The Crimes of the U.S. Intelligence Agencies.* A Report by the Center for National Security Studies. New York: Penguin Books, 1976.

Hammond, Paul Y. *The Cold War Years: American Foreign Policy Since 1945.* New York: Harcourt, Brace and World, 1969.

Herman, Edward S. *The Real Terror Network: Terrorism in Fact and Propaganda.* Boston: South End Press, 1982.

Hildebrand, George H. *Growth and Structure in the Economy of Modern Italy.* Cambridge: Harvard University Press, 1965.

Holland, Stuart K. *Capitalismo e squilibi regionali* (Capitalism and regional disequilibria; published originally in English). Bari: Laterza, 1976.

———. *Le regioni e lo sviluppo economico europeo* (The regions and European economic development; published originally in English). Bari: Laterza, 1977.

———. "Regional Underdevelopment in a Developed Economy: The Italian Case." *Regional Studies* 5 (1971): 71–90.

Iannettone, Giovanni. *Politica regionale comunitaria* (Community regional policy). Naples: A. Conte, 1979.

Istituto per l'Assistenza allo Sviluppo Meridionale. *Iniziative industriali a partecipazione estera nel Mezzogiorno* (Industrial initiatives with the participation of foreign capital in the Mezzogiorno). Rome: IASM, 1981.

Istituto Nazionale di Sociologia Rurale. *La riforma fondiaria: Trent'anni dopo* (The Land Reform: Thirty years later). Milan: Franco Angeli/INSOR, 1979.

Johnstone, Diana. "Integrating Europe to Disintegrate the Left." In *The Politics of Eurocommunism: Socialism in Transition*, edited by Carl Boggs and David Plotke. Boston: South End Press, 1980.

Joseph, Paul. "American Policy and the Italian Left." in *The Politics of Eurocommunism: Socialism in Transition*, edited by Carl Boggs and David Plotke. Boston: South End Press, 1980.

Jossa, Bruno, ed. *Economia del sottosviluppo* (The economy of underdevelopment). Bologna: Il Mulino, 1973.

Kay, Geoffrey. *Sviluppo e sottosviluppo: Un'analisi marxista* (Development and underdevelopment: A Marxist analysis; published originally in English). Milan: Feltrinelli, 1976.

Keeble, David; Peter L. Owens; and Chris Thompson. "Regional Accessibility and Economic Potential in the European Community." *Regional Studies* 16 (December 1982): 419–31.

Keohane, Robert O., and Joseph S. Nye. *Power and Interdependence: World Politics in Transition*. Boston: Little, Brown, 1977.

Kidron, Michael. *Il capitalismo occidentale del dopoguerra* (Western capitalism of the post war era; published originally in English). Bari: Laterza, 1969.

Kogan, Norman. "The Italian Communist Party: The Modern Prince at the Crossroads." in *Eurocommunism and Detente*, edited by Rudolf L. Tokes. New York: New York University Press, 1978.

La Francesca, Salvatore. *La politica economica del Fascismo* (Fascism's economic policy). Bari: Laterza, 1972.

Lamont, Douglas F., and Robert Purtshert. *Managing Foreign Investments in Southern Italy: U.S. Business in Developing Areas of the EEC*. New York: Praeger, 1973.

Lange, Peter, and Sidney Tarrow, eds. *Italy in Transition: Conflict and Consensus*. London: Frank Cass, 1980.

La Palombara, Joseph. *Italy: The Politics of Planning*. Syracuse, N.Y.: Syracuse University Press, 1966.

La Repubblica. Rome. Various issues, 13 December 1983–13 February 1987.

Leanza, Umberto. *Legislazione per il Mezzogiorno e Mercato Comune Europeo* (Legislation for the Mezzogiorno and the European Common Market). Rome: Guiffrè, 1963.

Legg, W. J., and E. F. Szczepanik. "EEC Food Policies for the 1990s." *Futures* 10 (August 1978): 342.

Libertini, Lucio. *Integrazione capitalistica e sottosviluppo: I nuovi termini della questione meridionale* (Capitalist integration and underdevelopment: The new terms of the southern question). Bari: Laterza, 1968.

Lougheed, A. L. "The Common Agricultural Policy and International Trade." *National Westminster Bank Quarterly Review*, November 1971, 22.

Lowe, C. J., and F. Marzari. *Italian Foreign Policy 1870–1940*. London: Routledge and Kegan Paul, 1975.

Lutz, Vera. *Italy: A Study in Economic Development*. Oxford: Oxford University Press, 1962.

Macaluso, Emanuele. "The Agricultural Policy of the EEC." *World Marxist Review* 20 (March 1977): 110.

———. "A New Development for the South." *The Italian Communists*, no. 4 (October/December 1980): 50.

MacEwan, Arthur. "Nuova luce sulla dipendenza e lo sviluppo dipendente" (New light on dependence and dependent development). *Monthly Review* (Italian ed.), no. 2 (March/April 1983): 11–16.

Machiavelli, Niccolò. *Il principe* (The prince; first printed in 1532). In *The Portable Machiavelli*, edited by Peter Bondanella and Mark Musa. New York: Penguin Books, 1979.

Mammarella, Giuseppe. *Italy After Fascism: A Political History 1943-1965*. Notre Dame, Ind.: University of Notre Dame Press, 1966.

Manaresi, Alfonso. *Storia medioevale* (Medieval history). Milan: Trevisini, 1936.

———. *Storia moderna* (Modern history). Milan: Trevisini, 1936.

Marsh, John, and Christopher Ritson, *Agricultural Policy and the Common Market*. European series no. 16, PEP. London: Chatham House, 1971.

Martellaro, Joseph A. *Economic Development in Southern Italy 1950-1960*. Washington, D.C.: Catholic University of America Press, 1965.

Martinengo, Giancarlo, and Piercarlo Padoan. *Lo SME e il dollaro: Interdipendenza e gerarchia nei rapporti tra aree valutarie* (The European Monetary System and the dollar: Interdependence and hierarchy in the relationships between currency areas). Rome: Edizioni Scientifiche Italiane, 1983.

Martins, Mario Rui, and John Mawson. "The Programming of Regional Development in the EEC: Supranational or International Decision-making?" *Journal of Common Market Studies* 20 (December 1982): 229-344.

Marzani, Carl. *The Promise of Eurocommunism*. Westport, Conn.: Lawrence Hill, 1980.

Meldolesi, Luca. *Disoccupazione ed esercito industriale di riserva in Italia* (Unemployment and the industrial reserve army in Italy). Bari: Laterza, 1972.

Morviducci, Claudia. *Il Parlamento italiano e le comunità europee* (The Italian Parliament and the European communities). Milan: Giuffrè, 1979.

Mottura, Giovanni, and Enrico Pugliese. "Observations on Some Characteristics of Italian Emigration in the Last Fifteen Years." *International Review of Community Development*, nos. 27-28 (Summer 1972): 3-20.

Mouffe, Chantal, ed. *Gramsci and Marxist Theory*. London: Routledge and Kegan Paul, 1979.

Mountjoy, Alan B. *The Mezzogiorno*. London: Oxford University Press, 1973.

Mutti, Antonio, and Irene Poli. *Sottosviluppo e meridione* (Underdevelopment and the Italian south). Milan: Mazzotta, 1975.

Nappa, Anna, ed. *Il Mezzogiorno e la politica mediterranea della CEE* (The Mezzogiorno and the EEC's Mediterranean policy). Naples: FORMEZ, 1978.

Nisticò, Ulderico. *Storia delle Calabrie* (History of the Calabrias). Cosenza: Walter Brenner Editore, 1984.

Nurkse, Ragnar. *La formazione del capitale nei paesi sottosviluppati* (Capital formation in underdeveloped countries; published originally in English). Turin: Guilio Einaudi, 1965.

Olivi, Bino. *Il tentativo Europa: Storia politica della Comunità Europea* (The attempt to make Europe: A political history of the European community). Milan: ETAS, 1979.

Paba, Antonello. "I poli di sviluppo: Un riesame" (Development poles: Another look). *Quaderni dell'economia sarda*, nos. 3-4 (September/December 1976): 111-26.

Padovani, Gigi. *L'Europa a due velocità* (Europe at two speeds). Turin: Stampatori, 1979.

Palma, Gabriel. "Dependency: A Formal Theory of Underdevelopment or a Methodology for the Analysis of Concrete Situations of Underdevelopment?" *World Development* 6 (1978): 881.

Papanice, Leonardo. *Il problema dell'agricoltura italiana ed il Mercato Comune* (The problem of Italian agriculture and the Common Market). Putignano: De Robertiis e Figli, 1966.

Papisca, Antonio. *Comunità Europea e sviluppo politico: Contributo all'analisi del sistema comunitario europeo* (The European community and political development: a contribution to the analysis of the European community system). Reggio di Calabria: Editori Meridionali Riuniti, 1974.

Parboni, Riccardo. *The Dollar and Its Rivals* (Published originally in Italian as *Finanza e crisi internazionale* [Milan: Etas Libri, 1980]). London: Verso, 1981.

Pelkmans, Jacques. "Economic Theories of Integration Revisited." *Journal of Common Market Studies* 18 (June 1980): 333–54.

Petriccione, Sandro. *Politica industriale e Mezzogiorno* (Industrial policy and the Mezzogiorno). Bari: Laterza, 1976.

Pinder, John. "Positive and Negative Integration: Some Problems of Economic Union in the EEC." *The World Today*, March 1968, 88–110.

Podbielski, Gisele. "The Common Agricultural Policy and the Mezzogiorno." *Journal of Common Market Studies* 19 (June 1981): 331–50.

———. *Italy: Development and Crisis in the Post-war Economy*. Oxford: Clarendon Press, 1974.

———. *Venticinque anni di intervento straordinario nel Mezzogiorno* (Twenty-five years of extraordinary intervention in the Mezzogiorno; also available in English). Rome: Giuffrè/SVIMEZ, 1978.

Ponzo, Ettore. "Il finanziamento della politica agricola comune nel periodo 1962–1974" (The financing of the Common Agricultural Policy in the 1962–1974 period). *Rivista di economia agraria*, no. 3 (September 1976): 523–46.

Pugliese, Aldo. "Prodotti agricolo-alimentari e manufatti nella bilancia commerciale italiana: Una proposta d'interpretazione" (Foodstuffs and manufactured goods in Italy's balance of payments: A proposed interpretation). *Rivista di economia agrari*, no. 4 (December 1976): 705.

Quadrio Curzio, Alberto. *Riflessioni sulle imprese multinazionali e la Comunità Economica Europea* (Reflections on multinational corporations and the European Economic Community). Bologna: Cooperativa Libraria Universitaria Editrice, 1975.

Reuter, Peter. *Disorganized Crime: The Economics of the Visible Hand*. Cambridge, Mass.: MIT Press, 1983.

Reviglio, Franco. *Spesa pubblica e stagnazione dell'economia italiana* (Public spending and the stagnation of the Italian economy). Bologna: Il Mulino, 1977.

Robbins, Bill. "EEC Social Policy and Its Effect on National Industrial Relations." *Management Decision* 20 (1982): 23–41.

Robinson, Joan. *Sviluppo e sottosviluppo* (Development and underdevelopment; published originally in English as *Aspects of Development and Underdevelopment* [Cambridge: Cambridge University Press, 1979]). Bari: Laterza, 1981.

Robson, Peter. *The Economics of International Integration*. London: George Allen and Unwin, 1980.

Rodgers, Allan. *Economic Development in Retrospect: The Italian Model and Its Significance for Regional Planning in Market-oriented Economies*. Washington, D.C.: V. H. Winston and Sons, 1979.

Rossi-Doria, Manlio. "Limiti e prospettive della trasformazione agraria del Mezzogiorno" (The limits of and the prospects for the Mezzogiorno's agrarian transformation). *La questione meridionale*, vol. 16, monograph 95, of *I problemi di Ulisse* (The problems of Ulysses), 62–70. Florence: Sansoni Editore Nuova, 1983.

Rother, Klaus. "L'attuale sviluppo demografico nel Mezzogiorno" (The current demographic development in the Mezzogiorno). *Rivista Trimestrale Mezzogiorno d'Europa* (Mezzogiorno d'Europa Quarterly Review; also available in English), no. 4 (October–December 1984): 537.

Saba, Andrea. *La politica di incentivazione degli investimenti industriali in Italia e in Europa* (Incentives policy for industrial investments in Italy in Europe). Rome: Ateneo, 1967.

Sabella, Domenica. *L'Europa e il Mezzogiorno*. Rome: Editoriale di cultura e di documentazione, 1959.

Sabetti, Filippo. *Political Authority in a Sicilian Village*. New Brunswick, N.J.: Rutgers University Press, 1984.

Saccomandi, Vito. "Crisi economica, integrazione europea e politica agraria nel periodo 1973–1976" (Economic crisis, European integration, and the Common Agricultural Policy from 1973–76). *Rivista di economia agraria*, no. 3 (September 1976): 561–94.

Salvemini, Cosmo Giacomo Sallustio. *Gli squilibri regionali nella Comunità Economica Europea* (Regional Disequilibria in the European Economic Community). Milan: Guiffrè, 1977.

―――. *Gli squilibri regionali nella Comunità Economica Europea e insufficienza dello SME* (Regional disequilibria in the European Economic Community and the insufficiency of the EMS). Milan: Giuffrè, 1979.

Sampson, Gary P., and Alexander J. Yeats. "An Evaluation of the Common Agricultural Policy as a Barrier Facing Agricultural Exports to the European Economic Community." *American Journal of Agricultural Economics* 59 (February 1977): 99.

Saraceno, Pasquale. *Il meridionalismo dopo la ricostruzione 1948–1958* (Conceptualizations of the Mezzogiorno's underdevelopment after the reconstruction 1948–1957). Rome: Giuffrè/SVIMEZ, 1974.

Sarti, Roland. *Fascism and the Industrial Leadership in Italy 1919–1940: A Study in the Expansion of Private Power Under Fascism*. Berkeley and Los Angeles: University of California Press, 1971.

Saville, Lloyd. *Regional Economic Development in Italy*. Durham, N.C.: Duke University Press, 1967.

Schettini, Giacomo. "Il partito della Cassa" (The Cassa's plight). *Rinascita*, no. 33 (25 August 1984): 5.

Serfaty, Simon, and Lawrence Gray, eds. *The Italian Communist Party: Yesterday, Today, and Tomorrow*. Westport, Conn.: Greenwood Press, 1980.

Seroni, Adriano. Introduction to *La città del sole*, by Tommaso Campanella. Milan: Giangiacomo Feltrinelli Editore, 1979.

Shaw, Timothy M. "EEC-ACP Interactions and Images as Redefinitions of Eurafrica: Exemplary, Exclusive, and/or Exploitative?" *Journal of Common Market Studies* 18 (December 1980): 135.

Signorile, Claudio. *Il nuovo Mezzogiorno e l'economia nazionale* (The new Mezzogiorno and the national economy). Bari: Laterza, 1982.

Singer, Hans W. "The Distribution of Gains Between Investing and Borrowing Countries." *American Economic Review, Papers and Proceedings* 40 (May 1950): 473–85.

Siotis, Jean; Luigino Scricciolo; and Georges N. Yannopoulos. *La CCE ed il Sud Europa: Verso l'allargamento* (The EEC and southern Europe: Toward enlargement). Rome: Istituto Affari Internazionali, 1979.

Spencer, Milton H. *Contemporary Economics.* New York: Worth Publishers, 1971.

Spinetti, Gastone Silvano, ed. *Italy Today.* Rome: Documentation Center of the Presidency of the Council of Ministers of the Republic of Italy, 1955.

Stati Uniti e Italia negli anni della crisi (The United States and Italy in the years of the crisis). *Dossier,* monograph no. 16 (October–December 1981).

Stern, Robert M. *Il commercio estero italiano e la sua influenza sullo sviluppo economico nazionale* (Italy's foreign trade and its influence on national economic development; published originally in English). Milan: Etas Kompass, 1968.

Sylos Labini, Paolo. *Sindacati, inflazione e produttività* (Trade unions, inflation, and productivity). Bari: Laterza, 1972.

———. *Il sottosviluppo e l'economia contemporanea* (Underdevelopment and the contemporary economy). Bari: Laterza, 1983.

Tagliacarne, Guglielmo. "Le regioni forti e le regioni deboli della comunità allargata: Indicatori socio-economici per la politica regionale della comunità" (The strong and the weak regions of the enlarged community: socio-economic indicators for the community's regional policy). *"Note economiche" del Monte dei Paschi di Siena,* no. 4 (July–August 1973): 31–51.

Tamburini, Gualtiero. *Teoria e pratica di politica regionale in alcuni paesi della CEE* (The theory and practice of regional policy in some EEC countries). Bologna: Centro universitario di studi europei, 1977.

Templeman, Donald C. *The Italian Economy.* New York: Praeger, 1981.

Togliatti, Palmiro. *Lectures on Fascism* (published originally in Italian as *Lezioni sul Fascismo*). New York: International Publishers, 1976.

Toniolo, Gianni. *L'economia dell'Italia fascista* (Fascist Italy's economy). Bari: Laterza, 1980.

Triffin, Robert. "The European Monetary System." In *Integration and Unequal Development: The Experience of the EEC,* edited by Dudley Seers and Constantine Vaitsos. New York: St. Martin's Press, 1980.

Turone, Sergio. *Partiti e mafia dalla P2 alla droga* (The political parties and the Mafia from the P2 [Masonic lodge scandal] to drugs). Bari: Laterza, 1985.

Ungerer, Horst; Owen Evans; and Peter Nyberg. *The European Monetary System: The Experience, 1979–1982.* Occasional Paper No. 19. Washington, D.C.: International Monetary Fund, 1983.

Velo, Dario, ed. *Le imprese multinazionali* (Multinational corporations). Milan: Giuffrè, 1974.

Vetrone, Mario. "Revisione della politica agraria comune ed attuazione delle direttive comunitarie" (The revision of the Common Agricultural Policy and the implementation of community directives). *Bari economica,* nos. 7–8 (July/August 1975): 11–19.

Vicarelli, Fausto. "Il processo d'integrazione reale-finanziaria dell'economia italiana nella CEE" (The process of the real-financial integration of the Italian economy in the EEC). In *Contributi alla ricera economica/Servizio studi della Banca d'Italia* (Contributions to economic research/Research service of the Bank of Italy), 285–320. Rome: Banca d'Italia, 1973.

Villani, Pasquale. "Le città meridionali" (The southern cities). *La questione meridionale*, vol. 16, monograph 95, in *I problemi di Ulisse* (The Problems of Ulysses), 71–76. Florence: Sansoni Editore Nuova, 1983.

Villari, Luigi. *Italian Foreign Policy Under Mussolini*. New York: Devin Adair, 1956.

Vinci, Salvatore. "L'agricoltura italiana nell'integrazione europea" (Italian agriculture in European integration). *Rivista di politica agraria*, no. 1 (June 1983): 13–22.

———. "Il quadro macroeconomico per lo sviluppo del Mezzogiorno" (The macroeconomic framework for the Mezzogiorno's development). *Rivista Trimestrale Mezzogiorno d'Europa* (Mezzogiorno d'Europa Quarterly Review; also available in English), no. 4 (October–December 1984): 547.

Wallace, Helen; William Wallace; and Carole Webb, eds. *Policy-making in the European Community*. 2d ed. Chichester: John Wiley and Sons, 1983.

Waltz, Kenneth N. *Theory of International Politics*. Reading, Mass.: Addison-Wesley, 1979.

Welk, William G. *Fascist Economic Policy: An Analysis of Italy's Economic Experiment*. Cambridge: Harvard University Press, 1938.

Whitman, Marina von Neumann. "International and Interregional Payments Adjustment: A Synthetic View." Princeton Studies in International Finance No. 19. Princeton: Princeton University, Department of Economics, 1967.

Wiarda, Howard J. "From Corporatism to Neo-syndicalism: The State, Organized Labor, and the Changing Industrial Relations Systems of Southern Europe." *Comparative Social Research* 5 (1982): 3–57.

Willis, Frank Roy. *Italy Chooses Europe*. New York: Oxford University Press, 1971.

Wiskemann, Elisabeth. *Europe of the Dictators 1919–1945*. Ithaca, N.Y.: Cornell University Press, 1966.

———. *Fascism in Italy: Its Development and Influence*. London: Macmillan & Co., 1969.

———. *Italy Since 1945*. London: Macmillan & Co., 1971.

Woolf, Stuart. *A History of Italy 1700–1860: The Social Constraints of Political Change*. London: Methuen, 1979.

Zijlstra, J., and B. Goudzwaard. *Politica economica e problemi della concorrenza nella CEE e negli stati membri* (Economic policy and problems of competition in the EEC and in the member states). Brussels: CEE, 1966.

Zurlo, Giuseppe. "Enti di sviluppo ed il loro ruolo nell'attuazione delle direttive comunitarie" (Development agencies and their role in the implementation of community directives). *Bari economica*, nos. 7–8 (July–August 1975): 24–29.

Index

Abruzzo, 89, 180n.7, 182n.7, 183n.4
Active internationalization of the Italian economy, 137–39, 140
Amin, Samir, 25
Anomalous consumerism, 119–21
Anomalous urbanization, 119
Anschluss, 37
Areas of industrial development: defined, 49; and the establishment of the dependent industrialization policy, 48–49; and the intensification of the Mezzogiorno's underdevelopment, 102–3, 106
Australia, and investments in the Mezzogiorno, 81, 89
Austria: and the Kingdom of the Two Sicilys, 126, 190–91 nn. 23 and 25; and World War II, 37
Axis. *See* Rome-Berlin Axis

Banca d'Italia. *See* Bank of Italy
Banca Nazionale, 35
Banco di Napoli, 35
Banco di Sicilia, 35
Bank of Italy, 35, 74, 75, 122
Baran, Paul, 25
Bari, University of, 122
Basilicata, 89, 180n.7, 182n.7, 183n.4
Basle Accord, 74, 186n.7
Belgium: and the ERDF, 91; and the Group of Ten, 74; and the Kingston Agreement, 74; and the Smithsonian Agreement, 73–74
Bonn-Paris Axis, 140
Bretton Woods international monetary regime, 73
Brussels Accord, 74, 76

Calabria, 44, 89, 122, 124, 128, 180n.7, 182n.7, 183n.4
Camorra, 128

Campania, 71, 87, 89, 97, 180n.7, 182n.7, 183n.4
Canada: and the Group of Ten, 74; and investments in the Mezzogiorno, 81, 89; and the Kingston Agreement, 74; and the Smithsonian Agreement, 73–74
CAP: defined, 59; and Italy, 66, 91, 92–93, 102, 139, 140; and the Mezzogiorno, 66, 91, 92–93, 102, 116, 139, 140; and West Germany and France, 58–60, 92–93. *See also* EEC: and the CAP
CASMEZ: and the dependent industrialization policy, 49–51, 103–4, 107; established and life extended, 45; and extraordinary intervention in the Mezzogiorno, 56, 102, 103–5, 107, 110–11; and the public works policy, 45–46; refinanced and life extended, 51, 103–4; and United States hegemony over Italy, 45
Cassa per il Mezzogiorno. *See* CASMEZ
Christian Democratic Party. *See* DC
CIPE, 104, 106, 107
CNPE, 104
Commercial Bank of Italy, 75
Committee of Ministers for the Mezzogiorno: abolished, 106; and the dependent industrialization policy, 49–50; located within the CNPE, 104
Common Agricultural Policy. *See* CAP
Common Regional Fund, 137
Cosa nostra, 132
Cutolo, Raffaele, 132

DC: relations with the Mafia, 130, 133, 135; relations with the northwestern elite, 39–40, 48, 49, 61, 103, 106, 107, 130, 135
Denmark: and the Basle Accord, 186n.7;

207

and the ERDF, 91; and the Kingston Agreement, 74; and the Mafia, 135; and the Smithsonian Agreement, 74

De Pasquale, Pancrazio, 133

Dependent industrialization policy: and areas of industrial development, 48–49, 102–3, 106; and the CASMEZ, 49–51, 103–4, 107; and the Committee of Ministers for the Mezzogiorno, 49–50; and the creation of economic deserts in the Mezzogiorno, 117; and emigration from the Mezzogiorno, 123–24; established, 48–49; and the Mezzogiorno's hypertertiarization, 122; and the parastate industries, 49, 98; and relations between the Mezzogiorno and the Italian State, 98–101, 102–4, 106–7, 119

Depressed Areas Laws of 1934 and 1937, 43

Development: defined, 28; in relation to Marxist and liberal intellectual traditions, 26–27, 178 nn. 2 and 3. *See also* Positive, balanced development; Underdevelopment

Dollar (United States), and the Italian lira, 72–76

Dutch florin. *See* Florin (Dutch)

Economic deserts, 117

Economic development without employment, 115, 137

Economic planning, 48

Economic programming concept, 48, 103, 106

EEC: and the CAP, 58–60, 91, 92–93; and the *de jure* "rules of the game," 60; and the EIB, 91, 94–97; and the ERDF, 91–92; establishment of, and the United States, 56; and Greece, 139; and Italy, 55, 60, 69, 91–97, 115, 136, 138, 140; and the juridical dimension of integration, 55; and the Mafia, 133–35; membership of, 183 n.1; and the Mezzogiorno, 55, 81, 91–97, 100, 101–2, 115–16, 136; objective of, 55; and the political predominance of West Germany and France, 56–60, 69, 72–73, 77–80, 92–93, 136, 138, 139; and Portugal, 139; prescribed objective of, unattained, 136; Social Policy of, and intra-EEC immigrant workers, 124; and Spain, 139, 140; unbalanced integration of, 78, 99, 100, 116, 136, 137–38

EIB: defined, 94, 188 n.30; and EEC investments in Italy and in the Mezzogiorno, 91, 94–97, 188 nn. 31 and 32

Emanuel, Arghiri, 25

Emigration, 123–24

Emilia-Romagna, 180 n.6, 182 n.7, 183 n.4

EMS: created, 74; strengthened, 186–87 n.16; and the United Kingdom, 74

England. *See* United Kingdom

Enti di riforma. *See* Land Reform Agencies

Entrepreneurial Mafia, 130–32, 135. *See also* Mafia

ERDF: defined, 91; and EEC investments in Italy and in the Mezzogiorno, 91–92

EUA/ECU: defined, 76–77; and the Dutch florin, 80; and the French franc, 80; and the Italian lira, 76–80; strengthened, 186–87 n.16; and the West German mark, 77–80

European Economic Community. *See* EEC

European Investment Bank. *See* EIB

European Monetary Cooperation Fund. *See* FECOM

European Monetary System. *See* EMS

European Regional Development Fund. *See* ERDF

European Unit of Account/European Currency Unit. *See* EUA/ECU

EUROSTAT, 122

Fascism. *See* Italy, Fascism in

FECOM, 74

First National Economic Program, 103, 188 n.9

Florin (Dutch), and the EUA/ECU, 80

Foreign Trade Institute (Italian). *See* ICE

Franc (French), and the EUA/ECU, 80

France: and the Basle Accord, 186 n.7; and the CAP, 58–60, 92–93; and the ERDF, 91; and the Group of Ten, 74; and the Kingdom of the Two Sicilys, 126; and the Kingston Agreement, 74;

Index

political predominance in the EEC, 56–60, 69, 92–93, 136, 138, 139, 140; in relation to Italy, economically, 139; and the Smithsonian Agreement, 73–74
Frank, André Gunder, 25
Free enterprise ideology: and the EEC's "rules of the game," 60; and United States hegemony over Italy, 42. *See also* Mezzogiorno: ideological legitimation of the underdevelopment of; Modified free enterprise ideology
French franc. *See* Franc (French)
Friuli Venezia-Giulia, 180 n.6, 183 n.4

Germany, 37
Germany, West. *See* West Germany
Greece, and the EEC, 139
Group of Ten, 74

Hypertertiarization, 122

ICE, 69
IMF, 122
Immigrant workers, intra-EEC, and the Social Policy of the EEC, 124
Incentives policy: and the creation of economic deserts in the Mezzogiorno, 117; and emigration from the Mezzogiorno, 123–24; established, 48–49; and the Mezzogiorno's hypertertiarization, 122; modified, 50; and the parastate industries, 50, 98; and relations between the Mezzogiorno and the Italian State, 98–101, 102–4, 119
Integration: defined, 28; unbalanced, of the EEC, 78, 99, 100, 116, 136, 137–38. *See also* EEC: and the juridical dimension of integration
Interdependence: defined, 28; among Western Europe's major economies, 56
Interministerial Committee for Economic Programming. *See* CIPE
International division of labor: defined, 184 n.8; and Italy, 40, 66, 72–73, 75–76, 81, 137, 140
International Monetary Fund. *See* IMF
Ireland: and the Basle Accord, 186 n.7; and the ERDF, 91; and the Kingston Agreement, 74; and the Smithsonian Agreement, 74

Istituto Commercio Estero. *See* ICE
Italian Communist Party. *See* PCI
Italian lira. *See* Lira (Italian)
Italian Socialist Party. *See* PSI
Italy: and the active internationalization of its economy, 137–39, 140; and the Basle Accord, 74; and the CAP, 66, 91, 92–93, 102, 139, 140; and the development of a southern EEC bloc, 137, 139–40; emigration from, 123–24; and the EEC, 55, 60, 69, 91–97, 115, 136, 138, 140; and the EIB, 91, 94–97, 188 nn. 31 and 32; and the ERDF, 91–92; Fascism in, 36–38, 42, 129–30; foreign investment in, 82–86, 91–97, 138; and the Group of Ten, 74; initiatives of for greater autonomy, 40, 137–40; and the international division of labor, 40, 66, 72–73, 75–76, 81, 137, 140; Kingdom of, 33–36, 129, 180 n.1; and the Kingston Agreement, 74; and the Mafia as an agent of social control in the Mezzogiorno, 129, 130, 133–35; and the passive internationalization of its economy, 138–39; and the productive development of its work force, 137–38, 139, 140; and regional institutions of government, 55–56, 107, 180 nn. 5, 6, and 7, 183 n.4; in relation to France, economically, 139; in relation to the United Kingdom, economically, 139; in relation to West Germany, economically, 184 n.9; and the Rome-Berlin Axis, 37; and the Rome-Madrid Axis, 140; and the Smithsonian Agreement 73–74; three economic systems of, defined, 34, 180 nn. 5, 6, and 7; unification of, 33–35, 122, 129, 180 n.1; United States hegemony over, 38–41, 42–44, 45, 60–62, 69, 75–76, 130, 136, 137, 138, 140

Japan: and the Group of Ten, 74; and investments in the Mezzogiorno, 81, 89; and the Kingston Agreement, 74; and the Smithsonian Agreement, 73–74

Kay, Geoffrey, 25
Kingdom of Italy. *See* Italy: Kingdom of
Kingdom of Sardinia. *See* Italy: unifica-

tion of. *See also* Spain: Kingdom of, and relations with the Kingdom of the Two Sicilys
Kingdom of Spain. *See* Spain: Kingdom of, and relations with the Kingdom of the Two Sicilys
Kingdom of the Two Sicilys. *See* Two Sicilys, Kingdom of the
Kingston Agreement, 74

Land Reform Agencies, 45
Land reform policy, 44–45, 47, 52, 115–16
La Repubblica, 124
Latium. *See* Lazio
La Torre, Pio, 133
Law for the Sila (no. 230 of 12 May 1950), 44, 115
Lazio, 87, 89, 180 nn. 6 and 7, 182 n.7, 183 n.4
Lebanon, 81, 89
Left, Italian political: and the anti-Fascist resistance, 38–39; and counterbalanced U.S.-Soviet influence, 41; and the ideological legitimation of the Mezzogiorno's underdevelopment, 43–44; relations between components, 38–39, 40–41, 101; relations with the northwestern elite, 37–38, 41, 62, 99, 101, 123, 135
Legge Siciliana. *See* Sicilian Law (Sicilian Regional Government law no. 104 of 27 December 1950)
Legge Sila. *See* Law for the Sila (no. 230 of 12 May 1950)
Legge Stralcio. *See* Summary Law (no. 841 of 21 October 1950)
Liechtenstein, 81, 89
Liguria, 180 n.5, 183 n.4
Lira (Italian): and the EUA/ECU, 76–80; and the United States dollar, 72–76; and the West German mark, 72–75, 77–80
Lombardy, 180 n.5, 183 n.4
Lucania. *See* Basilicata
Luxembourg: and the Basle Accord, 186 n.7; and the ERDF, 91; and the Kingston Agreement, 74; and the Smithsonian Agreement, 74

Mafia: as an agent of social control in the Mezzogiorno, 129, 130, 133–35; as a characteristic and consequence of the Mezzogiorno's underdevelopment, 115; and the crisis of the traditional ethic, 129–30; and Denmark, 135; and the EEC, 133–35; as entrepreneur, 130–32, 135; and Fascism, 129–30; initiatives of the PCI against, 130, 133; meaning of the term, 128; and its model of capitalist accumulation, 131–32; new ethic of, 130–31; origins of, 124–28; relations with the DC, 130–33; relations with the PSI, 133; traditional ethic of, 128–30; and West Germany, 135
Marche, 89, 180 n.6, 183 n.4
Marches, The. *See* Marche
Mark (West German): and the EUA/ECU, 77–80; and the Italian lira, 72–75, 77–80
Mezzogiorno: and anomalous consumerism, 119–21; and anomalous urbanization, 119; and areas of industrial development, 48–49, 102–3, 106; and the CAP, 66, 92–93, 102, 116, 139, 140; consequences of underdevelopment for, 115; economic deserts in, 117; and economic development without employment, 115, 137; and the EEC, 55, 81, 91–97, 100, 101–2, 115–16, 136; and the EIB, 94–97, 188 n.31; emigration from, 123–24; and the entrepreneurial Mafia, 130–32, 135; and the ERDF, 91–92; and extraordinary intervention by the CASMEZ, 56, 102, 103–5, 107, 110–11; and Fascism, 36–37, 42; foreign investment in, 81–82, 86–97, 136–37; function of in the Italian economy, 34, 44, 47, 52, 53, 71, 100, 108–9, 115, 116, 121, 122–23, 130, 135, 136; and gap in economic development in relation to north-central Italy, 51, 101–2, 106, 109–10; hypertertiarization in, 122; ideological legitimation of the underdevelopment of, 42–44; and the Mafia as an agent of social control in, 129, 130, 133–35; under the political control of the northwestern elite, 35, 37, 42, 107, 108–9, 116, 130, 135, 136; and regional institutions of government, 55–56, 107, 180 n.7; and rural exodus, 115–16; and social disintegra-

tion, 117–18, 135; and "special projects," 106–7; the subordination of, 35–36; and the unproductive expenditure of capital under the policy of social control, 100, 102–4, 117–18, 121–22. *See also* Dependent industrialization policy; Free enterprise ideology; Incentives policy; Land reform policy; Modified free enterprise ideology; Parastate industries; Public works policy

Minister for Extraordinary Intervention in the Mezzogiorno, 107

Modified free enterprise ideology, 45, 47–48. *See also* Free enterprise ideology; Mezzogiorno: ideological legitimation of the underdevelopment of

Molise, 89, 180 n.7, 182 n.7, 183 n.4

National Committee for Economic Programming. *See* CNPE

National economic development programs. *See* First National Economic Program; Vanoni Plan

National Fund for the Development of the South, 111

'Ndrangheta, 128

Netherlands: and the ERDF, 91; and the Group of Ten, 74; and the Kingston Agreement, 74; and the Smithsonian Agreement, 73–74

New Family. *See* Nuova Famiglia

Northwestern elite: defined, 34; and political control over the Mezzogiorno, 35, 37, 42, 107, 108–9, 116, 130, 135, 136; relations with the DC, 39–40, 48, 49, 61, 103, 106, 107, 130, 135; relations with the Left, 37–38, 41, 62, 99, 101, 123, 135; relations with the "state bourgeoisie," 98–101, 119, 135; relations with the United States, 38, 40–41, 61–62. *See also* CAP; Dependent industrialization policy; Economic programming concept; Incentives policy; Land reform policy; Parastate industries; Policy of social control; Public works policy

Norway, and the Basle Accord, 74, 186 n.7

Nota Aggiuntiva La Malfa, 103

Nuova Famiglia, 132

Nuova Famiglia Organizzata, 132

OECD, 122, 184 n.9

Omertà, 128–29, 191 n.27

Organization for Economic Cooperation and Development. *See* OECD

Organized New Family. *See* Nuova Famiglia Organizzata

Parastate industries: and the dependent industrialization policy, 49, 98; and the incentives policy, 50, 98; investments of, 101, 104, 106, 108; and relations between the Mezzogiorno and the Italian State, 98–99, 119

Passive internationalization of the Italian economy, 138–39

PCI, and initiatives against the Mafia, 130, 133. *See also* Left, Italian political: relations between components

Pianificazione economica. See Economic planning concept

Piemonte, 180 n.5, 183 n.4, 190–91 n.23

Pitagora, 122

Policy of social control: emigration as the "safety valve" of, 123; the Mafia as an agent of, 129, 130, 133–35; and the unproductive expenditure of capital in the Mezzogiorno, 100, 102–4, 117–18, 121–22

Portugal, and the EEC, 139

Positive, balanced development, defined, 28. *See also* Development; Underdevelopment

Productive development of the Italian work force, 137–38, 139, 140

Programmazione economica. See Economic programming concept

Protocol concerning Italy. *See* EEC: and Italy

PSI, relations with the Mafia, 133. *See also* Left, Italian political: relations between components

Public works policy, 44–47, 52

Puglia, 71, 89, 97, 122, 180 n.7, 182 n.7, 183 n.4

Pythagoras. *See* Pitagora

Real income: and the complementarity of the Mezzogiorno's industrial and tertiary sectors, 122–23; consumption and investment of, in underdeveloped economic systems, 29; defined, 179 n.12; drained from the Mezzogiorno by anomalous consumerism, 119–21; and the Mezzogiorno's development, 136–37; use of, by the Kingdom of Sardinia's ruling class in determining the Italian economy's structure, 34; use of, in Western Europe, determined by West Germany and France, 57–58

Regional institutions of government: distinguished as "ordinary" and "special," 183 n.4; grouped according to the economic systems in which they are located, 180 nn. 5, 6, and 7; and legislative autonomy, 55–56; and "special projects," 107

Rognoni-La Torre Law (no. 416/416 bis of 13 September 1982), 133

Rome, Treaty of, 55, 60, 96, 136, 139, 183 n.1

Rome-Berlin Axis, 37

Rome-Madrid Axis, 140

Rural exodus, 115–16

Saraceno, Pasquale, 103

Sardegna, 89, 180 n.7, 182 n.7, 183 n.4

Sardinia. *See* Sardegna

Sardinia, Kingdom of. *See* Italy: unification of. *See also* Spain: Kingdom of, and relations with the Kingdom of the Two Sicilys

Schema Vanoni. See Vanoni Plan

Schumpeter, Joseph, 25

Seigniorage: defined, 73; gained by the United States and West Germany at Italy's expense, 75–76

Sicilia, 89, 97, 128, 133, 140, 180 n.7, 183 n.4

Sicilian Law (Sicilian Regional Government law no. 104 of 27 December 1950), 44–45, 115–16

Sicily. *See* Sicilia

Sila. *See* Law for the Sila (no. 230 of 12 May 1950)

Single Text (Law no. 1523 of 30 June 1965), 104

Smithsonian Agreement, 73–74

Social control policy. *See* Policy of social control

Social disintegration, 117–18, 135

Social Policy of the EEC, and intra-EEC immigrant workers, 124

Southern Development Fund. *See* CASMEZ

Southern EEC bloc, 137, 139–40

Soviet Union: and the strategic equilibrium with the United States, 56; and the strategic military posture of the United States, 38. *See also* Left, Italian political: and counterbalanced U.S.-Soviet influence

Spain: and the EEC, 139–40; Kingdom of, and relations with the Kingdom of the Two Sicilys, 124–26, 190–91 nn. 23 and 24

"Special projects," 106–7

State bourgeoisie: defined, 44; relations with the northwestern elite, 98–101, 119, 135

Statistical Office of the European Communities. *See* EUROSTAT

Summary Law (no. 841 of 21 October 1950), 44, 115

Sweden: and the Basle Accord, 74, 186 n.7; and the Group of Ten, 74; and investments in the Mezzogiorno, 81, 83, 89; and the Kingston Agreement, 74; and the Smithsonian Agreement, 73–74

Switzerland: and the Group of Ten, 74; and investments in the Mezzogiorno, 81, 89; and the Kingston Agreement, 74; and the Smithsonian Agreement, 74

Tecnopolis, 122

Tennessee Valley Authority, 43

Testo Unico. *See* Single Text (Law no. 1523 of 30 June 1965)

Treaty of Rome. *See* Rome, Treaty of

Trentino-Alto Adige, 180 n.6, 183 n.4

Two Sicilys, Kingdom of the: and agricultural capitalism's genesis, 125, 191 n.25; and Austria, 126, 190–91 nn. 23 and 25; and France, 126, and piloted industrialization, 125–28; under Spanish domination, 124–26, 190–91 nn. 23 and 24; and the United Kingdom, 126. *See also* Italy: unification of

Tuscany, 180 n.6, 182 n.7, 183 n.4

Umbria, 180 n.6, 183 n.4

Underdevelopment: consequences of, for the Mezzogiorno, 115; defined, 28–29; intellectual debate on, 25–27. *See also*

Development; Positive, balanced development
United Kingdom: and the EMS, 74; and the ERDF, 91; and the Group of Ten, 74; and the Kingdom of the Two Sicilys, 126; and the Kingston Agreement, 74; in relation to Italy, economically, 139; and the Smithsonian Agreement, 73–74
United States: and the establishment of the EEC, 56; and the Group of Ten, 74; hegemony over Italy, 38–41, 42–44, 45, 60–62, 69, 73, 75–76, 130, 136, 137, 138, 140; hegemony over Western Europe, 56–57, 60, 61, 69, 73, 136, 138; investments in the Mezzogiorno, 81, 82, 83, 86, 89; and the Kingston Agreement, 74; relations with the northwestern elite, 38, 40–41, 61–62; and the Smithsonian Agreement, 73–74; and the strategic equilibrium with the Soviet Union, 56; strategic military posture of, 38. *See also* Left, Italian political: and counterbalanced U.S.-Soviet influence
United States dollar. *See* Dollar (United States)
Unity of Action Pact of 1934, 40

Valle d'Aosta, 180 n.5, 183 n.4
Vanoni Plan, 48, 103, 188 n.9
Veneto, 71, 180 n.6, 183 n.4

Wallerstein, Immanuel, 25
Western Europe: and interdependence of its major economies, 56; United States hegemony over, 56–57, 60, 61, 69, 73, 136, 138; use of real income in, determined by West Germany and France, 57–58
West German mark. *See* Mark (West German)
West Germany: and the Basle Accord, 186 n.7; and the CAP, 58–60, 92–93; and the ERDF, 91; and the Group of Ten, 74; and the Kingston Agreement, 74; and the Mafia, 135; political predominance of in the EEC, 56–60, 69, 72–73, 77–80, 92–93, 136, 138, 139, 140; in relation to Italy, economically, 184 n.9; and the Smithsonian Agreement, 73–74
World Bank, 45
World War II, 36–41, 42, 56, 115, 130

Zaza, Michele, 132